TSONGKHAPA

His Holiness the Dalai Lama with the participants in the international conference "Jé Tsongkhapa: Life, Thought, and Legacy" at Ganden Shartsé Monastery in Mundgod, Karnataka State, India, on December 20, 2019. Photo by Lobsang Tsering.

TSONGKHAPA

The Legacy of Tibet's Great Philosopher-Saint

Edited by David B. Gray

Wisdom Publications
132 Perry Street
New York, NY 10014 USA
wisdomexperience.org

Library of Congress Cataloging-in-Publication Data
Names: Jé Tsongkhapa: Life, Thought, and Legacy (Conference) (2019: Mundgod,
     India) | Gray, David B., 1969– editor.
Title: Tsongkhapa: the legacy of Tibet's great philosopher-saint /
     edited by David B. Gray.
Description: First edition. | New York: Wisdom Publications, 2024. |
     Includes bibliographical references and index.
Identifiers: LCCN 2023035969 (print) | LCCN 2023035970 (ebook) |
     ISBN 9781614297550 (paperback) | ISBN 9781614297710 (ebook)
Subjects: LCSH: Tsong-kha-pa Blo-bzang-grags-pa, 1357-1419—Criticism and
     interpretation—Congresses. | Dge-lugs-pa (Sect)—Doctrines—Congresses. |
     Mādhyamika (Buddhism)—Congresses. | Tantric Buddhism—Congresses.
Classification: LCC BQ7950.T755 J428 2024 (print) | LCC BQ7950.T755 (ebook) |
     DDC 181/.043—dc23/eng/20231025
LC record available at https://lccn.loc.gov/2023035969
LC ebook record available at https://lccn.loc.gov/2023035970

ISBN 978-1-61429-755-0   ebook ISBN 978-1-61429-771-0

28 27 26 25 24
5   4   3   2   1

Cover design by Jess Morphew. Interior design by KGDKBG.

Printed on acid-free paper that meets the guidelines for permanence and durability of the Production Guidelines for Book Longevity of the Council on Library Resources.

Printed in United States of America.

Please visit fscus.org.

Contents

MOVING MINDS

Editor's Preface

THIS VOLUME IS the product of an important recent conference focusing on the intellectual legacy of the Tibetan philosopher, yogi, and saint Tsongkhapa (1357–1419). Entitled "Jé Tsongkhapa: Life, Thought, and Legacy," the conference commemorated the sixth hundredth anniversary of Tsongkhapa's passing and was held on December 21–23, 2019, at Ganden Monastery in Mundgod, India. The conference was convened by His Holiness the Dalai Lama and as a result was attended by a large and diverse audience of scholars, practitioners, local Indians and Tibetans, and pilgrims from around the world. Conference presentations were made in Tibetan and English as well as Hindi. Collected herein are the English presentations by the authors who were able and willing to revise and expand their conference presentations. Donald S. Lopez Jr. also revised and contributed his keynote address, "Tsongkhapa in Global Context," which serves as a very fine introduction to this volume. In his essay, Dr. Lopez reflects upon the global significance of Tsongkhapa's legacy, both through the lens of his own experience as a scholar studying Buddhism at Ganden Monastery in 1979 and through comparison with major figures in the history of Christian thought.

The essays contributed to this volume fell into three broad areas, which enable the division of the book into three sections. The first, not surprisingly, is Madhyamaka, a natural reflection of the very important and well-known contributions Tsongkhapa made to the study of Indian philosophical thought in Tibet and his advocacy in particular of the Prāsaṅgika Madhyamaka school of Nāgārjuna, Buddhapālita, and Candrakīrti. Four chapters focus on Tsongkhapa's contributions in these areas. The first, Guy Newland's "Start Making Sense: Finding Tsongkhapa's Middle Way," provides a straightforward and clear introduction to Tsongkhapa's interpretation of Madhyamaka philosophy, showing how Tsongkhapa played an essential role in clarifying Candrakīrti's contributions to Madhyamaka thought. The essay focuses on the two truths, especially Candrakīrti's critique of the concept of the intrinsic nature or reality of persons and things and the implications of this with respect to how conventional reality is properly understood, an epistemological understanding that was central to Tsongkhapa's unique approach.

A closely related issue, the nature of the self, is explored in the second chapter, "Tsongkhapa and Candrakīrti on Uprooting Saṃsāra: The Two-fold Object of the Identity View." In this essay, Dr. Dechen Rochard explores Tsongkhapa's understanding of Candrakīrti's negation of individual identity. After first exploring the issue of the *identity view* (*satkāyadṛṣṭi*), a crucial but often poorly understood topic in Buddhist philosophy, the essay presents Candrakīrti's and Tsongkhapa's argument, which connects this with a central existential problem, namely self-grasping, which can be alleviated via analytical meditation in which inherent identity is sought and not found. The essay neatly demonstrates the centrality of the practitioner's view of self to the path to spiritual awakening.

In the third chapter, "Thinking Beyond Thought: Tsongkhapa and Mipham on the Conceptualized Ultimate," Jay L. Garfield explores Tsongkhapa's views on the nature of ultimate reality, specifically Tsongkhapa's argument that this entails a movement from inferential to direct awareness of emptiness. He also discusses later contributions to the debate regarding the nature of ultimate reality and the possibility of its realization made by nineteenth- and twentieth-century Nyingma thinkers Ju Mipham and Bötrul Dongak Tenpai Nyima.

The fourth and final entry in this section is "Tsongkhapa on the Importance of Ascertainment in Meditation on Emptiness" by Thupten Jinpa. In this chapter, Jinpa notes Tsongkhapa's emphasis on the need for ascertainment (*nges pa*), or the correct apprehension of a given truth—in this case, emptiness—as a necessary consequence of sustained meditation practice. The essay explores the need for accurate philosophical analysis in the context of meditation practice so as to directly realize the truths about the nature of self and reality that are the objects of the practice. It thus nicely points to the integration of Buddhist theory and practice.

While Tsongkhapa is best known in the West as a philosopher, as Donald Lopez points out in his introduction to this volume, about two-thirds of his writings focus on the tantras and their associated practices. The second section of this volume is thus dedicated to his writings on the tantras. In the first chapter in this section, "Tsongkhapa's Masterful Exegesis of Cakrasaṃvara Tantra," I elucidate Tsongkhapa's approach to the study of tantric literature with a focus on his commentary on the

Cakrasaṃvara Tantra. I argue that Tsongkhapa's exegetical approach was broadly based, taking into account the available translations, explanatory tantras, and commentaries. He also advocated an ecumenical approach to tantric commentary, since drawing on diverse tantric traditions advances one's understanding.

Chapter 6 is Gavin Kilty's contribution, "A Lamp to Illuminate the Five Stages: Tsongkhapa's Reformatory Work on Guhyasamāja Tantra." Kilty first surveys the Guhyasamāja tradition and its transmission to Tibet and the two main Indian exegetical traditions, the Ārya and Jñānapāda schools. Outlining Tsongkhapa's approach to the *Guhyasamāja Tantra*, he then focuses on how the tradition conceptualizes the generation-stage and completion-stage practices.

The final contribution in this section is chapter 7, "The Shadow of Heshang: Tsongkhapa on Chan, Dzokchen, and Mahāmudrā Meditation" by Roger R. Jackson. Jackson explores the claim that Tsongkhapa received and secretly transmitted esoteric instructions on advanced meditation practices to realize the nature of mind and awakening. He explores the evidence for this claim in Tsongkhapa's writing and contemporaneous works. In so doing, he also details Tsongkhapa's positions with respect to the Nyingma dzokchen and Kagyü mahāmudrā traditions, as well as with the Chinese Chan tradition associated with the eighth-century master Heshang Moheyan, with which the former traditions were sometimes linked.

The volume concludes with a section entitled "Moving Minds," which explores Tsongkhapa's legacy and impact both in Tibet and beyond. It opens with "Jé Tsongkhapa's Contribution to Buddhist Hermeneutics" by Geshé Ngawang Samten. Buddhist hermeneutics, as understood here, is a response to the challenge posed by scriptures that appear to contradict one another. Geshé Ngawang Samten first reviews the interpretive strategies employed by Buddhists to get a definitive sense of what the Buddha actually taught. He then turns to Tsongkhapa's groundbreaking contributions to this field of study in Tibet in the *Essence of Eloquence*.

Chapter 9, "Tsongkhapa's Hermeneutics and the Perfection of Wisdom," contributed by Gareth Sparham, takes a more focused look at the interpretation of the Perfection of Wisdom literature in both India and Tibet. Sparham first introduces the literature and the major Indian commentaries on it, focusing on debates regarding the authorship and validity of two important commentaries that were attributed to Vasubandhu and hence could be linked to the authoritative figure of Maitreya. Sparham then discusses Tsongkhapa's interpretation of this literature, as well as his evaluations of the authorship of the two commentaries, only one of which he attributes to Vasubandhu. Sparham distinguishes Tsongkhapa's views on these issues from other influential Tibetans such as Dölpopa Sherab Gyaltsen.

The tenth chapter is "Jé Tsongkhapa's Teachings and Translations in Mongolian" by Bataa Mishig-Ish, who surveys the dissemination of Tsongkhapa's oeuvre to Mongolia. Dr. Bataa first briefly surveys the introduction of Buddhism to Mongolia, particularly the formal adoption of the Geluk school of Tibetan Buddhism by the Western Oirat Mongols in the seventeenth century. He then turns to the dissemination of Tsongkhapa's works in the Mongolian context, with a focus on Tsongkhapa's famous texts on the stages of the path (*lam rim*) and their publication as woodblock texts in the eighteenth century. He argues that Tsongkhapa's *lam rim* teachings were an important spiritual resource that helped preserve the Buddhist teachings in Mongolia during the era of oppressive Communist rule in the twentieth century.

The final chapter is Bhikṣuṇī Thubten Chodron's "Learning, Living, and Teaching Bodhicitta: Jé Tsongkhapa's Contribution to Spreading Compassion in the World." Venerable Chodron argues that Tsongkhapa's approach to teaching compassion is particularly suited for the modern Western context. She begins with a discussion of the bodhisattva path and compares Tsongkhapa's spiritual journey with that of Sudhana, the hero of the *Gaṇḍavyūha Sūtra*. She observes that Tsongkhapa emphasizes the exchange of self and other when discussing the "spirit of awakening" (*bodhicitta*). She argues that the current Dalai Lama, following Tsongkhapa, emphasizes this contemplative exercise. The author then turns to Candrakīrti's discussion of three types of compassion as well as Tsongkhapa's commentary on this and its special relevance for modern practitioners.

While this volume does not come close to exhausting the limits of what might be said concerning the impact of Tsongkhapa's work in Tibet and beyond, it does reunite contributions to this study that briefly converged in Mundgod, India, just before the global pandemic ushered in a new awareness of our profound human interdependence. Hopefully these essays will advance the appreciation of Tsongkhapa's intellectual legacy in the wider English-speaking world, where he remains a little understood figure of Asian religious history, unlike in the Tibetan-speaking world, where his impact is justly celebrated.

Introduction: Tsongkhapa in Global Context

Donald S. Lopez Jr.

This is an edited transcript of a keynote address delivered to His Holiness the Dalai Lama and an audience of monks, nuns, and laypeople in the assembly hall at Ganden Shartsé Monastery in Mundgod, India, on December 20, 2019.

YOUR HOLINESS, VENERABLE members of the sangha, distinguished guests. Please forgive me if I begin with a personal reminiscence. Professor Jeffrey Hopkins, who is here today, founded the Buddhist studies program at the University of Virginia in 1976. In designing the program, he sought to incorporate several elements of the geshé curriculum into the graduate program. To that end, His Holiness kindly selected a series of geshés to teach at the University of Virginia over the next decade. The first of these was Lati Rinpoché (1922–2010), who arrived in 1976. Because his longtime attendant Ngawang Tsultrim could not accompany him, I served as Rinpoché's assistant, bringing him his meals and his tea and asking him each afternoon, "Shall we go for a walk?" (*cham cham la 'phebs kyi yin pas*).

In October 1978, I came to India on a Fulbright Fellowship to work on my dissertation, a translation and study of the Svātantrika section of *Lcang skya grub mtha'*, or *Beautiful Adornment of Mount Meru*, the famous work on tenets by Changkya Rölpai Dorjé (1717–86), remembered by history as the preceptor and confidante of the Qianlong emperor. I had my first audience with His Holiness that fall. I remember that I asked him about such topics as "the imaginary lacks the entityness of nature" (*kun btags la mtshan nyid ngo bo nyid med*) and "being established from the side of the object without being posited by the power of appearing to a nondefective awareness" (*blo gnod med la snang ba'i dbang gis bzhag pa ma yin par don gyi sdod lugs kyi ngos nas grub pa*). In January 1979, forty years ago, my wife and I made our way south here to Ganden, where my teacher, Lati Rinpoché, was then abbot of Ganden Shartsé.

Back then, conditions in Mundgod were difficult, especially for an American visiting India for the first time. But here at Ganden were Lati Rinpoché, Song Rinpoché, and Dzemé Rinpoché, with Kyabjé Trijang Rinpoché visiting during Losar. At Drepung were Khensur Pema Gyaltsen, Ngawang Nyima, Gen Nyima, and the geshé who became my closest teacher, Loseling Khensur Yeshé Thupten. Tara Rinpoché also visited. After Losar, the monks from the School of Dialectics in Dharmsala came down, and I remember Gen Losang Gyatso debating with Ngawang Nyima one night in the debating courtyard at Gomang. Although the facilities at the monasteries back then were very primitive, and everything was hot and dusty, I realize in retrospect that these places called Lama Camp #1 (Ganden) and Lama Camp #2 (Drepung) were in fact a pure land and that I was in the presence of buddhas. These were the most important days of my life. Today, I return to Ganden, having just completed a translation of all of *Lcang skya grub mtha'*. I have brought the first copy with me to present to His Holiness.

These were the days when His Holiness was concerned that the monks were devoting too much of their studies to the monastic textbooks (*yig cha*) of their colleges and not to the writings of the master himself, and so he had printed hundreds of copies of a two-volume set of Tsongkhapa's writings on emptiness, with the rather understated title, *The Master's Statements on the View* (*Rje gsung lta ba'i skor*). I still have those dark-green books on the shelf in my study in America.

One afternoon in the spring of 1979, I was circumambulating a small stupa at Gomang College at Drepung, reciting the famous five-line prayer to Tsongkhapa known simply by its first three syllables: *dmigs rtse ma*. The Buryat geshé Ngawang Nyima (or Agvan Nyima, 1907–90), then abbot of Gomang, walked over and asked me what I was doing. When I told him, he said, "You're an American, I'm a Mongolian. Here we are in India, speaking Tibetan, talking about someone from Amdo. There must be karma." I think he was right. And now, forty years later, when all of these masters, except one, are gone, I am here at Ganden again, to talk about the "crown ornament of scholars of the Land of Snows."

What can we say about this man? We can say that more than ten thousand people here at Ganden, with tens of thousands more watching around the world, have gathered today, six hundred years after he passed into nirvāṇa, entirely because of him. Because of him, there are the monasteries known simply as "the three foundations" (Ganden, Sera, and Drepung); because of him, there is Tashi Lhunpo, Labrang, and Kumbum. Because of him, there is the Ganden Phodrang. Because of him, there is the Panchen Lama. Because of him, there is the Dalai Lama. Because of him, this man who was not a king, not an emperor, not a warlord, not a politician. Because of him, this man who was an itinerant yogin, traveling from one retreat site to another, accompanied by a few disciples and four *dzo* (a cross between a yak and a cow) loaded down with volumes of the Kangyur and Tengyur, a man who had visions of Mañjuśrī, the bodhisattva of wisdom, a man who wrote some of the most sophisticated philosophical works in history.

The title of my comments today is "Tsongkhapa in Global Context." But this is a topic for an entire book. Therefore, let me limit my remarks to the realm of religion. When the term *world religion* was first coined in German in the nineteenth century, there were only two: Buddhism and Christianity. And indeed, the two religions have a long history of interaction. In early European descriptions, Buddhism is often compared to Roman Catholicism, and not always in a flattering way. Indeed, that comparison is most often made by Protestants, based on the presence of monks, monasteries, rosaries, incense, and chanting, as well as a pope, in the two religions. Today, we dismiss much of this. But perhaps we can return to the comparison in a different light.

In the history of the Roman Catholic Church, there is no thinker more important than St. Thomas Aquinas, who provided the philosophical foundation for Catholicism. Tsongkhapa's *Great Treatise on the Stages of the Path* (*Lam rim chen mo*) is sometimes compared to the *Summa Theologica* of Aquinas, although they are very different works. Still, there is a comparison to be made: Just as Thomas went back to the works of Aristotle to reshape Christian theology, arguing that reason is a path to God, so Tsongkhapa went back to the works of Nāgārjuna and Candrakīrti to provide the most influential exposition of Madhyamaka in the history of Buddhism, arguing that reason is essential even at the most exalted stages of the path to buddhahood.

Although Thomas Aquinas wrote five short hymns, including the famous "Adoro Te Devote," he is remembered for his genius as a philosopher. For the devotional side of the religious life, the Catholic Church reveres above all *The Imitation of Christ* by St. Thomas à Kempis, a contemporary of Tsongkhapa. This work provides detailed instruction for daily practice, intended to return monastic life to its spiritual foundations, foundations from which Thomas à Kempis felt many monks had strayed. *The Imitation of Christ* was the inspiration for another important work, the *Spiritual Exercises* by St. Ignatius Loyola, the founder of the Jesuits, the Christian order most often compared to the Geluk and the order with the most extensive interaction with Buddhism. In the case of Tibet, we think especially of the Italian Jesuit Ippolito Desideri (1684–1733), who studied at Sera Monastery in Lhasa and wrote lengthy refutations of rebirth and emptiness, in Tibetan. Like Thomas à Kempis and Ignatius Loyola, Tsongkhapa wrote many important devotional works, hymns, and instructions on practice—especially in his many works on tantra, which comprise some two-thirds of his collected works (*gsungs 'bum*)—but also in works on Madhyamaka, such as his several "instructions on the Madhyamaka view" (*dbu ma'i lta khrid*).

A final figure to mention is St. Benedict, author of yet another seminal work of the Roman Catholic Church, the *Rule of St. Benedict*, which provided the foundation for the organization and governance of monastic life. Benedict himself did not seek to establish his own religious order. However, the Benedictine order would develop over the centuries, eventually building thousands of monasteries across Europe. Tsongkhapa has been referred to as a "reformer" in European-language books about Buddhism for more than a century. There are several problems with the use of this term. However, his commitment to monastic discipline is clear throughout his biography, from his Dharma festival on the Vinaya in 1397 at Sengé Dzong to his composition of rule books (*bca' yig*) that would form the foundation for much of Tibetan monastic life, first at Ganden and later for hundreds of Geluk institutions across Inner Asia and today around the world.

With this brief comparison, I seek to make a simple point. One might argue that the Roman Catholic Church is built on the work of three saints, each towering in his importance: Thomas Aquinas, Thomas à Kempis, and Benedict of Nursia, who, respectively, provided the philosophical, spiritual, and institutional foundations of the church. For the Geluk, we find these three foundations provided by a single monk, Losang Drakpa from

Tsongkha. And furthermore, for Tsongkhapa, these three foundations were not separate domains. Indeed, one of the hallmarks of his work is his call for the importance and the synergy of the three spheres, the *'khor lo gsum*: *lta ba*, *sgom pa*, and *spyod pa*: philosophy, meditation, and action. To this remarkable achievement, accomplished in a life of only sixty-two years, we should add that these foundations were expressed in some of the most beautiful poetry and prose in the vast literature of the Tibetan language.

I mentioned at the outset that my translation of *Lcang skya grub mtha'* has just been published. Along with Jamyang Shepa's *Great Exposition of Tenets* (*Grub mtha' chen mo*), Changkya's is the most famous *grub mtha'* text and certainly the more widely read. As I was working on the translation, I was continually struck by the presence of Tsongkhapa, or "the foremost great being" (*rje bdag nyid chen po*), as Changkya usually refers to him. Although there is no *grub mtha'* text among the eighteen volumes of his collected works, nor in those of his two chief disciples, Gyaltsab and Khedrup, there is hardly a single topic on which Tsongkhapa does not offer essential insight, whether it is the refutation of Sāṃkhya in the chapter on non-Buddhist traditions; the question of whether the Pudgalavāda of the Saṃmitīya sect—the famous (and infamous) proponents of an "inexpressible person"—are really "proponents of Buddhist tenets" (*nang pa'i grub mtha' smra ba*) in the Vaibhāṣika section; to the extensive discussion of substantial existence (*rdzas yod*) and exclusion of the other (*gzhan sel*) in the Sautrāntika chapter. The lengthy Cittamātra chapter, which Changkya seems to have written first, is based largely on Tsongkhapa's *Essence of Eloquence* (*Legs bshad snying po*), and the two Madhyamaka chapters are based on many of his works, but especially his *Great Commentary on the Mūlamadhyamakakārikā* (*Rtsa shes ṭik chen*) and his *Illuminating the Intent* (*Dgongs pa rab gsal*), his commentary on Candrakīrti's *Entering the Middle Way* (*Madhyamakāvatāra*).

If one were to characterize the writings of Tsongkhapa with a single term, it might be "integration" (*zung 'jug*). When we read his works, we notice immediately that he is not only a master of the "five books" (*gzhung lnga*) that form the basis of the Geluk curriculum—Maitreya's *Ornament for Realization* (*Abhisamayālaṃkāra*), Candrakīrti's *Entering the Middle Way*, Dharmakīrti's *Commentary on Reliable Cognition* (*Pramāṇavārttika*), Vasubandhu's *Treasury of Abhidharma* (*Abhidharmakośa*), and Guṇaprabha's *Discourse on Discipline* (*Vinayasūtra*)—and their vast related literature, but that he is able to see deep connections among them. For example, in his *Notes on Ornament for the Middle Way* (*Dbu ma rgyan gyi zin 'bris*), he takes up the category of "reasoning about the unestablished" (*gzhi ma grub pa'i gtan tshigs*), the question of whether something that does not exist can be the subject of a syllogism. At first sight, this appears to be a technical question deriving from Indian Buddhist logic, and in many ways it is. However, Tsongkhapa understands that in Madhyamaka, it is essential to be able to reason about things that do not exist, most importantly the self of persons and the self of phenomena. This is just one of many examples of the ways in which he integrates Dharmakīrti's logic into Madhyamaka ontology.

Yet another example of integration is Tsongkhapa's weaving of Indian sources into his works. As a young monk, he spent four full years at Tsal Gungthang, essentially in a reading retreat, immersing himself in the Tsalpa edition of the Kangyur and Tengyur. The most immediate result of his study was his first major work, *Golden Rosary of Good Explanation* (*Legs bshad gser phreng*), his magnum opus on the Perfection of Wisdom, where he famously cites twenty-one Indian commentaries on Maitreya's *Ornament for Realization*. As Thupten Jinpa notes in *Tsongkhapa: A Buddha in the Land of Snows*, from this point on, Tsongkhapa would rely almost exclusively on Indian sources in the many works that would follow; it was Indian works that he loaded on to the backs of the four *dzo* that accompanied him from one retreat to another. It was from this point that he styled himself "the Well-Read Losang Drakpai Pal from Tsongkha in the East" (*mang du thos pa shar tsong kha pa blo bzang grags pa'i dpal*).

The most famous, and perhaps the most consequential, integration that we find in the collected works of Tsongkhapa is his integration of sūtra and tantra. In some ways, this derives from Atiśa and his *Lamp for the Path to Enlightenment* (*Bodhipathapradīpa*). However, Tsongkhapa's engagement with the question is far more extensive and sophisticated, where, for example, in the first chapter of his *Great Exposition of Secret Mantra* (*Sngags rim chen mo*) he takes up the crucial question of the distinguishing feature of tantra. He concludes that it is not to be found in the realm of wisdom because there is no wisdom more profound than that set forth by Nāgārjuna and Candrakīrti. All those who achieve liberation, whether by the path of the *śrāvaka* or the path of highest yoga tantra, must realize the subtle selflessness of persons and phenomena as set forth in Prāsaṅgika.

Instead, Tsongkhapa argues, the difference must be found in the realm of method, in the practice of *lha'i rnal 'byor*, deity yoga. As always, he has an Indian source, the *Vajra Canopy Tantra* (*Vajrapañjara Tantra*), to support his argument: "The method is to bear the Teacher's form" (*thabs ni ston pa'i gzugs can no*).

Each of these examples, however, are instances of the most important form of integration that we find in Tsongkhapa's works: the integration of study and practice, the conviction that what might seem arcane, technical, even pedantic in the vast corpus of the Buddhist canon always offers an occasion for practice—in his words, an opportunity to see all teachings as *man ngag*, as personal instructions.

At the beginning of his *grub mtha'*, Changkya writes:

> A state of degeneration beyond degeneration
> has become full blown.
> That the secrets of the teachings of the Sage
> still have not declined is due to his kindness.[1]

Changkya wrote those words almost three hundred years ago. If the degenerate age was full blown then, what is our fate today? There are surely many lessons that the works of Tsongkhapa have to offer to the modern world. But the one that occurs to me today is his commitment to reason, analysis, and evidence in all elements of the Buddhist path, from going for refuge to the most advanced stages of tantric practice, his conviction that it is only through the exercise of the highest powers of the intellect that we can attain direct perception of the real.

In 1979, I finished my study of the Svātantrika chapter of Changkya several weeks before I had to return to America. I asked Loling Khensur Yeshé Thupten what I should study next, and he said, without hesitation, the *Essence of Eloquence*. And so he began to teach me. We did not finish. On the day of my departure from Mundgod, I came to say goodbye, tears streaming down my face. As I began to do a prostration, he said, "Don't bow down," *phyag ma tshal*. He explained that if I did not bow down, it meant that the teaching was not concluded and that we would meet again to continue the study of this precious text, the text that was recited by

---

1. Changkya Rölpai Dorjé 2019, 71.

the monks of Ganden six hundred years ago to honor the passing of this great master. And so I end with this prayer, that we will all meet again in the future, where our teacher will appear before us once again, to teach us how to understand the teachings of the "crown ornament of scholars of the Land of Snows, Tsongkhapa" (*gangs can mkhas pa'i gtsug rgyan tsong kha pa*).

MADHYAMAKA

1. Start Making Sense:
Finding Tsongkhapa's Middle Way

Guy Newland

> Avalokiteśvara, great treasure of non-objectifying compassion;
> Mañjuśrī, master of stainless wisdom;
> Vajrapāṇi, destroyer of the entire host of demons:
> crown jewel of the sages of the Land of Snow,
> Tsongkhapa Losang Drakpa, at your feet I pray.[1]

The name of this traditional prayer, *miktsema* (*dmigs rtse ma*), refers to "non-objectifying compassion," which means "loving care that has no real object." Edward Conze, having translated the Perfection of Wisdom sūtras, summarized that vast corpus in these lines:

> A Bodhisattva is a being compounded of the two contradictory
> forces of wisdom and compassion. In his [*sic*] wisdom, he sees no
> persons; in his compassion, he resolves to save them all.[2]

Perhaps this is profound, but *as stated* it is also a perfect bit of nonsense. It is easy to liberate zero beings, so it is fortunate for bodhisattvas that zero would seem to be their correct and complete count per the highest wisdom of the cosmos.

The *Teaching of Vimalakīrti* (*Vimalakīrtinirdeśa*) and other Mahāyāna sūtras stress that there is no intrinsic superiority between silence and speech; in each moment the bodhisattva prefers whatever is most skill-

---

1. My translation. The prayer, according to tradition, was originally offered by Tsongkhapa to his teacher Rendawa but was rewritten in this form by Rendawa and offered back to Tsongkhapa.

2. Conze 1951, 130.

ful for liberation. And so it is with sensible speech and paradoxical speech; each, according to context, may be most skillful. As a manner of pointing out the profound, mystery and paradox have a special power for the human mind. On the other hand, so also does a sensible clarity.

Tsongkhapa penetrated the profound and explained it, extensively, in the clearest and most sensible way. In sum: *Only things that are empty of inherent existence can function as causes and effects.* Only living beings who are empty can liberate or be liberated; non-empty things or persons could never function as causes or agents. Tsongkhapa quotes Candrakīrti's *Clear Words* (*Prasannapadā*):

> [In the context of emptiness,] proper and improper conduct and their consequences make sense; all worldly conventions make sense. Hence Nāgārjuna says: "For those to whom emptiness makes sense, everything makes sense."[3]

In this passage, Tsongkhapa comments that "what makes sense" means that *these things exist.* Experiencing awakening, Tsongkhapa eloquently expressed this insight in his ecstatic poem "Praise to Dependent Arising."[4]

So that this insight might become a source of vast benefit, he set out to explain exactly *how* emptiness and dependent arising are compatible; to do that, he needed plausible solutions to some bedeviling philosophical problems. He had to explain how things that cannot be found under analysis can nonetheless *actually exist* and *be reliably known* to function. And in order to safeguard the functioning of conventional phenomena, he also had to show how to avoid reifying the ineffable ultimate as an absolute that collapses all else to mere illusion. He had to dispel any notion that the ultimate cancels and supersedes conventional existence rather than *being its necessary condition.*

Here I will summarize (1) how Tsongkhapa avoids reifying the ultimate as a monistic mystical absolute, (2) how he shows that Madhyamaka analysis does not even slightly refute the existence of conventional phenomena, and (3) perhaps most controversially and least understood, how he explains

---

3. As cited in Tsongkhapa 2002, 136.
4. See Tsongkhapa, "In Praise of Dependent Origination," n.d.

reliable cognition of conventional phenomena (*tha snyad pa'i tshad ma*) within Candrakīrti's Prāsaṅgika Madhyamaka.

The Ultimate Exists Conventionally

Candrakīrti's reading of Madhyamaka gained ascendance in eleventh-century Tibet, but Tibetans—leaning on Jayānanda's commentary—struggled to make sense of it. Many understood Candrakīrti to be teaching an absolutely *unknowable* ultimate. Some, such as Chapa Chökyi Sengé, criticized Candrakīrti on that basis. Chapa argued that the ultimate mind must finally, through analysis, come to *know* the final reality of all things—or else liberation will not be attainable. He faulted Candrakīrti for apparently teaching otherwise.[5]

Others, like Maja Jangchup Tsöndrü and Patsap Nyima Drak, looked with favor on Candrakīrti's supposed notion of an ultimate beyond the realm of cognition. Some saw this as harmonious with tantric evocations of a pristine ultimate unsullied by the inevitable dualism of human consciousness.[6] On this reading of Candrakīrti, dualistic distinctions are kindly concessions to the needs of ordinary, frightened people; they provide no reliable knowledge. Yet if this is correct, how can any of the dualism-based practices of ordinary beings bring them closer to awakening?

In response to these problems, Tsongkhapa explains exactly what the ultimate reality is and how it is that we *can* know it—but also how this derives from, rather than contradicts, Candrakīrti. The ultimate is a total negation, the sheer absence or lack of a very particular kind of status that is superimposed on things by delusion. Emptiness, this negative ultimate, is therefore an existing quality or nature possessed by all phenomena, including all conventional phenomena. Yet, like all other phenomena, it is a dependent arising and exists only conventionally. We can study it. We can understand it. Deep meditative familiarity with this particular aspect of phenomena will root out all delusion, culminating in the inexpressible, nonconceptual, and nondual yogic insight that unwinds the needless misery of cyclic existence.

Following Candrakīrti, Tsongkhapa argues that we become attached

5. Newland 1992, 28.
6. Vose 2009, 28–29.

to things by the power of an afflictive misunderstanding, a particular consciousness that hypostatizes by superimposing intrinsic reality.[7] Delusion-based attachment leads to karma; one stops cyclic existence by totally and finally stopping that afflicted mind. To do that, one must know oneself, and all things, *as lacking intrinsic existence.*

To accomplish this, one must rely on a qualified teacher and, following that person's instructions, find the Madhyamaka view through analysis. One carefully analyzes the meaning of authoritative scriptures and classic texts. Then, internalizing their meaning, and in accordance with it, one analyzes whether it is reasonable or possible for the person and the psychophysical aggregates to exist as they now appear.

Therefore Tsongkhapa repeatedly stresses that *study is practice.* He quotes a Kadam master:

> [W]hether you show off or conceal that you studied only a handbook, you cannot get anywhere without reading a yak's load of books.[8]

The fault of separating scholarship from yogic practice is a constant theme in Tsongkhapa's writing. He laments:

> Nowadays those making effort at yoga have studied a few scriptures, while those who have studied much are not skilled in the key points of practice.[9]

He sets out to remedy this situation by teaching exactly how the classic texts work as the best and most authentic instructions for personal practice.[10] Study of the scriptures and commentaries is, he says, "the unexcelled cause that gives rise to the discriminating wisdom which is the sacred life-force of the path."[11]

Study is critical because the liberating insight of knowing the ultimate

7. Tsongkhapa 2002, 211–13.

8. Tsongkhapa 2004, 219.

9. Tsongkhapa 2002, 33.

10. Tsongkhapa 2000, 51.

11. Tsongkhapa 2004, 219.

reality can be achieved only by meditating on precisely that which you have studied and then reflected upon. It is not that one studies one sort of thing and then later realizes or awakens to something else. In his *Great Treatise on the Stages of the Path*, Tsongkhapa three times cites the same verse from the *King of Samādhis Sūtra* (*Samādhirājasūtra*):

> If you analytically discern the lack of self in phenomena
> and if you cultivate that very analysis in meditation
> this will cause the result, attainment of nirvāṇa;
> there is no peace through any other means.[12]

Tsongkhapa names only Heshang Moheyan as an advocate of the contrary view that all thinking, all conceptualization, is the root source of our problems and thus the practice should be to abandon such. However, through the character of Heshang he is intending to refute views held by many prior and *later* Tibetans. Quoting Kamalaśīla, Tsongkhapa argues that if you aspire to and teach utter nonthinking, you abandon correct analytical discrimination, thereby cutting off the only pathway to sublime wisdom.[13]

Furthermore, Tsongkhapa goes on to say that even when one has established the Madhyamaka view via analysis, one still must return, after a period of stabilizing meditation, to analyze again and again.[14] It is not that some initial analysis sets the stage for some trans-analytical bliss. Rather, through repeatedly alternating analysis and stabilization, one eventually reaches the deepest and most powerful kind of insight. He tells us to remember this critical point: "You must distinguish between (1) not thinking about true existence and (2) *knowing* the lack of true existence."[15] Only the latter is a path to liberation.

---

12. Tsongkhapa 2002, 23, 108, and 345.

13. Tsongkhapa 2002, 332.

14. Tsongkhapa 2002, 344.

15. Tsongkhapa 2002, 344.

Identifying the Object of Negation

Tsongkhapa explains that to know that a particular person is absent, one must know that person; likewise, in order to know emptiness—the lack of inherent existence—one must know exactly what this inherent existence *would* be like if it were real. He carefully explains this subtle object of negation:

> There is with regard to objects a conception that things have ontological status—a way of existing—in and of themselves, without being posited through the force of an awareness. The object of that conception is the hypothetical "self" or "intrinsic nature." To exist intrinsically or autonomously means having its own unique manner of being.
>
> Take the case of an imaginary snake mistakenly ascribed to a rope. If we leave aside how the snake is ascribed from the perspective apprehending a snake, and instead try to analyze what the snake is like in terms of its own nature, since a snake is simply not there in that rope, its features cannot be analyzed.
>
> Like that, suppose we leave aside analysis of how things appear to a conventional awareness and analyze the objects themselves, asking what is the manner of being of these things? They are not established in any way. Ignorance is that which, instead of seeing this, apprehends each thing as having a way to exist such that it can be known in and of itself, without being posited through the force of a conventional awareness.[16]

This means that—contrary to an alternative Madhyamaka view that things have their own nature conventionally—for Candrakīrti and Tsongkhapa there is simply no way that things *are* in and of themselves; they have no manner of existing on their own side. Contrary to the Yogācāra view, there *are* external objects, but they exist only relative to the perspectives of *conventional consciousnesses*. So it is that they may be very different things for the beings of different realms.

All phenomena exist nominally, as mere imputations, relative to conven-

16. Tsongkhapa 2002, 212–13.

tional minds. Importantly, Tsongkhapa does *not* restrict this explanation to conventional phenomena. He says that all objects of knowledge—even the ultimate reality, emptiness—are posited as existing in relation to conventional consciousnesses. Thus all things exist only conventionally; all things exist as mere imputations. There is nothing—even emptiness—that exists ultimately.

But what about nirvāṇa? What about the ultimate mind of nondual, trans-conceptual, liberating wisdom? If such an ultimate mind knows emptiness, then must that not establish emptiness as the one truly real object?

Tsongkhapa says: NO.[17] Emptiness exists conventionally insofar as it is recognized as existing by the conventional mind of a practitioner who has just arisen from meditation on emptiness. The ultimate mind that nondualistically knows emptiness does not regard emptiness as existing or as not existing; it knows only emptiness.

Yet still: If the profound emptiness is the final nature, the actual reality, of all things, must that not entail that it is *its own final nature*? For if it were not its own final nature, what else could be? And in that case, would it not be *self-existent*, the one truly self-sufficient entity?

Again: no. Tsongkhapa twice quotes Candrakīrti's statement that the ultimate "is not established by way of its own selfhood."[18] Rather, it is identifiable as the object of a sublime wisdom perceiving reality. No emptiness is its *own* final nature. If we ask regarding any conventional phenomenon, "What is its final nature?" we arrive at last at the emptiness of that particular phenomenon. But if we then ask of that emptiness what is *its* final nature, we find the emptiness of that emptiness. This means that any emptiness, every emptiness, is—like everything else—a dependent arising; it does not exist by way of its own nature. Emptinesses are all exactly "of the same taste" (*ro gcig*)—the absence of inherent existence—but they do not exist on their own. An emptiness exists only in relationship to the particular phenomenon of which it is the final nature—and in relation to the conventional mind that posits it to *exist as such* in the wake of deep analysis of that particular phenomenon.

<hr>

17. Tsongkhapa 2002, 190–92 and 198.

18. Hopkins 2008, 218; also, Tsongkhapa 2021a, 224.

Madhyamaka Analysis Is Intent on Seeking Essential Nature

A second issue: Madhyamaka analyses show that the closer we scrutinize how any particular object exists, the less clear the object becomes. Carried to completion, Madhyamaka analyses such as those of Nāgārjuna seem to refute *every single thing imaginable*, insofar as there is nothing irreducible upon which analysis can fix. How then do we avoid Conze's paradox: "In his wisdom, [the bodhisattva] sees no living beings; in his compassion, he vows to save them all"?

Tsongkhapa approaches this question by having an interlocutor ask: How can any reasonable person, how can any philosopher—Madhyamaka or otherwise—analytically refute things and yet still claim they exist? How is it possible for something to exist—as the object of our compassion, for example—when reason has refuted it?

Tsongkhapa responds by saying the question conflates two very different things: (1) being unable to withstand rational analysis and (2) being found by reason not to exist. Of the former he explains, "To ask whether something withstands rational analysis is to ask whether it is found by reasoning analyzing reality."[19] In Madhyamaka analysis we are seeking to discover whether forms and so forth have an intrinsic nature. The fact that such analysis comes up empty does not mean forms do not exist. And it does not mean that reason refutes them. Rather, the inability to withstand rational analysis refutes just that which—if it did exist—would have to be found by reasoning. It refutes self-existence, intrinsic nature. And Tsongkhapa quotes Candrakīrti's commentary on Āryadeva's *Four Hundred Stanzas* (*Catuḥśatakaṭīkā*) to show that this is exactly what Candrakīrti meant. Candrakīrti says, "[O]ur analysis is intent upon seeking intrinsic nature," and adds:

> When reason analyzes in this way, there is no essential nature that exists in the sensory faculties . . . they have no essential existence. If they did, then under analysis by reason their status as essentially existent would be seen more clearly, but it is not.[20]

19. Tsongkhapa 2002, 156.

20. Tsongkhapa 2002, 156–57 and 160.

To make this clear, Tsongkhapa explains that this is analogous to the fact *we cannot see sounds*. Seeing and hearing are two different epistemic channels, each finding its appropriate objects but not finding (no matter how carefully it searches) other kinds of objects that are also present. So it is with ultimate analysis and conventional awareness. Each has its own domain, neither superseding nor canceling the other. And so Candrakīrti says, "We refute things that exist essentially; we do not refute that eyes and such are products and dependently arisen results of karma."[21]

Conventional Knowledge in Prāsaṅgika

In a particularly important section of his *Great Treatise*, Tsongkhapa explains exactly how and why Candrakīrti (1) asserts reliable cognition while also (2) refuting reliable cognition as taught by Buddhist realists. He does this through cogent and meticulous commentary on the relevant passages from four of Candrakīrti's texts: *Entering the Middle Way* (*Madhyamakāvatāra*), *Clear Words*, *Commentary on the Four Hundred Stanzas*, and *Commentary on Sixty Verses of Reasoning* (*Yuktiṣaṣṭikāvṛtti*). As Tsongkhapa notes, some of these passages—which focus on the refutation of reliable cognition as asserted by Buddhist realists—had been a source of grave doubt prior to Tsongkhapa. This is because they can easily be construed as completely refuting the existence of reliable cognition. Even after Tsongkhapa shows that Candrakīrti *does* provide for reliable cognition, his critics focus their attacks with particular vehemence on this exact point, insisting that the (1) profound emptiness and (2) reliable knowledge of the conventional are contradictory and irreconcilable.[22] For that reason, it is important to explore this in some depth.

In brief, the term *reliable cognition*, or *pramāṇa* (*tshad ma*), plays a central role in Buddhist epistemology, especially due to the work of Dharmakīrti. In his *Commentary on Reliable Cognition* (*Pramāṇavārttika*), we learn that one kind of reliable cognition (epistemic instrument) is perception, wherein a sense faculty ascertains irreducible characteristics in its object,

21. Cited in Tsongkhapa 2002, 160.
22. Tsongkhapa 2002, 163–75; Yakherds 2021, passim.

particularly the object's intrinsic capacity to perform a function (*don byed nus pa, arthakriyā*).[23] Eltschinger explains that for Dharmakīrti,

> [A] real entity gives rise to a direct perceptual awareness of it thus projecting an image of itself into cognition . . . The image it displays provides a vivid and isomorphic perceptual counterpart of the . . . real entity it takes as its object . . .[P]erception [thereby] provides direct, unbiased and non-conceptual access to ultimate reality."

It is the nature of water to function to moisten, the nature of fire to burn. Tactile perception attests to these characteristic natures.

Tsongkhapa's critics, Tibetan and otherwise, fail to take full account of the fact that Tsongkhapa explicitly agrees with them that reliable cognition, understood in this way, cannot work in Prāsaṅgika because there is no self-existent nature, even conventionally. There is nothing irreducible; there is no way that things are in and of themselves. Tsongkhapa must show that while nothing—including reliable cognition—exists ultimately, Candrakīrti does allow that reliable cognition of the conventional exists. He will have to explain how reliable cognition is possible even when there is no objective nature for such a mind to certify.

Is the World Reliable in Any Way?

Tsongkhapa begins his explanation of conventional reliable cognition in Prāsaṅgika by analyzing critical passages where Candrakīrti seems to say that ordinary sense consciousness can never be a source of reliable knowledge. An interlocutor quotes Candrakīrti's *Entering the Middle Way* as saying, "The world is not reliable in any way."[24] Is this not a straightforward denial of conventional reliable cognition?

Tsongkhapa quickly demonstrates that this is not the case. He does this by placing the passage in context and showing how Candrakīrti himself explained it in his autocommentary. There Candrakīrti explains, "Only noble beings are authorities on the *contemplation of reality* [emphasis

---

23. Eltschinger 2010, 402–3.
24. Tsongkhapa 2002, 164.

added]," and proceeds to argue that "if a mere visual consciousness could ascertain reality, there would be no point in training in ethics, study, reflection, or meditation." Everyone would already see things just as they are. On this basis, Candrakīrti concludes, "Because the world is not reliable in any way, the world has no critique *in the context of reality*." Tsongkhapa continues, showing that Candrakīrti's *Commentary on Nagarjuna's Sixty Verses on Reasoning* makes the same point: the Buddha taught that the sense consciousnesses are not reliable in the specific sense that they are not reliable with regard to the reality that is the final nature of things.

Thus, in context, Candrakīrti's point is that ordinary eye consciousnesses and so forth do not and will never discredit the profound truth that the path uncovers. They are not reliable in any way *in the context of knowing reality*, how it is that things finally exist. It is unreasonable to interpret these passages as meaning that Candrakīrti was somehow refuting the notion that an eye consciousness can give us reliable information about shapes and colors. If we had no reliable information at all from our senses, then how would we even begin to study, reflect, and meditate? How would we find our way to food and shelter?

Tsongkhapa drives this point home by considering the absurd implications of reading Candrakīrti otherwise: Suppose Candrakīrti meant: "If the eye were a reliable knower of forms, there would be no need to make an effort to practice the path in order to realize emptiness."[25] Tsongkhapa argues that this would be as senseless as saying that if the eye is reliable regarding forms, there is no need for the ear to hear sounds. In other words, again, just as the eye and ear have distinct epistemic pathways—each with its own respective objects, neither impeding the other—so it is with the ordinary eye consciousness seeing forms and the analytical wisdom knowing the emptiness of those forms.

Worldly Consciousnesses Are Deceptive

Tsongkhapa then takes on what he acknowledges as a tougher exegetical nut. It appears that Candrakīrti is giving a general refutation of conventional reliable cognition when his *Commentary on the Four Hundred Stanzas* says:

25. This and the above quotations occur at Tsongkhapa 2002, 164.

> The Buddha said that even consciousness . . . has a false and deceptive quality. . . . That which has a false and deceptive quality . . . is not nondeceptive because it exists in one way and appears in another. It is not right to designate such a reliable cognition because in that case all consciousnesses would be reliable cognitions.[26]

Tsongkhapa explains that this passage very specifically refutes conventional reliable cognition *as advocated by those who follow Dharmakīrti*. He proves this by quoting at length a passage where Candrakīrti specifically refers to his opponents here as "logicians utterly unpracticed in the sensibilities of the world" whom you must train "as though they were young children." As Tsongkhapa explains, for these logicians, sense perception is non-mistaken because it apprehends, it *gets at*, the actual intrinsic character of the object. Here Candrakīrti is refuting them because in Prāsaṅgika, even conventionally there is no intrinsically existent character that perception could apprehend. When one fully sets aside how an object exists from the perspective of minds apprehending it, there is nothing we can say about the characteristics of the object itself.

Nonetheless, Candrakīrti cites the Buddha as saying that consciousness is deceptive. Since reliable cognition means being a reliable, nondeceptive source of information, does this not rule out any kind reliable consciousness?

Tsongkhapa says no. Candrakīrti here explains deceptiveness as the quality of existing in one way and appearing in another. Tsongkhapa takes this to refer to the fact that for Candrakīrti, even ordinary, normal sense perception is deceived in the particular sense that things appear to it as inherently existent and yet are not. This is another way of saying that our senses misinform us—*not* about everything but about the ultimate nature of things. They are not reliable *in the context of reality*; they are mistaken about reality.[27]

So the kind of reliable cognition Candrakīrti accepts operates in an environment very different from the one Dharmakīrti seems to envision. Tsongkhapa quotes Candrakīrti's *Commentary on the Four Hundred Stan-*

---

26. Cited in Tsongkhapa 2002, 164–65.

27. Tsongkhapa 2002, 165–67.

zas: "Worldly perceptions cannot cancel the perception of reality because *worldly perception is reliable only for the world* and because the objects it observes have a false and deceptive quality."[28]

Candrakīrti thus seems to allow that, operating *within* this environment of deceptively appearing objects, the world—that is to say, the conventional mind—can have perceptions that are conventionally reliable. These are sure to be mistaken about only one thing: the presence or absence of intrinsic nature in their objects. Thus Candrakīrti is not giving a general refutation of conventional reliable cognition.

Conventional Reliable Cognition in Prāsaṅgika

Tsongkhapa also proves that Candrakīrti definitely does assert conventional reliable cognition. He quotes Candrakīrti's *Clear Words*:

> [Reliable cognition and its objects] are established through mutual dependence. When reliable cognitions exist, then there are things that are objects of comprehension. When there are things that are objects of comprehension, then there are reliable cognitions. However, neither reliable cognitions nor objects of comprehension exist essentially.[29]

As Tsongkhapa explains, this shows that Candrakīrti's apparent refutations of reliable cognitions are in fact refutations of an *essence-based epistemology*; Candrakīrti clearly asserts reliable cognitions and objects of comprehension that are contingently posited phenomena.

To confirm that this exegesis is the best possible reading of Candrakīrti, Tsongkhapa points to a well-known passage in *Clear Words*: "We therefore posit that the world knows objects with four reliable cognitions," referring to perception, inference, scripture, and analogy. Of course, ultimately, in the context of analyzing reality and so forth, there is no reliable cognition. Also no cars, dogs, or boats. In such a context, we also cannot find any *absence* of reliable cognition. Nothing truly exists, nothing inherently exists, nor do things inherently not exist; everything is equally

---

28. Cited in Tsongkhapa 2002, 166.
29. Cited in Tsongkhapa 2002, 167.

and completely empty. But as we address one another with words, seeking to organize conferences or to make arguments, Candrakīrti clearly specifies that *there is reliable cognition.* Amid the continuous deceptive appearance of things as inherently real, there are nonetheless reliable sources of information.

This leaves the most critical question: If Candrakīrti denies any essential character in the object for a reliable cognition to apprehend, then *in what sense can we say that it knows its object at all?* What does it mean to say that one mind is a reliable source of information and another is not, when in fact there is exactly zero independent objective reality against which to judge?

To spell out the answer to this, Tsongkhapa quotes Candrakīrti's *Entering the Middle Way*:

> Also, perceivers of falsities are of two types:
> those with clear sensory faculties and those with impaired sensory
>   faculties.
> A consciousness with an impaired sensory faculty
> is considered wrong in relation to a consciousness with a good sen-
>   sory faculty.
>
> Those objects known by the world
> and apprehended with six unimpaired sensory faculties
> are true for the world. The rest
> are posited as unreal for the world.[30]

If a sensory consciousness is unimpaired—unaffected by superficial causes of error such as eye disease—then it is accurate in conventional terms. It is still mistaken in terms of appearance because, under the influence of ignorance, its object appears as though it were intrinsically existent. Yet this does not contradict conventional accuracy. Except in the context of considering the ultimate reality, ordinary unimpaired minds *are* reliable sources of information about what does and does not exist. They are reliable cognitions.

---

30. *Madhyamakāvatāra* 6.24–25, cited in Tsongkhapa 2002, 167.

Candrakīrti, as cited by Tsongkhapa,[31] lists examples of internal and external impairment—echoes, reflections, and so forth—and nowhere hints that the fundamental ignorance is an instance of such. Candrakīrti apparently takes it for granted, implicit in the qualification "for the world," that we know that none of these distinctions—in fact, no distinctions at all—hold up in an ultimate sense. If we did count the fundamental ignorance as a cause of impairment here, then we would always perceive everything through impaired faculties, and thus everything we know would be utterly unreal even conventionally. This is a view that perhaps some critics of Tsongkhapa would accept. But if Candrakīrti intends to rule out any kind conventional reliable cognition, he could easily include the fundamental ignorance among the causes of impairment in these verses or commentary, and yet he does not.

And indeed, if there were no conventionally reliable information at all, then how could we distinguish virtue and nonvirtue? How would we determine what texts to study or which teacher to rely upon? And again, how would we find food and so forth if we had no reliable way to make distinctions? There are Buddhists who posit that there is no possibility of knowing conventional objects because all that appears is a web of delusion. They have quite a few philosophical problems of their own.[32] We cannot make improvements in our minds or our world if we have not the slightest foothold on reality, no first step to stand upon. And thus it is that they will say, and in fact they *must* say, that we are *already* buddhas. For if we were not, we never would be. The idea of gradual progression makes no sense when everything that appears is totally delusory.

Certified Testimony versus Unimpeached Testimony

From this we see Candrakīrti's notion of conventional reliable cognition—by which we mean sources of accurate information about what does and does not exist conventionally—is very different from that of Dharmakīrti. Candrakīrti never posits a mind certifying the presence or absence of some intrinsic quality in its object. This is impossible in his system. But by reading Candrakīrti carefully—not leaning too heavily on Jayānanda but closely

31. Tsongkhapa 2002, 168.
32. Yakherds 2021, passim.

reading what Candrakīrti actually says and does not say—Tsongkhapa shows us that *Candrakīrti does assert conventional reliable cognition*. He asserts minds that are accurate, reliable, "for the world," which means at the conventional level. *And there is no other level at which any positive or negative statement can be affirmed*. Reliable minds are just those unaffected by superficial causes of error. Those unaffected by superficial causes of error can impeach or discredit those that are. Those impaired by superficial error cannot discredit those that are not.

So the conventional reliable knowledge of Candrakīrti and Tsongkhapa does not operate by way of certifying the presence of some essential character in its objects. It is rather that, having apprehended an object, its apprehension of that object is not falsified or discredited by some other mind. It is not that its testimony is notarized by the impression of the aspect of some nature in its object; there is no self-existent nature in the object. Rather, it simply stands as *unimpeached*—and that very lack of impeachment is warrant for relying on that information. Tsongkhapa's *Illuminating the Intent* puts it this way:

> The positing of a conventional object—apprehended by the six consciousnesses without such impairment—as real and the positing of an object opposite to that as unreal is done only in relation to worldly consciousnesses because those are, respectively, unimpeached and impeached by worldly consciousnesses with respect to their existing as they appear.[33]

Conventional objects are never real or true in the sense of existing just as they appear; their fundamental mode of existence is discordant with the manner in which they seem to exist. But they do exist, and we can know them. Reliable knowledge comes from conventional consciousnesses that are free from superficial causes of error and are thus not impeached by other conventional minds.

For example: We can know that, conventionally, water is wet. But this is not because our sense powers detect the nature of wetness out there in the water. If we claim this, then we are asserting conventional reliable

---

33. Tsong kha pa, *Dgongs pa rab gsal*, 148. Other translations in Hopkins 2008, 228, and Tsongkhapa 2021a, 231.

cognition in a Dharmakīrtian mode—and validating Tsongkhapa's critics. Candrakīrti and Tsongkhapa do not assert this. Instead, they say, we know that water is wet because it is perceived that way by a conventional mind that lacks a superficial cause of error and, for that very reason, is not impeached by another conventional mind.

Conventional Existence

We can see how this principle of falsification works when Tsongkhapa defines conventional existence. If his critics were correct that he imported an essentialist notion of cognition, then he would perhaps say that to exist means to be certified as existing by one of the four types of reliable cognition. Instead, he goes directly to Candrakīrti's notion of impeachment or falsification:

> How does one determine whether something exists conventionally? We hold that something exists conventionally (1) if it is known to a conventional consciousness (*tha snyad pa'i shes pa*); (2) if no *other*[34] conventional reliable cognition contradicts its being as it is thus known; and (3) if reason that accurately analyzes reality—that is, analyzes whether something intrinsically exists—does not contradict it. What fails to meet those criteria does not exist. [emphasis added][35]

Since nothing exists ultimately in Madhyamaka, to know what conventionally exists is to know what exists. And here we see that, whatever others may say, for Tsongkhapa *conventional existence is NOT defined via the incontrovertible certification of perception or inference.* Rather, Tsongkhapa follows Candrakīrti in delineating the class of existing objects by (1) first

---

34. This is the word *gzhan* in the Tibetan (Tsong kha pa, *Lam rim chen mo*, 560–61; see Tsongkhapa 2004, 178, for English). On the next page, Tsongkhapa uses the word *other* (*gzhan*) again in the same or a similar sense when explaining this definition: "Other conventional reliable cognitions do not contradict that which exists conventionally." Other than . . . what? He means that if something actually exists conventionally, no new conventional cognition will discredit it. So if "another" (later) conventional cognition *does* discredit it, this means that—contrary to what we had thought—the prior "reliable" cognition was not really such.

35. Cited in Tsongkhapa 2002, 178.

placing in view every object known by any conventional consciousness, and then (2) seeing which of those apprehensions can be impeached. Within the broad sphere of what living beings apprehend, those things that cannot be ruled delusory are exactly those that we may take to exist.

Note particularly Tsongkhapa's use of the word *other* (*gzhan*) in the second criterion, when he states that something may conventionally exist only if no *other* conventional reliable cognition contradicts the consciousness apprehending it. If a mirage's being water is contradicted by conventional reliable cognition, then it turns out that the prior conventional consciousness was not reliable. So why does Tsongkhapa say (and repeat in other places) this apparently unnecessary use of the word *other*? The implication is quite clear: He is accounting for a situation where we actually *believe* that we do have a reliable cognition, but later—looking at the matter more closely, in a different light, or upon further analysis—find that the early perception was incorrect due to an error of which one was originally unaware.

A person may see a mirage to the west of them and take it to be water. They may believe that they have knowledge of the presence of water via reliable perception. And yet as they proceed to the west, they find that there is no water. They then realize that what they reasonably took to be a reliable perception was in fact not such. The traditional examples of this sort are all comprehended within Candrakīrti's category of superficial causes of error—echoes, reflections, intoxication, disease, bad philosophy.

Many things that conventional consciousness take as true may in fact be false—and yet that mistakenness may not be recognized until much later. It cannot be that older, actually reliable cognitions are refuted by other, later occurring cognitions. The fact is that what we reasonably count as reliable knowledge now may later come to be understood to have never been such. Tsongkhapa does not stress this point, but it is implicit in his use of the word *other* in his definition of conventional existence.

Instability and Progress in Science and Mind-Training

It appears Tsongkhapa has here created circular definitions. Believed-in things can be taken as real if uncontradicted by reliable minds, reliable cognitions. These reliable minds are taken as reliable precisely insofar as they are unimpeached. By what might they be impeached? By reliable minds—

to wit, minds unimpaired by superficial causes of error such as eye disease, echoes, mirrors, or bad philosophy. Of course we could only know which minds are, and which are not, so impaired by relying upon the investigations of reliable minds.

Such circularity is surely inevitable in any epistemology that proposes to describe knowledge without positing an absolute ground or foundation. Because there is no essential nature at all, there can be no correspondence theory of what it means to know; instead, Prāsaṅgika epistemology is coherentist. Whatever it is that we suppose we know may later have to be revised. The present Dalai Lama—who counts himself a staunch follower of Tsongkhapa—extends this notion of revisable knowledge into his perspective on science. He says that if science proves something different than what is found in scripture, then we should trust science, understanding that the Buddha was skillfully teaching in terms of what his audience understood at that earlier time. The Dalai Lama writes:

> If scientific analysis were conclusively to demonstrate certain claims in Buddhism to be false, then we must accept the findings of science and abandon those claims.[36]

And he says that Abhidharma cosmology

> gives very exact measurements of the distance from the earth to the moon and sun and the stars, as well as the size of the sun and moon. The problem is, these measurements are wrong from the modern scientific point of view.[37]

And from this the Dalai Lama concludes, "My own view is that Buddhism must abandon many aspects of the Abhidharma cosmology."[38]

Before germs were discovered, disease was inevitably associated with many other causes. There was as yet no conventional reliable cognition that could challenge such postulations. The invention of microscopes and telescopes did not eliminate superficial causes of error but instead enhanced

---

36. Dalai Lama 2005, 3.

37. Zajonc 2004, 97.

38. Dalai Lama 2005, 80.

perception so that it became possible to impeach previously unimpeached conventional beliefs. What had been reasonably taken as knowledge about the cause of disease and the movement of the stars came to be understood as fiction. In this way, the philosopher of science Karl Popper sees science as an "*evolutionary process* in which hypotheses or conjectures are imaginatively proposed and tested in order to explain facts or to solve problems."[39]

As has been argued, this instability—this lack of *final* certainty about what constitutes knowledge—is not a lamentable quagmire.[40] Rather, it is exactly what makes evolutionary progress, both material and spiritual, possible. For whatever plausible purpose we have, we may seek improvements to the methods through which we pursue it and the beliefs associated with those methods. Even things that are very widely believed may come to be discredited through the further use, or amplification, of conventional epistemic instruments—that is to say, through better empirical evidence and/or better analysis.

Through a process of impeaching past beliefs and abandoning behaviors associated with such, we can refine ways of living—modes of practice—better suited to our situation, including our bodies, minds, and total environments. Apparently successful interactions with other living beings and the physical environment lead to assumptions or beliefs associated with a new way of acting. And these have verisimilitude, standing as fact unless discredited by some further deployment—or enhancement (through technology or non-ordinary power)—of the unimpaired observer's conventional faculties.

It is thus quite reasonable that the Dalai Lama, a scholar-yogi with truly profound insight into the teaching of Tsongkhapa, would advocate the refinement of knowledge—even when it supersedes scripture—through subsequent analysis and investigation. The gradual transformation of the mind, culminating in awakening, depends on the idea of progress, the possibility of improvement, as distinct from alternative Buddhist notions that we are all perfectly awakened already. The Dalai Lama understands that there is congruence between the scientific method and the successive refinement that takes place in Buddhist mind-training. In each case, we start with models or presumptions about how to proceed, what matters,

---

39. Zalta 2017.
40. Cowherds 2011, 71.

and how the world works—and these models are refined or superseded through subsequent insight or discovery.

By attentive conventional practice we can become gradually more skillful in acting to promote happiness. Concepts, models, ideas, stories, maps: they are never the world itself. But then again, there is never any natural way the world is just in itself, apart from some perspective upon it. All things are empty of such nature. So what we need, and what we can develop, are better models, stories more conducive to healing and transformation. Never idling in the swamp of popular opinion or custom, we can hone our ways of working as physicians, scientists, and spiritual teachers. We can become deeply attuned in our responses, knowing quickly which test to run, which question to pose to which student, what dose to give which patient, even though *all things are equally empty.*

Because *only empty things work.* It is *because* of emptiness—not despite it—that there are better and worse ways of doing things in terms of the outcomes we seek. As Tsongkhapa says:

> "All of this is devoid of essence,"
> and "From this arises that effect"—
> these two certainties complement
> each other with no contradiction at all.
> What is more amazing than this?
> What is more marvelous than this?[41]

41. Tsongkhapa, "In Praise of Dependent Origination," n.d., vv. 20–21ab.

2. Tsongkhapa and Candrakīrti on Uprooting Saṃsāra: The Twofold Object of the Identity View

Dechen Rochard

THE GREAT MASTER Jé Tsongkhapa made an enormous contribution to the study and practice of the Buddhadharma. Among the topics we are celebrating here is his contribution to Madhyamaka philosophy. It is evident that Jé Tsongkhapa closely followed Candrakīrti's commentaries on Nāgārjuna's Madhyamaka treatises. In this paper I discuss Tsongkhapa's interpretation of Candrakīrti's negation of the self, in particular his analysis of the object of the *identity view* (Skt. *satkāyadṛṣṭi*), what Tibetans call the "view of the perishable collection" (*'jig tshogs la lta ba*). Jé Tsongkhapa's interpretation of the object (*yul*)[1] of the identity view, based on Candrakīrti's presentation, is among his greatest contributions to the exegesis of Madhyamaka in Tibet and subsequently, through his followers, around the world.

Candrakīrti's Presentation

In *Entering the Middle Way (Madhyamakāvatāra)* 6.120, Candrakīrti introduces the negation of the self as the very path to liberation from suffering and its cause:

> Seeing with wisdom that all afflictions and faults without exception
> arise from the identity view,

---

1. The terms *yul* (Skt. *viṣaya*) and *dmigs pa* (Skt. *ālambana*) are used interchangeably by Candrakīrti in this context. The ambiguity of latter term, however, might be seen to have contributed to diverging interpretations by later commentators.

and having understood the self to be its object,
the yogin negates the self.[2]

nyon mongs skyon rnams ma lus 'jig tshogs la
lta las byung bar blo yis mthong gyur cing
bdag ni 'di yi yul du rtogs byas nas
rnal 'byor pa yis bdag ni 'gog par byed

This verse identifies the root cause of saṃsāra as the *identity view*. In his autocommentary, Candrakīrti describes the identity view as "an afflictive intelligence that grasps in a manner of thinking *me* or *mine*."[3] He explains its object and functioning:

> Its object (*dmigs pa*) is just the self because self-grasping has the self as its object (*yul*). Here, one who wishes to completely abandon all the afflictions and faults of saṃsāra must abandon the identity view, and one will abandon it by fully understanding the selflessness of the self; therefore, initially the yogin negates just the self. For, having negated it, the identity view is abandoned, and the afflictions and faults are thereby completely reversed. So the thorough analysis of the self is the method to attain liberation. Therefore the yogin initially scrutinizes just the self, asking: What is this so-called self that is the object of the identity view?[4]

Candrakīrti gives a very similar account in his *Clear Words* (*Prasannapadā*) when commenting on chapter 18 of Nāgārjuna's *Fundamental Verses on the Middle Way* (*Mūlamadhyamakakārikā*):

> Seeing that saṃsāra is rooted in the identity view and seeing that the object (*dmigs pa*) of the identity view is just the self, it is by way of not seeing the self that the identity view is aban-

---

2. Candrakīrti, *Madhyamakāvatāra*, 6.120. Pedurma 60:532. Also cited in Candrakīrti's *Prasannapadā*, where I refer to La Vallée Poussin's Sanskrit edition and incorporate de Jong's 1978 adjustments (La Vallée Poussin 1970, 340.8–11): *satkāyadṛṣṭiprabhavān aśeṣān kleśāṃś ca doṣāṃś ca dhiyā vipaśyan / ātmānam asyā viṣayaṃ ca buddhvā yogī karoty ātmaniṣedham eva //*.

3. Candrakīrti, *Madhyamakāvatārabhāṣya*. Pedurma 60:774.

4. Candrakīrti, *Madhyamakāvatārabhāṣya*. Pedurma 60:775.

doned. Seeing that all the afflictions and faults are reversed by abandoning that view, initially one must scrutinize just the self, asking: What is this so-called "self" that is the object (*yul*) of self-grasping?[5]

When we look at these two passages together, we can see that Candrakīrti equates the identity view with self-grasping. Likewise, he equates the object of the identity view with the object of self-grasping. He states here and elsewhere[6] that the self is the object of the identity view, just as it is of self-grasping. This differs from accounts given by certain other masters, such as Vasubandhu, who say in his *Treasury of Abhidharma Autocommentary* that the aggregates are the object of self-grasping.[7] Jé Tsongkhapa fully embraces the distinction between the interpretations of Candrakīrti and other masters. However, certain other commentators on Candrakīrti, such as Shākya Chokden, do not embrace this distinction and gloss Candrakīrti's *Entering the Middle Way Autocommentary* passage above as saying that the object of the identity view is the perishable collection of aggregates, as its Tibetan name suggests.[8] To understand what accounts for such a difference in interpretation of the object of the identity view, and what this difference entails, let us look at how the identity view is treated in other traditions.

What Is the Identity View?

All the Abhidharma traditions classify *satkāyadṛṣṭi* (Pali, *sakkāyadiṭṭhi*) as a mental factor—specifically, a mental affliction. The Theravāda tradition classifies it as a nonvirtuous mental factor, and specifically as a wrong view. The Sarvāstivāda tradition classifies it not as nonvirtuous but as

---

5. Candrakīrti, *Prasannapadā*. Pedurma 60.270. Skt. (La Vallée Poussin 1970, 340.13–15): *kāyadṛṣṭimūlakameva saṃsāramanupaśyamastasyāśca satkāyadṛṣṭerālambhanamātmānameva samanupaśyannātmānupalambhācca satkāyadṛṣṭiprahāṇaṃ tatprahāṇācca sarvakleśavyāvṛttiṃ samanupaśyana prathamataramātmānamevopaparīkṣate / ko 'yamātmā nāmeti yo 'haṃkāra-viṣayaḥ //.*

6. Candrakīrti, *Madhyamakāvatārabhāṣya*. Pedurma 60:783: *bdag dang bdag gi ba'i rnam par zhugs pa'i lta ba la 'jig tshogs la lta bar gsungs so zhes smra'o //.*

7. Vasubandhu, *Abhidharmakośabhāṣya*, chap. 9. Pedurma 79:905: *bdag tu 'dzin pa 'di'i yul gang zhig yin / yul ni phung po yin no //.*

8. Shākya mchog ldan, *Dbu ma rnam nges*, 263–64: *'o na 'jig tshogs la lta ba'i dmigs pa yang 'jig tshogs nyid yin pa la su yang mi rtsod pas / de dpyod mi dgos so //.*

neutral.[9] The Mahāyāna traditions, beginning with that of Asaṅga, consider *satkāyadṛṣṭi* to be ambiguous between an intellectually acquired *satkāyadṛṣṭi*, which is nonvirtuous, and an innate *satkāyadṛṣṭi*, which is neutral.[10] According to the Prāsaṅgika-Madhyamaka tradition, it is the innate *satkāyadṛṣṭi* that is the root obstacle to liberation, while its imprints obstruct omniscience, or complete enlightenment. Therefore the object as held by this mental factor is the one that the yogin negates.

Steven Collins notes that the Pali term *sakkāyadiṭṭhi* literally means "belief in a (really) existing body," and given that *body* stands here for all five aggregates upon which a person is imputed, he translates it as "personality belief."[11] Rupert Gethin describes it as "the view that the individual exists."[12] Bhikkhu Ñāṇamoli translates it as "the false view of individuality."[13] Bhikkhu Bodhi translates it as "identity view,"[14] and Paul Fuller follows him in this. Fuller presents a most extensive account of *view* (*diṭṭhi*) according to the Theravāda tradition and provides sources showing *sakkāyadiṭṭhi* to be the root of all wrong views and a fundamental cause of other mental afflictions, which is similar to the point made by Candrakīrti above.[15]

Bhikkhu Dhammajoti, in his extensive study of Sarvāstivāda Abhidharma, translates *satkāyadṛṣṭi* as "Self-view" and provides two etymologies of *satkāya* as follows:

> The Vaibhāṣika explains *sat* to mean "real/existent," and *kāya*, "accumulation." *Satkāya-dṛṣṭi*, therefore, refers to the view of a real Self superimposed on the impermanent *skandha*-s.... Vasubandhu, however, presents the Sautrāntika view which interprets *sat* as "perish"; accordingly, this view is the false belief with

---

9. Dhammajoti (2007, 51) cites the *Mahāvibhāṣāśāstra* (extant only in Chinese translation) as a source asserting *satkāyadṛṣṭi* to be neutral (*avyākṛta*) rather than unwholesome.

10. Schmithausen 1987, 148.

11. Collins 1982, 93.

12. Gethin 1998, 148.

13. Buddhaghosa 1991, 895.

14. Bodhi 2000, 2037.

15. Fuller 2005, 26.

regard to the "perishing accumulation".... The Tibetan rendering as *'jig tshogs la lta ba* reflects this interpretation.[16]

Richard Gombrich argues that the Pali Text Society's *Pali-English Dictionary* definition of *sakkāya* as "the body," or "individuality," or "identified with the five khandas," and so on does not fit the commentarial gloss of this term. Referring to fourteen sutta passages and their commentaries, Gombrich argues that the meaning of *sakkāya* changes and in some places is ambiguous. He arrives at identifying the meaning of *sakkāya* in terms of the notion of *sakkāyadiṭṭhi* in his final example, where it indicates grasping at permanence, and concludes:

> Here at last we clearly see that *sakkāya* is being interpreted as "the category 'existent,'" with "existent" implying permanence; existence as opposed to change, being as opposed to becoming.[17]

In this context, the phrase "the category 'existent'" refers to the Brahmanical notion of pure *being*, which, according to the Vedānta, is one of the three qualities of ultimate reality (the others are *consciousness* and *bliss*), as well as to the Upaniṣadic notion of permanent existence (and *existence* here could mean "self").[18] Gombrich argues that it is this notion of *existent* that the Buddha's teachings on the negation of *sakkāya* and the abandoning of *sakkāyadiṭṭhi* originally opposed. So it seems that *sakkāyadiṭṭhi* is not restricted to a personality view. This is an important point to consider when addressing Tsongkhapa's interpretation of Candrakīrti.

Peter Harvey, relying on Theravāda sources, draws attention to two types of belief in a self, one gross and one subtle, the former being a type of view and the latter being a type of conceit:

> The first is Self-identity view: to take any of the aggregates as (1) Self, (2) the property of Self, (3) in Self, or (4) containing Self. It

---

16. Dhammajoti 2007, 435–36. Citing the Ejima edition of the *Abhidharmakośabhāṣya* (281), Dhammajoti gives Vasubandhu as saying *ātma-dṛṣṭir ātmīya-dṛṣṭir vā satkāya-dṛṣṭiḥ / sīdatīti sat / cayaḥ kāyaḥ saṃgātaḥ skandha ityarthaḥ /*.

17. Gombrich 2003, 238.

18. Gombrich 2009, 64–65: "*ātman* is *brahman*," "*brahman* is existence," "existence, in this ideology, implies absence of change."

is to view something specific as "this am I" (S. III.128). . . . Second, there is a more deep-rooted "I am conceit" (*asmi-māna*), which remains even once a person becomes a Stream-enterer. This is a vague attitude of "I am" with respect to *all* of the aggregates, just as the scent belongs to the whole flower, not just to a particular part of it (S III.130).[19]

According to certain sources within the Theravāda tradition, the mental factor *view* (*diṭṭhi*) and the mental factor *conceit* (*māna*), while they are both accompanied by attachment (*lobha*), never accompany each other. So it seems that *asmimāna* and *sakkāyadiṭṭhi* are contradictory (in the Buddhist logical sense, where there is no shared basis). However, Fuller suggests another way of interpreting this situation:

> In developed Abhidhamma, conceit and view cannot occur in the same type of consciousness. This suggests that they are either completely incompatible, or that the two terms refer to the same processes. If the latter option is true, as I think it is, then we may imagine that right view, as the contemplation of rise and fall, continues the process of cleansing body, speech, and (primarily) mind, in the higher stages of the path. Wrong view, on the higher stages of the path, is the subtle conceit of selfhood. Right view is a contemplation which rids the mind of this conceit.[20]

Fuller supports his interpretation with detailed reference to Buddhaghosa's *Visuddhimagga* and other sources, noting that Buddhaghosa's *Sāratthappakāsinī* interprets "the notion 'I am' (*asmīti*) as the triple proliferation of craving, conceit, and views."[21] So, according to this interpretation, *asmimāna* in the developed Theravāda tradition is an instance of both conceit and view.

Other mental factors closely related to *satkāyadṛṣṭi* are grasping and ignorance. Fuller's interpretation rests on an intimate connection between view and grasping. He considers two well-established interpretations of

19. Harvey 2009, 268.
20. Fuller 2005, 102.
21. Fuller 2005, 119. See also Bodhi 2000, 1057n61.

views presented in the Theravāda tradition: the "opposition understanding," in which a right view corrects a wrong view, where only the latter is to be abandoned; and the "no-views understanding," in which all views, whether right or wrong, are considered unwholesome and to be abandoned. He suggests that neither of these interpretations, as ordinarily understood in terms of right and wrong doctrines, presents an accurate picture, and he argues for an alternative approach.[22] His thesis here—that wrong view is the grasping aspect of ignorance—is a further development of an approach previously expressed by Gethin:

> What all this implies is that (false) view is as much a matter of the psychology and emotional attitude of the person holding a view as it is of the formal content of the view. The Buddhist tradition recognizes that what is formally Buddhist theory can be grasped and held in a manner such that it constitutes wrong view.[23]

This point is crucially important and especially relevant to Jé Tsongkhapa's interpretation of Candrakīrti. It is the *manner of holding* the object that constitutes the identity view.

Jé Tsongkhapa's Interpretation of Candrakīrti

The above introduction to the identity view shows how open it is to interpretation. Candrakīrti's presentation of it seems to have inherited this trait, in that different Tibetan masters offer different characterizations of it. Jé Tsongkhapa's interpretation is penetrating and brilliant, for he does not negate the conventional self but negates the self as it is held by the identity view. What does this mean?

In *Illuminating the Intent*, his commentary on Candrakīrti's *Entering the Middle Way*, Tsongkhapa identifies the innate identity view as "an afflictive intelligence that, in a manner of thinking *me* or *mine*, grasps those two as inherently existent."[24] This is very close to Candrakīrti's own words (see above). However, it is noticeable that Tsongkhapa adds the term

22. Fuller 2005, 8.

23. Gethin 1997, 222.

24. Tsong kha pa, *Dgongs pa rab gsal*, 293.

inherently existent (rang bzhin gyis grub pa) and explicitly states that holding *me* or *mine* as inherently existent is the root of the problem. This is based on a passage in Candrakīrti's *Commentary on the Four Hundred Stanzas (Catuḥśatakaṭīkā)*, which Tsongkhapa quotes on more than one occasion:

> Regarding that, the so-called *self (bdag)* refers to an inherent nature *(rang bzhin)* of things that does not depend upon something else. Since that does not exist, the self does not exist. Understanding this in terms of the twofold division of persons and phenomena, there is the selflessness of persons and the self-lessness of phenomena.[25]

Here Candrakīrti employs the term *self* to refer to an inherent nature, and this plays a very influential role in Tsongkhapa's understanding of self-lessness. Indeed, this notion of *self* seems to coincide with the notion of *sakkāya* in the Pali canon, interpreted by Gombrich as "the category existent" or "intrinsic being" in the Brahmanical sense, as discussed above. Such an intrinsic nature, whose existence does not entirely depend on being imputed by thought or terminology, is the notion of *self* that is being negated by Candrakīrti—according to Tsongkhapa.

In his *Great Treatise on the Stages of the Path*, commenting on Candrakīrti's *Entering the Middle Way* 6.120, Tsongkhapa spells out two notions of self—one that exists and the other that does not:

> Of these two—the self considered to be just an inherently existent nature and the self considered to be the object of awareness merely thinking "I"—the former is the object of negation of ultimate analysis, and the latter is accepted conventionally and thus not negated. This shows that the object *(dmigs pa)* of the innate identity view is not negated. However, as it is held *(de'i rnam pa'i 'dzin stangs)* it is the inherently existent I, therefore it is not the case that this is not negated.[26]

---

25. Candrakīrti, *Catuḥśatakaṭīkā*, chap. 12. Pedurma 60:1381. Quoted in Tsong kha pa, *Legs bshad snying po*, 398–99, *Lam rim Chen mo*, 592, and *Dgongs pa rab gsal*, 116.
26. Tsong kha pa, *Lam rim chen mo*, 593.

In this passage Tsongkhapa distinguishes between the *object* (*dmigs pa / ālambana*) of the innate identity view, and the *aspect* (*rnam pa / ākāra*) of that view, which is the way that the object is held (*'dzin stangs*) by that mind. This is a distinction made by Candrakīrti himself. In *Clear Words*, at the beginning of the chapter analyzing the self, Candrakīrti says, "The existent appears in the aspect of reality to the spiritually immature."[27] This means that things appear as real (that is, as inherently existent) to ordinary beings. In the context of Candrakīrti's analysis of the self, the term *aspect* indicates the manner in which the object is cognized by the mind apprehending it. Then, based on Candrakīrti's distinction between the object and the aspect of the identity view, Tsongkhapa draws a more explicit distinction between two kinds of object of the identity view: the *focal object* (*dmigs pa'i yul*)[28] and the *held object* (*rnam pa'i yul / 'dzin stangs kyi yul*) (literally, the *object as held* or the *object as cognized*).

The striking point that Jé Tsongkhapa makes in the above passage is that "the object of the innate identity view is not negated." The term *object* here is highly ambiguous. In this context Tsongkhapa interprets it to mean the focal object of that view. He considers this to be the mere self, which is imputed on the aggregates. This focal object is not negated. What is negated is the held object of the identity view, which Tsongkhapa considers to be the self held to be inherently existent. This is the inherently existent self, which does not exist at all. Other masters, such as Shākya Chokden, accept a distinction between the focal object and the held object of the identity view, but they do not agree with what Tsongkhapa considers them to be. Shākya Chokden considers the focal object of the innate identity view to be the aggregates, and the held object of that view to be the mere self. Both Tsongkhapa and Shākya Chokden agree that the held object of the identity view is negated while the focal object of that view is not negated. But their accounts of what these objects are yield entirely different outcomes. Shākya Chokden interprets Candrakīrti to be denying even the conventional existence of the mere self, whereas Tsongkhapa interprets him to be denying the conventional existence of an inherently existent self.

---

27. Candrakīrti, *Prasannapadā*. Pedurma 60:270. Skt. (La Vallée Poussin 1970): 340.4: *sattattvākāreṇa pratibhāsate bālānāṃ //*.

28. Tsong kha pa, *Legs bshad snying po*, 404.

Jé Tsongkhapa's differentiation between the focal object and the held object of the identity view is the main point that I wish to highlight in this paper. It is a most useful tool for understanding the crucial quotation from Candrakīrti's *Entering the Middle Way Autocommentary* cited above: "One . . . must abandon the identity view, and one will abandon it by fully understanding the selflessness of the self; therefore, initially the yogin negates just the self." Tsongkhapa gives the following explanation of these sentences:

> [Candrakīrti] says that one abandons [the identity view] through reversing its way of grasping by realizing the selflessness, or non-inherent existence, of the self that is its object.[29]

This passage contains two occurrences of the word *self.* Each has a different meaning. Given that Tsongkhapa glosses *selflessness* as "noninherent existence," the occurrence of *self* in the compound *selflessness* refers to inherent existence. In the case of the solitary word *self,* this refers to the self that is the object of the identity view. Now, is this the focal object or the held object of that view? If it were the held object of the identity view— that is, the inherently existent self—then the phrase "the selflessness of the self" would mean that the inherently existent self does not inherently exist. This is absurd and would be useless for one's meditation practice. Instead, according to Tsongkhapa, it is the focal object of the identity view. Inherent existence is negated on the basis of the mere self, which conventionally exists, not on the basis of an inherently existent self, which does not exist at all.

The crucial understanding that purifies the identity view is a *non-seeing* (Tib. *ma dmigs pa*) of inherent existence. I suggest that this notion of inherent existence is best understood as *inherent identity.* Although things seem to bear an identity from their own side, nothing does so. When such an identity is sought, it cannot be found. According to Tsongkhapa's understanding, ultimate reality is the absence of inherent identity, and it is due to perceiving this reality directly that the mental afflictions and faults of saṃsāra are gradually and completely purified. In the *Clear Words* passage cited above, Candrakīrti's words *ma dmigs pa* indicate that

---

29. Tsong kha pa, *Lam rim chen mo,* 593.

the object-not-seen is not an ordinary kind of object. It is an object such that its nonappearance to the meditator's mind reveals ultimate reality. One does not experience that kind of effect by not seeing a mere ordinary object. The object or appearance in question obscures ultimate reality and pervades every ordinary perception of sentient beings. Sentient beings do not have any mundane perceptual experience that is not influenced by the subtle propensity of grasping at inherent identity; and we have no way of even noticing it—unless we are yogins who have directly realized selflessness. So, the *non-seeing* in this context is not just the non-seeing of the mere self. It is the non-seeing of the false appearance of inherent identity. When this is not seen, it alters the understanding of the perceiver completely.

If one adheres to Jé Tsongkhapa's interpretation of Candrakīrti and engages in analytical meditation practice accordingly, then one will arrive safely at this understanding. For at the end of this ultimate analysis, one will arrive at the nonperception of inherent identity and see its mere absence. Conversely, by engaging in other approaches to analyzing the self, while one may succeed in not finding the self, one might instead find the aggregates, which would be the perception of yet another mundane object. A perception of the aggregates would not have the capacity to remove from one's mindstream the obstructions to liberation and to omniscience, for the aggregates would still appear to bear their identity from their own side. There are different ways of interpreting the renowned and much-cited teaching given by a venerable nun disciple of the Buddha:

> Just as we refer to a chariot
> based on the group of parts,
> so, based on the aggregates,
> we have the convention "sentient being."[30]

Candrakīrti's interpretation is especially profound. The self and the aggregates are mutually dependently imputed, and neither bears its

---

30. Candrakīrti, *Madhyamakāvatārabhāṣya*. Pedurma 60:784. This verse is attributed to the nun Arhantī Śailā in chapter 9 of Vasubandhu's *Abhidharmakośabhāṣya* and to Bhikkhunī Vajirā in *Saṃyutta-nikāya* 1.10 (Bodhi 2000, 230). On the difference in attribution, see Bingenheimer 2008, 5–26.

identity from its own side. This in itself is an analytical meditation. Using this method the yogin eventually perceives the absence of inherent identity with a mind of meditative wisdom. This perception is what gradually removes the innate identity view, along with its seeds and imprints, from the yogin's mindstream.

Inappropriate Attention

Meditation on selflessness, or identitylessness, has the effect of lessening one's disturbing emotions in daily life. According to Tsongkhapa's account, the identity view holds its object in a distorted manner—as bearing its identity from its own side—which generates inappropriate attention and unrealistic projections. Geshé Lhundub Sopa explains:

> First there is a mind of ignorance that holds the object wrongly—as inherently existent. Then there is a mind of inappropriate attention that holds the object in a further wrong way—as attractive, ugly, and so on. Then other mental afflictions arise on the basis of inappropriate attention. Seeing things as ugly usually gives rise to aversion and hatred; seeing things as beautiful usually gives rise to attachment and desire.[31]

The way of holding the object determines whether any action following from it is virtuous or nonvirtuous, as Geshé Sopa further explains:

> What is the difference between love, which is a virtuous mind, and attachment, which is not? . . . If desire arises on the basis of inappropriate attention, which holds its object in a distorted way, then it is attachment, which is a nonvirtuous consciousness. In contrast, if desire arises on the basis of a mind that holds its object correctly, then it is a virtuous consciousness. So the difference between them concerns whether we hold the object correctly.[32]

31. Sopa with Rochard 2017, 210.
32. Sopa with Rochard 2017, 211.

This is how the identity view continuously propagates saṃsāra. It holds its object in a distorted manner—as inherently existent, where the object is cognized to exist as it appears, appearing to bear its identity from its own side. From this kind of grasping, other mental afflictions arise. His Holiness the Dalai Lama has said, "We take for granted that everything is there objectively: good is good, bad is bad, from the side of the object. So then inappropriate attention arises. Based on that, attachment, hatred, and so on arise. That is very clear." Later he adds, "My great friend Aaron Beck, according to his experience over several decades, observed that when we develop anger, the object of our anger appears very negative—and 90 percent of that negativity is mental projection."[33] His Holiness also reports that some of his quantum physicist friends, having taken to heart their discovery that nothing can be found objectively, witnessed a reduction of their mental afflictions as a result of this understanding over a period of time. I find this to be a most interesting observation.

However, it remains to be seen how much connection there might be between a scientific analysis of the object under scrutiny and a philosophical analysis of the object under scrutiny, where the former is a search for the object itself or its parts and the latter is a search for the object's identity based on its parts, and how the effects of each type of search might relate to those of the other. It is beyond the scope of the present paper to address this point with the attention it deserves, though it could be the subject of further research. In any case, the reduction and eventual removal of all mental afflictions along with their traces is the final goal of practicing the Buddhist path. Gradual removal of mental afflictions from an individual's mindstream may be regarded as the main tool for arriving at a stable state of inner peace and, if others successfully accomplish this too, a corresponding state of peace in the world.

33. Personal communication, November 23, 2015; trans. Dechen Rochard.

3. Thinking Beyond Thought: Tsongkhapa and Mipham on the Conceptualized Ultimate[1]

Jay L. Garfield

I N TIBETAN DISCUSSIONS of the two truths, the nature of our knowledge of the ultimate truth leads to interesting epistemological and ontological problems. This is particularly the case in Geluk discussions, inflected as they are by both Dharmakīrti's and Candrakīrti's epistemologies, which, however different they are, agree on the necessity of epistemic warrant for genuine knowledge and on the appropriateness of particular epistemic warrants or instruments to their respective objects of knowledge. Given that the ultimate truth must be a possible object of knowledge, there must be a *pramāṇa* by means of which it is known. But only buddhas or bodhisattvas on the path of seeing or above are capable of directly perceiving the ultimate truth. So for the rest of us, our knowledge of the ultimate is conceptual and hence mediated by inference (*rjes dpag, anumāna*) and so must be conceptual in nature. But the ultimate transcends all concepts, conceptions, and signs. And so it would appear that we can know nothing about it. But that would suggest that we can't even know this, or that there are two truths to be known, including one about which we can know nothing.

Moreover, the idea that ordinary beings and lower-level bodhisattvas cannot know emptiness at all would wreak havoc with Geluk understandings of *lam rim* (the graduated path), and of the role of study on the path, according to which our ability to verify our apparent perception of the ultimate depends upon the concordance of the object of direct perception in meditative equipoise with the understanding achieved in conceptual

---

1. This essay was previously published in *Philosophy East and West* 70, no. 2 (2020): 1–16. Reprinted here with permission.

47

meditation and in subsequent realization (*bcad shes*). This raises important questions: Is the object of inferential insight into the ultimate the ultimate truth itself or merely some surrogate? If it is the ultimate, since the ultimate realized by buddhas and by bodhisattvas in advanced meditative equipoise transcends all conception but can in some sense be known conceptually, are there two ultimates or one? If two, what is their relationship to one another? If conceptual realization grasps only a surrogate, given that that surrogate is deceptive, is it knowledge at all? And if so, in what sense?

The rubric through which these questions are addressed by Geluk scholars and their interlocutors (such as Gorampa Sönam Sengé and Taktsang Loden Sherab) relies on the distinction between the *don dam rnam grangs ma yin pa* and the *don dam rnam pa* (sometimes *rnam grangs ma yin pa'i don dam* and *rnam grangs pa'i don dam*) or the "uncategorized vs. categorized ultimate." These terms are sometimes translated as the "non-nominal vs. nominal ultimate" or as the "conceptualized vs. nonconceptualized ultimate," or as the "figurative or metaphorical ultimate vs. the genuine or literal ultimate."

As this set of pairs of terms indicates, it is hard to find a precise English translation for *rnam grangs* in this context. But the family of options on which various translators have settled helps us to fix on the relevant semantic range. The general idea is this: The *categorized* is that which is apprehended conceptually, that which is seen in terms of sets of distinctions or, as we might put it in the language of Sellarsian epistemology, that which is *seen as*;[2] the *uncategorized* is that which is apprehended in the absence of the drawing of distinctions, the applications of concepts, or that which is merely *seen,* not seen *as* anything, not verbalized. In this discussion, I will consistently use *categorized* and *uncategorized ultimate* to translate *rnam grangs pa'i don dam* and *rnam grangs ma yin pa'i don dam,* respectively, unless in direct quotation from scholars using alternative vocabulary.[3]

Here I explore the resources that this distinction and the accounts grounded thereon provide for an understanding of the distinction between conceptual and nonconceptual knowledge of ultimate truth and for an

2. We leave aside here the vexed question of just *what* it might be seen as.

3. The Tibetan vocabulary is grounded in Bhāviveka's distinction between the *aparyaya-paramārtha* and the *paryayaparamārtha* introduced in *Tarkajvālā,* but Tibetans are unanimous in urging that their distinctions are not Bhāviveka's, as that would run the risk of admitting that their position is in fact a *rang rgyud pa* (Svātantrika) position.

account of ultimate truth and its role in epistemology more generally. I will begin with an exploration of the Geluk position as developed by Tsongkhapa and his commentators and will then consider responses to that position by Mipham Rinpoché and Bötrul from the Nyingma perspective. I will conclude with some reflections on what we learn from this literature about rival Tibetan understandings of the relation between conceptual and nonconceptual knowledge.

The topic is of interest not only because it occupies so much of the attention of so many of Tibet's most eminent philosophers but because it focuses questions about the relation between the conceptual and the nonconceptual in the context of the most important and most recondite kind of knowledge recognized in the Tibetan Buddhist tradition—knowledge of the ultimate enabled by ultimate *pramāṇas* (that is, epistemic instruments capable of giving access to ultimate truth)—and so raises questions about the role of direct perception and conceptual understanding in realization. We will see that examination of these issues gives us more reason to believe that paradoxical understandings of the ultimate are the most rational understandings and the only way to avoid a dismal mysticism about ultimate reality.

The Geluk Position

Tsongkhapa argues (2002 and 2006) for a particularly strong understanding of the identity of the two truths and therefore for a particularly intimate connection between knowledge of the ultimate and knowledge of the conventional—that to understand the ultimate is to understand dependent origination and, hence, to understand the conventional. He takes the basis of division of the two truths to be objects of knowledge: To know the conventional truth is to know dependently originated phenomena; to know the ultimate truth is to know the emptiness of those phenomena. While conventional and ultimate phenomena are not different *phenomena extensionally*, they are, in this view, different intentionally, just as Hesperus and Phosphorus are extensionally, but not intensionally identical.[4]

In the special insight (*lhag mthong*) section of the *Great Treatise on the*

---

4. *Ngo bog cig la ldog pa tha dad.* Also see Cowherds 2011, Thakchoe 2007, and Garfield 2015 for more on this issue.

Stages of the Path (*Lam rim chen mo*), Tsongkhapa argues that the basis of division of the categorized versus the uncategorized ultimate is not objects of knowledge (*shes bya*) but kinds of cognitive states (*blo*). That is, whereas the two truths are divided based on objects of knowledge—with the conventional comprising dependently arisen phenomena and the ultimate comprising the emptiness of those phenomena, regardless of the nature of the cognitive state or status of the subject apprehending them—in the case of the distinction between the categorized and uncategorized ultimate, he argues, we are distinguishing not between two distinct objects of knowledge but between two distinct modes of subjectivity in reference to a single object—namely, *emptiness,* the ultimate truth.

Tsongkhapa is adamant that there is a single ultimate in the objective sense,[5] although there are two distinct modes of apprehension, one conceptual and one nonconceptual, and that the latter is the goal. Nonetheless, it is crucial to his framework that each is served by *pramāṇa*, and that each constitutes genuine, nondeceptive insight into ultimate truth. In the *Great Treatise,* referring directly to Bhāviveka's distinction, he says:

> Commenting on this, in his *Blaze of Reasons* [Bhāviveka] says:
>
> > [Ultimate] means that which is concordant with (*mthun pa*) the ultimate. Because that ultimate exists for a wisdom that is concordant with direct knowledge of the ultimate, it is said to be concordant with the ultimate.
>
> When we say that something "does not exist ultimately" or "is "nonexistent ultimately," it has [this meaning], because that same text says:
>
> > *Qualm:* The ultimate is beyond all awarenesses, but the refutation of an essence of things is in the realm of letters. Thus, would not the refutation be nonexistent for that reason?
> >
> > *Reply:* There are two types of ultimate. One of these operates without conceptual activity; it is supramundane, stainless, and without elaborations. The second operates

---

5. Remembering that this single object is apprehended by two very different kinds of subjective cognitive states.

with conceptual activity and is concordant with the collections of merit and wisdom; it is called "sublime wisdom in the world," and it does involve elaborations. Here we hold this latter to be the qualifier in the thesis "does not exist ultimately," and so there is no fallacy.

> Take this as referring to wisdom based on study and reflection that properly analyzes reality and to consciousnesses above that; it does not refer only to a noble being's post-equipoise condition.[6]

Bhāviveka, using the language of *concordance* (*mthun pa*) to refer to the categorized ultimate, suggests, at least in Tsongkhapa's reading, that the two kinds of apprehension of ultimate truth agree with respect to their object. The distinction between them must then be on the subjective side. And so Bhāviveka continues (with Tsongkhapa's agreement) by explaining that when explicit claims are made about the ultimate, one is engaging with the categorized ultimate; when one engages nonconceptually, one engages with the uncategorized ultimate. Since these two kinds of apprehension engage with the same object, there is nothing wrong with understanding the claims made about the categorized ultimate to be true of the uncategorized ultimate, although it cannot be apprehended in terms of those claims or the concepts they implicate.

In his *Ocean of Reasoning*, Tsongkhapa draws this distinction explicitly in the context of the discussion of the nature of ultimate truth in the commentary on *Fundamental Verses on the Middle Way* (*Mūlamadhyamakakārikā*) 24.9:

> According to other treatises, the ultimate is twofold: the primary [noncategorized] ultimate truth and the secondary [categorized] ultimate truth. For instance, Jñānagarbha's *Distinguishing the Two Truths* (*Satyadvayavibhaṅga*) says,
>
> > Since the refutation of such things as arising
> > is consistent with reality,
> > we assert that it is ultimate.

---

6. Tsongkhapa 2002, 220–21, citing the *Tarkajvālā*.

And Kamalaśīla's *Light of the Middle Way* (*Madhyamakāloka*) says:

> Since *nonarising* is consistent with the ultimate, it is called "ultimate." But it is not actual [*yang dag*]. The actual is that ultimate which is free from all fabrication.
>
> Here "fabrication" refers not only to the fabrication that is the object of negation through reasoning but also to the fabrication of appearance. The freedom from fabrication of appearance is the vanishing of all fabrication of dualistic appearances in the perspective of one directly perceiving reality.[7]

Here Tsongkhapa emphasizes both the fact that conceptual understandings of the ultimate, such as those deriving from Prāsaṅgika arguments, are understandings of the ultimate itself and not of something else, *and* that the *actual*—that is, the actual *realization*—of the ultimate is a realization free from fabrication, including not only the fabrication of subject-object duality but also the fabrication of appearance—that is, the imputation of conceptual categories to the object of perception. Once again, we have a single object but two distinct modes of apprehension of it; each is correct, but one is more salutary than the other.

The challenge to this framework is twofold. First, we require an account of what it is to apprehend and to *know* without the application of conceptual categories. Second, we require an account of the *correctness* of conceptual apprehension despite its implication in fabrication. We will see that it is the latter issue that preoccupies Tsongkhapa's critics. Tsongkhapa then turns to the relation between the categorized ultimate and conventional truth, emphasizing that while they are distinct with respect to their objects, they are intimately related:

> However, in the case of the emptiness that is the negation—that is, the internal negation—of the ultimate arising of the person and the aggregates, the bases of emptiness must appear to conventional authoritative cognition, such as a visual consciousness that sees things directly. Therefore it appears to a dualistic

---

7. Tsongkhapa 2006, 495.

appearance from the perspective of the cognizing mind that sees it directly but does not appear without dualistic appearance. Therefore it is a secondary ultimate, but it is a genuine conventional truth. . . .

Through this argument, one should understand that the objects perceived through the wisdom through which the Buddha perceives empirical phenomena and the object posited through the wisdom of the other āryas in the post-meditative state, which are perceived through internal negation as illusion-like, are also secondary (categorized) ultimates.[8]

The point here is that when one perceives emptiness as the categorized (secondary) ultimate, one perceives it as the emptiness of conventional phenomena. That requires that conventional phenomena are apprehended by conventional reliable cognition (*pramāṇa*), and as their emptiness and their dependently originated status are one and the same, their emptiness appears to the same conventional reliable cognition.

While that might appear to be inconsistent with Tsongkhapa's commitment to the division of the two truths on the basis of objects of knowledge, and his commitment to conventional *pramāṇas* for conventional phenomena and ultimate *pramāṇas* for ultimate phenomena, it is not. The ontological union of the two truths entails that ultimate truth is in an important sense identical to the conventional. Moreover, Tsongkhapa asserts that the *secondary*—or *categorized*—ultimate is also genuine conventional truth; the uncategorized, he maintains, transcends all convention.

But this entails neither that the uncategorized and the categorized ultimates are extensionally distinct nor that the uncategorized ultimate is not in any sense identical to the conventional. This is because he also argues that even the uncategorized ultimate is identical to the conventional *extensionally (ngo po gcig)*, although distinct *intensionally (ldog pa tha dad)*. This preserves the two bases of division—objects of knowledge for the two truths and subjects for the two classifications of the ultimate—while preserving the identity of the two truths. The distinction is epistemological while the identity is ontological. The categorized ultimate is the bridge: it is identical in object with, but subjectively distinct from, the uncategorized

---

8. Tsongkhapa 2006, 495–96.

ultimate; and it is subjectively identical with, but distinct in object from, the genuine conventional truth.

Tsongkhapa explains this idea further in *Illuminating the Intent*. Here he is commenting on Candrakīrti's analogy of floaters in the visual field of someone afflicted by ophthalmia for conventional truth and the absence of the floaters ("falling hairs" in the Sanskrit and Tibetan traditions) as analogous to the emptiness of intrinsic nature:

> [Candrakīrti's use of the ophthalmia analogy indicates] only the listener's failure to realize exactly what is explained; it does not rule out the listener's conceptual realization of the nonexistence of hair. . . .
>
> Although the explanation of ultimate truth through an analogy does not lead to its realization in the way ultimate truth is seen by those free from the affliction of the cloud of ignorance, this does not mean that Candrakīrti accepts reality as nonrealizable in a general sense.
>
> Ultimate truth is not ineffable, for definite scriptural texts and their verbal descriptions do embody its profound meanings. Furthermore it is not the case that ultimate truth is unrealizable by the mind associating with verbal descriptions. Therefore every single statement explaining the meaning of reality as beyond the scope of consciousness and verbal description must be understood in the same light.[9]

This is a very helpful passage for understanding Tsongkhapa's insistence that the categorized ultimate must be taken seriously *as ultimate truth*. Suppose I suffer from the relevant ophthalmia and go to see the doctor. When my ophthalmologist explains to me that there really are no falling hairs in the air around me and that I am simply suffering from an illusion due to injury to my retina, I both *come to know* that there are no such hairs and *fail to stop seeing them*. Only after the surgery (I hope) will I stop seeing them altogether. But the transformation effected by the surgery is a transformation of my subjectivity not of my cognitive attitude toward the rel-

---

9. Tsong kha pa, *Dgongs pa rab gsal*, 196; translated in Thakchoe 2007, 84–85, and Tsongkhapa 2021a, 248.

evant object of knowledge (the absence of hairs.) I already *knew* that there are no hairs; otherwise, I would not seek treatment. Only later did I come to *see* the world without hairs.

It follows, Tsongkhapa argues, that when my ophthalmologist said that it was my retina, not the environment, that was the problem, she spoke the *truth*. Even if I could not *see* that there are no hairs, I could *believe* what she said and so consent to the surgery. Once the surgery was completed and perception delivers to me a world that accords completely with what she said, I come to *know directly* that which I once merely *knew inferentially,* and moreover, what I knew only inferentially accords with what I now see to be the case perceptually. By analogy, Tsongkhapa insists that ultimate truth is expressible; when we say or think things about it, we are in the position of the patient prior to surgery—correct, but not yet affirmed in our correctness by perception, knowing only discursively. Part of what we know about it is that it is inexpressible, but we can know that conceptually; so, to say that it is inexpressible is, paradoxically, to express something ultimately true.[10]

Drakpa Shedrup (1675–1748), in his commentary on Tsongkhapa's *Essence of Eloquence*, clarifies this point nicely:

> We can distinguish between the categorized and the uncategorized ultimate in terms of how they are expressed in language. The categorized ultimate is twofold: the objective ultimate and the subjective ultimate. The first is like the emptiness of the sprout, which has an illusory appearance. The second is like the reliable inferential cognition that ascertains that emptiness. These two are both called "ultimate," but this is just a designation, and they are not actual ultimates.
>
> One can also distinguish between an objective and a subjective uncategorized ultimate in term of how it is expressed in language. The first is emptiness, and so is the ultimate. It is just as it is: emptiness, the consummate, the absolute truth, the same as

---

10. There is another issue lurking here, that of paradox in the ultimate. To be fair, Tsongkhapa, because of his allegiance to Dharmakīrti's logic, never countenances the possibility of true contradictions. Nonetheless, as a follower of Candrakīrti, he is certainly committed to paradoxes of this kind, even if he does not acknowledge that. See Garfield and Priest 2003; Deguchi, Garfield, and Priest 2013; and Garfield 2015.

the dharmadhātu. The second is the mental continuum of one
on the path of learning that directly realizes emptiness like the
wisdom of realization. This is said by some to be truly called the
noncategorized ultimate, but it is not. (362)[11]

Drakpa Shedrup argues that there is no difference in *object* between the
categorized and noncategorized ultimate; rather, the difference lies in its
mode of appearance. It is emptiness in each case, although in the case of
the categorized ultimate, it appears in an illusory fashion. The uncategorized ultimate is emptiness itself; the categorized is, on the object side, that
emptiness as it appears to a mundane subject, and on the subject side, like
the premises and inferences by means of which we come to know it. The
consciousness of one directly apprehending emptiness is called an *uncategorized ultimate* by courtesy, but, he emphasizes, it is not the actual ultimate but only a mode of apprehension of it. It is, however, a mode free from
illusory appearance, and hence the appellation. In any case, the final goal of
practice is not the realization of a *new object of knowledge* but the *transformation of subjectivity*; the transformation from inferential to direct awareness, and from the apprehension of emptiness with an illusory appearance
to an apprehension without that appearance.[12]

We should note several important consequences of Tsongkhapa's

11. My translation from Co ne Grags pa bshad sgrub, *Legs bshad snying po*, 362 (print edition)
384 (BDRC digital edition). The text occurs as follows: *sgras brjod rigs kyi sgo nas dbye na/ rnam
grangs pa'i don dam dang / rnam grangs ma yin pa'i don dam bden pa gnyis/ dang po la/ mthun
pa'i yul dang / yul can don dam bden pa gnyis/ dang po ni/ myu gu bden stong sgyu ma bzhin du
snang ba'i cha lta bu/ gnyis pa ni/ de rtogs pa'i rjes dpag tshad ma lta bu ste/ 'di gnyis la don dam
bden pa zhes btags pa tsam ma gtogs/ de dgnos ni min no// rnam grangs ma yin pa'i don dam bden
pa la yang sgras brjod tshul gyis dbye na/ yul don dam bden pa dang / yul can don dam bden pa
gnyis/ dang po ni/ stong nyid lta bu ste/ don dam bden pa/ ji lta ba/ stong nyid/ yongs grub/ yang
dag mtha'/ chos dbyings rnams don gcig// nyis pa ni/ slob pa'i rgyud kyi stong pa nyid mngon sum
du rtogs pa'i ye shes lta bu ste/ 'di rnam grangs ma yin pa'i don dam dngos yin zhe ga cig bzhed kyang
/ don dam dngos ni min no//*.

12. It is also worth noting the affinities of Grags pa bshad grub's views to Yogācāra thought as
articulated in the seventh chapter of the *Unraveling the Intent Sūtra* (*Saṃdhinirmocanasūtra*)
and in Vasubandhu's *Commentary on Distinguishing the Middle from the Extremes* (*Madhyānta-
vibhāgabhāṣya*), according to which the consummate nature (*pariniṣpanna / yongs su grub pa*)
is regarded as the ultimate in contradistinction to the dependent nature (*paratantra / gzhan
dbang*)—which is also taken to be reality as it is—because it is an object of purification by
observation, a foundation of the so-called progressive model of the three natures.

account at this point before considering the positions of his critics. First, his account explains the role of conception and language in the process of realization. They are, he says, more than mere ladders to be cast aside. Language and thought can truly characterize ultimate reality, even if ultimate reality is characterized as uncharacterizable. Setting aside Tsongkhapa's aversion to paradox, we note simply that he has the clarity of mind to see that one cannot back away from true assertions about the nature of reality, or undermine the accuracy of a position to which one subscribes, without undermining one's own cogency and claim to correctness. To deny the correctness of the Madhyamaka texts, in Tsongkhapa's view, would be to give up not just on conceptuality but also on the fact that nonconceptual thought directly perceives the ultimate.

Second, as Drakpa Shedrup notes, Tsongkhapa draws the distinction between the categorized and the uncategorized in terms of the distinction between inference and perception. This distinction is marked both in the epistemological (*pramāṇavāda*) tradition of Dignāga and Dharmakīrti and in the more Madhyamaka-inflected epistemology of Candrakīrti, each of which informs Geluk epistemology. But Tsongkhapa is not simply following an Indian epistemological tradition; he is working out how we can ever be warranted in our understanding of an ultimate truth that cannot be conceptualized since our own epistemic activity is always conceptual. This requires a cogent understanding of a non-categorical mode of apprehension, an idea that may seem mystical but need not be—although we will see that certain of Tsongkhapa's Tibetan critics take it in that direction.

Categorical apprehension on this view is simply inferential, discursive apprehension, mediated by explicit judgment. Uncategorized apprehension, then, is perceptual apprehension; spontaneous preconceptual engagement. Western philosophers since Kant and Buddhist philosophers from Sautrāntika on up both argue that perception of the phenomena we experience is always conceptually mediated; to perceive is to perceive-as, and to perceive-as is to mobilize concepts. Nonetheless, there is a clear difference between perception and inference, and Tsongkhapa's citation of Candrakīrti's example makes that plain. To perceive is to come to believe in what one perceives without thinking, without inference (even in cases where one knows that one is deceived). It is not to believe *that* that in which one believes spontaneously is actual. Inference begins with the data of perception but then involves the mediation of purely conceptual thought. Just being told that my eyes are bad doesn't get me to stop seeing the floaters, even though it gets me to stop believing in them. By locating the uncategorized ultimate as akin to perception *as opposed to inference* in that sense, Tsongkhapa ratchets down the mystical understanding of the nonconceptual, reducing it to the spontaneous, as opposed to the deliberate. The uncategorized ultimate is, then, simply the ultimate seen spontaneously; the categorized is the same ultimate understood conceptually but not really seen; believed-that, but not believed-in.

The Late Nyingma Critique

The Nyingma scholar Ju Mipham Rinpoché (1846–1912) takes a very different position, more sharply distinguishing the categorized from the uncategorized ultimate. In his view, the categorized ultimate is ultimate in name only, a mere simulacrum of the ultimate, referred to as ultimate only by analogy with the genuine, uncategorized ultimate. In *Speech of Delight* he writes:

> To begin with, it may be said that origination occurs at a conventional level, within the domain of the words and thoughts of learning and reflection, but that ultimately, there is no arising. When two modes are paired in this way, the latter is the categorized ultimate. Because it is categorized in the correspondence with its partner, relative existence, and because it pertains to the category of the ultimate, it is called *categorized*. This is what is categorized as the partner to the relative when speaking of the two truths.
>
> Since it is merely an entrance point that accords with the final ultimate truth, and since familiarization with this can overcome the apprehension of entities that is due to the habitual tendencies that have solidified since the beginning of time, it should be understood that this is the ultimate, and that this is also a perspective from which the claim of no origination is positive. One should know that even when having perfected the investigation

into this, it is no more than a way of having certainty during the ensuing attainment.

In terms of the final abiding way of authenticity, the deduction of no origination based on origination is mere mental other—exclusion, a mere conceptual reflection. Beyond all extremes of origination, no origination, and so forth, and leaving all objects of word and thought behind, the meaning perceived by the stainless wakefulness of the meditative equipoise of the noble ones is the unsurpassable uncategorized ultimate. From this perspective, no claim whatsoever is made.

Since the categorized ultimate is near to and in accord with this, it belongs to the category of the ultimate and is given the name the *according ultimate*.[13]

Here Mipham says that the categorized ultimate is a mere concept, not reality. It is not placed on the subject side, as it is for Tsongkhapa, as a distinct perspective on ultimate truth but is rather an object—a conceptual reflection or a universal—that is called *ultimate* only by courtesy of its proximity to the actual ultimate.[14] It is not *authentic*. It is not a *true* perspective on reality. He emphasizes the gulf between the categorized and the uncategorized ultimate in *Lion's Roar*:

> The context such as the analysis whether the ultimate is within the domain of mind or not refers to the uncategorized ultimate; the categorized ultimate is not the expressed meaning because the categorized ultimate is in the context of a novice progressively engaging in emptiness from merely a conceptual perspective. As such, the categorized ultimate cannot roam in the territory of a mind like the nonconceptual meditative wisdom of a sublime one, for which duality has subsided, like a beggar that has no power to sit on the universal emperor's throne.

13. Mipham 2004, 63–65.

14. "Proximity" here denotes, as Mipham makes clear, not that the categorized ultimate is even *like* the uncategorized but rather that it is an "entrance point" in contemplation and meditation that makes it possible to realize the uncategorized eventually.

Duckworth comments:

> The categorized ultimate concerns a perspective within a conceptual framework. In the content of discursive analysis, the categorized ultimate is known within that framework, where there is no such framework demarcating the uncategorized ultimate. In this way, Mipam portrays a provisional nature to conceptual categories.[15]

We can understand what drives Mipham in this direction. One can fairly ask about ultimate truth: Is it correctly captured by conceptual categories or not? Is there a truthmaker for claims about ultimate truth or not? Whereas Tsongkhapa unwillingly and unwittingly walks into paradox by answering both yes and no to the first and embraces the unity of the two truths by answering the second question in the affirmative, Mipham dodges explicit paradox by retreating to mysticism by answering a flat no to the first, and divorces the ultimate from the conventional by answering the second in the negative.

By taking the fact that the ultimate transcends all conception and expression to mean that no conception or expression can possibly be true of the ultimate (and therefore *denying* that nonetheless conception and expression *is* true of it), Mipham must render the categorized ultimate entirely conventional and, hence, a different object from the uncategorized ultimate. It therefore is entitled to the label merely in virtue of its similarity to, or utility in approaching, the genuine ultimate. Since nothing can be said of the genuine ultimate, no statement about it can be true, and so everything in the categorized ultimate is simply false. The contrast with Tsongkhapa's position is stark.

Bötrul (ca. 1900–1959) develops Mipham's views further. In *Distinguishing the Views and Philosophies* he writes:

> The two ultimate valid cognitions are:
> those that analyze the categorized in the uncategorized.
> The two conventional valid cognitions are:
> valid cognitions of confined perception and purity.

---

15. Duckworth 2008, 31–32.

> The Lord Mipam elucidated these delineations
> in accord with the quintessential instructions of the school of early
>   translations
> and the intended meaning of sūtras, tantras, and śāstras
> in the elegant discourse *Sword of Insight*.
>
> The categorized valid cognition analyzing the ultimate
> establishes the temporary categorized ultimate;
> the valid cognition that analyzes the uncategorized
> establishes the consummate uncategorized.
>
> The conventional valid cognition of confined perception
> establishes the mode of appearance—the impure relative;
> the conventional valid cognition of purity
> establishes the mode of reality—the pure relative.[16]

Here we see Bötrul distinguishing between the *temporary* categorized ulti-mate and the *consummate* (*yongs su grub pa*).[17] The objects themselves are distinct, and the *pramāṇa* that gives us access to the categorized gives us no knowledge of the uncategorized.

> Our tradition asserts that the categorized ultimate is
> an emptiness that is a negation of constructed extremes only par-
>   tially, and that
> the uncategorized ultimate is
> free from all subtle and gross constructed extremes.[18]

Here Bötrul explicitly distinguishes between the categorized and the uncategorized from the side of the object. The categorized is a kind of emp-tiness, but an emptiness that is not free from all extremes: there are still

16. Bötrul 2012, 34.

17. Again, note the Yogācāra language that intrudes when these topics are under discussion. One should hesitate before drawing too bright a line between the Yogācāra and Madhyamaka positions.

18. Bötrul 2012, 39.

things true and false of it. The uncategorized is a different kind of emptiness, one of which nothing can be said at all, and so free of all extremes:

> Our tradition asserts that the uncategorized ultimate
> is free from all assertions.
> Therefore the arguments of the great middle way
> are the great consequences.[19]

At this point we should note the subtle but important difference between the approaches of Tsongkhapa and his Geluk followers and Mipham and his new Nyingma followers regarding this issue. As I noted, Tsongkhapa is committed against his will to a contradiction, a paradox of expressibilty and characterization that emerges at the limits of language in the Madhyamaka tradition. This does not render him irrational but perspicacious. And the paradox is explained by the fact that the categorized and uncategorized ultimate are the same object taken from distinct subjective standpoints.[20] As a consequence, the transcendence of the ultimate of conceptual thought does not preclude its being conceptualized. But for Mipham and Bötrul, the objective distinction between the categorized and uncategorized ultimate means that its transcendence of conception and expression is unmitigated by the paradoxical fact that we can express that and we can conceive of it as the inconceivable. All of that is sent over to the categorized side and so is effectively denied. In attempting to avoid paradox, they are forced into mysticism. We see this consequence in the following passage:

> Our tradition asserts ultimate emptiness
> as the great uncategorized ultimate,

---

19. Bötrül 2012, 41.

20. Those familiar with debates about dialetheism in Madhyamaka might at this point think that this distinction between two standpoints amounts to a kind of parameterization and hence a retreat from a dialethic approach. One should resist this reading. Despite the fact that the contradictory properties of the object become evident from two distinct subjective perspectives, it does not follow that they are not two contradictory properties of the common object. See Deguchi, Garfield, and Priest 2013.

the expanse beyond the constructed phenomena
of the relative objects found by a valid cognition of confined
    perception.

Emptiness is not an entity;
while appearance is not reified,
that appearance abides as the great emptiness—
this is a critical point that destroys the clinging to entities.

Emptiness is not an entity;
while emptiness is not reified,
the self-lucidity of emptiness is appearing phenomena—
this is a critical point of the dawning of dependent arising.

Since it is not an entity, it is free from being a permanent entity;
since it is not a nonentity, it is free from being the extreme of
    annihilation.
The expansive luminous clarity—profound, peaceful, and free from
    constructs—
is asserted as the great ultimate, the abiding reality.

This way is neither the domain of an analysis of the categorized
    ultimate nor
the domain of analysis of the conventional valid cognition of
    confined perception.
The great valid cognition that analyzes the uncategorized ultimate
is the unique meaning established by Prāsaṅgika reasoning.[21]

Bötrul is explicit here about the radical disjuncture between the categorized and uncategorized ultimate, and that this disjuncture represents the distinction not between two subjective modes of apprehension but between two distinct objects of knowledge, only one of which—the uncategorized—is real and so a proper object of *knowledge.* The difference is between a real nonentity and a non-real but imagined entity. From the Geluk point of view—and, I might say, from the point of view of reason—

---

21. Bötrul 2012, 42.

this locates the ultimate outside of the domain of objects of knowledge entirely. If the goal of practice is to come to know ultimate truth, this is a disastrous consequence. Nonconceptuality may have been taken too far if that which we are to attain is in principle unattainable.

What Do We Learn from This?

This is not the first time that I have argued that one of the virtues of Madhyamaka philosophy, and of Tsongkhapa's adumbration of Candrakīrti's interpretation of that system, is rationally paradoxical. By attending closely to this debate about how to understand the distinction between the categorized and the uncategorized, we see how important these paradoxes are, and how rational. One might think that the embrace of paradox is the first step from rationality to mysticism. On the contrary (and Tsongkhapa himself to the contrary notwithstanding), we discover that it is when one attempts to save the ultimate from paradox by distinguishing objectively the characterized from the noncharacterized, and valorizing the noncharacterized as the only genuine ultimate, that one slides into a position where the most important thing to realize becomes unknowable and where the relationship between conventional and ultimate reality falls into mystery.

All Buddhist traditions struggle with the idea that conceptual thought is shot through with fabrication and that it engages with unreal universals, and with the idea that ultimate truth is beyond the reach of language and conception. The struggle is made more poignant because Buddhist scholars of all schools also work so hard to conceive and to describe just what that inconceivable and indescribable ultimate is like, and to show why it is inconceivable and indescribable. That task is necessary if there is to be any real content to Buddhist metaphysics, epistemology, and soteriology. And that task is further complicated by the thought that realization of the ultimate can have no connection to ordinary life. The debate between Geluk and Nyingma scholars in Tibet regarding how to reconcile these demands brings these difficulties into sharp relief. I have argued that in this debate, the Geluk tradition probably has things just right. Nonconceptual awareness makes perfect sense, so long as that of which one thereby becomes aware is also conceptualizable.

4. Tsongkhapa on the Importance of Ascertainment in Meditation on Emptiness

Thupten Jinpa

A KEY FEATURE IN Tsongkhapa's understanding of how effective spiritual transformation takes place, especially through sustained meditation practice, is the important role played by what he calls *ascertainment*. This is emphasized in the context of meditation aimed at cultivating insight (*vipaśyanā*) with respect to emptiness, the ultimate truth according to Madhyamaka philosophy. The Tibetan word for ascertainment, *nges pa*, is closely associated with *nges shes*, normally rendered as "certainty" or "conviction." Briefly, one could describe *ascertainment* as the function of a cognition endowed with *certainty*. Alternatively, one could view ascertainment as the cognitive aspect, in contrast to the perceptual aspect (*snang ba*), of the knowing subject. Differentiated in this way, the perceptual aspect relates to what the mind perceives or what appears to the mind, while ascertainment occurs at the level of cognition, what the mind comes to apprehend or ascertain. Despite this distinction, quite often Tsongkhapa uses the two Tibetan terms—*nges pa* and *nges shes*—interchangeably, as if they carry the same meaning. To complicate matters further, the same Tibetan word *nges pa* can also be used as an adjective, meaning "definite," "certain," or "determinate," used primarily to describe an attribute of an objective fact, something akin to being "final" or "true." Hence, in the context of scriptural interpretation, "definitive meaning" is the translation of the Tibetan phrase *nges don* (*nīthārtha*).

Tsongkhapa's usage of the word *nges pa* as "ascertainment" derives from how the term is used by Tibetan translators of Dharmakīrti's influential writings on epistemology. There, *nges pa* is used in a technical sense to render two distinct Sanskrit terms, *niścaya* and *adhyavaseya*, both of which mean "determination" or "perceptual judgment." In this technical sense, the term refers to the cognitive judgment that occurs after an instance of sensory perception. In this view, perception is immediate and indeterminate, while cognitive judgment is determinate and involves evaluation and activity of thought. Though drawing on this technical usage, Tsongkhapa seems to use the word, especially when explaining how enduring transformations occur through sustained meditation practice, in the sense of a *correct apprehension of a given truth gained through analysis and endowed with certainty with respect to that apprehended truth.*

Properly understood, ascertainment as defined by Tsongkhapa offers a compelling explanation of, to borrow contemporary scientific language, a "mechanism" by which lasting transformations take place through meditation practice. This important concept helps us also understand two theoretical frameworks of spiritual transformation found in classical Buddhist texts: (1) the *three levels of understanding* derived through study, critical reflection, and meditation and (2) the Tibetan Buddhist trio of *view, meditation, and conduct.* A key premise behind both frameworks is the idea that effective mental transformation is a function of cultivating correct view about the nature of self and reality and integrating such a view through prolonged contemplation and meditation.

Analysis as Key to Ascertainment

Given that Tsongkhapa's concept of ascertainment appears primarily in the context of meditation on emptiness or selflessness, my treatment of the concept here will relate to cultivating the view of emptiness. One possible reason why Tsongkhapa chose to emphasize the role of ascertainment may have been to underscore that insight into emptiness is not a passive disengagement or a nondiscursive withdrawal into a state of quietude. Rather, it is active form of knowing and understanding that *nothing whatsoever exists by virtue of intrinsic existence.* This understanding is completely at odds with the way we tend to perceive the world from our everyday naïve perspective, in which we instinctively assume that things possess objective existence definable through some kind of essence that establishes their existence and identity. This innate assumption—identified as fundamental ignorance (*avidyā*)—is the basis for our natural tendency for grasping, which in turn gives rise to the entire host of afflictions, including especially attachment and aversion.

Thus, according to Tsongkhapa, the ignorance that chains us to saṃsāric existence is not a passive *not knowing*; rather, it's an active *misknowing*, a distorted way of viewing. As such, its elimination should necessarily involve cultivating a perspective that directly opposes ignorance, in a way that challenges and negates its perspective—namely, the picture of the world that this fundamental ignorance portrays to us. Such a vision of the truth can only occur through a systematic deconstruction of the content constructed by our innate ignorance, revealing through careful and methodical analysis how nothing whatsoever possesses objective intrinsic existence as portrayed by our grasping mind.

In light of this, according to Tsongkhapa, the suggestion that meditation on emptiness should primarily take the form of nondiscursive disengagement is an error. Tsongkhapa describes this erroneous approach in his *Great Treatise on the Stages of the Path*:

> Some say that without discovering any sort of view that realizes selflessness, to [simply] hold the mind without thinking anything is to meditate on the way things are. Because emptiness, the way things are, is without any discernment of "this is" or "this is not," and that way of dwelling accords with the nature of things, one doesn't apprehend anything with the mind, because nothing whatsoever is established.[1]

In brief, Tsongkhapa rejects this view on the grounds that, if one has not gained the view of emptiness endowed with certainty first through intellectual understanding, it is impossible to meditate on it and attain insight. He sees in this view the mistaken assumption that any application of thought is necessarily deluded because of the belief that it involves grasping at intrinsic existence. Tsongkhapa warns that this kind of blanket rejection of thought and insistence on an exclusively nondiscursive approach in meditation could easily slide into the discredited view of the Chinese monk Heshang Moheyan at the Samyé Debate. Furthermore, if one shuns analysis and engages only in nondiscursive resting meditation, the most

---

1. My translation of Tsong kha pa, *Lam rim chen mo* (Jinpa 2019, 690). Tsongkhapa identifies four erroneous views and refutes them individually; the remaining three views are found in Tsongkhapa 2002, 337–39.

one could attain is *tranquil abiding*.[2] No matter how advanced, tranquil abiding alone cannot lead to the knowledge of the ultimate truth.

To stress this crucial point, Tsongkhapa cites the following stanzas from the *King of Samādhis Sūtra*:

> Although worldly persons cultivate samādhi,
> they do not destroy the notion of self.
> Their afflictions return and disturb them,
> as they did Udraka, who cultivated samādhi in this way.
>
> If you analytically discern the lack of self in phenomena
> and if you cultivate that analysis in meditation,
> this will cause the result, attainment of nirvāṇa;
> there is no peace through other means.[3]

Tsongkhapa reiterates these points later in his *Ocean of Reasoning*, in the following:

> And so, to know the facts regarding the way things exist is to understand the nonexistence of objects as they are grasped through ignorance. This is developed through arguments against the existence of that object and through arguments proving its nonexistence; but it is not developed just through the practice of refraining one's mind from engaging with the two selves. As it says in *Four Hundred Stanzas*, "Seeing selflessness in the object, the seed of existence is eliminated" (14.25cd). This means that one must understand the selflessness of the object grasped as having a self.[4]

---

2. In Tsong kha pa, *'Jam dbyangs kyi man ngag*, 492, for example, Tsongkhapa shares with his teacher Rendawa how Mañjuśrī has stated that the nondiscursive approach of not engaging in any form of mentation can only lead to tranquil abiding and never to insight. Thus, once one has found the stability of tranquil abiding, one then needs to engage in analytical meditation.

3. *Samādhirājasūtra*, cited in Tsong kha pa, *Lam rim chen mo*, 431. Tsongkhapa's teacher Rendawa also cites these two sūtra stanzas to underline the indispensability of analytical meditation and criticizes "today's proponents of mahāmudrā" for "regarding meditation without any thought through the cessation of all mental engagement to be flawless meditation." See Jinpa 2019, 93.

4. Tsongkhapa 2006, 41.

Thus ascertainment of emptiness endowed with certainty is crucial for effective meditation on emptiness.[5] And for this, analysis is indispensable.

Of the numerous forms of analysis for negating intrinsic existence presented in the great Indian Madhyamaka treatises, Tsongkhapa recommends in his *Great Treatise*, especially for the meditator at the beginner's stage, the reasoning of absence of identity and difference. Briefly, this involves analyzing the formal relationship between the *self* that we instinctively assume to exist as the basis of our personal identity, and the *aggregates*—the physical and mental constituents that make up our existence—in terms of whether they are identical or different. We are advised to frame the application of this reasoning of the *absence of identity and difference* within four key points: (1) identifying what exactly is to be negated;[6] (2) the logical entailment that were the self to possess intrinsic existence, it should exist either as identical with or distinct from the aggregates; (3) the absence of identity; and (4) the absence of difference. It is through this careful analysis that one arrives at the crucial conclusion that the self does not exist as endowed with intrinsic nature in any way. In other words, the self, which we so instinctively and with such conviction assume to be real, utterly lacks intrinsic existence.

Such knowledge of the self's absence of intrinsic existence—developed through analysis, sustained through contemplation, and endowed with a sense of certainty—is what Tsongkhapa means by *ascertainment*. Structurally, ascertainment entails (1) a *mode of apprehension*—namely, conscious awareness of emptiness or selflessness; (2) a *certainty* borne of knowing that the self is indeed devoid of intrinsic existence; and (3) the categorical or absolute nature of one's negation—what in technical Buddhist language is called *nonimplicative negation*. That is, nothing is implied in the place of

---

5. The influential nineteenth-century Nyingma thinker Ju Mipham agrees with Tsongkhapa on the importance of analytical meditation. The topic of analytical meditation is the fourth of the seven questions addressed in his *Torch of Certainty* (*Nges shes sgron me*), with the third addressing the question of whether the mind meditating on emptiness possesses a mode of apprehension. In these two sections, Mipham engages deeply with Tsongkhapa's views, especially as presented in the latter's *Great Treatise on the Stages of the Path*. In fact, one could argue that a large part of Mipham's *Torch of Certainty* was inspired by Tsongkhapa's explicit views on the important role of ascertainment in cultivating the view of emptiness. For a detailed analysis of Ju Mipham's engagement with Tsongkhapa's views, see Pettit 1999, especially chapters 6 and 7.

6. For a succinct presentation on this key point of identifying the object of negation according to the two Madhyamaka schools, see Tsongkhapa 2021a, chapter 9.

what is negated. To put in colloquially, there remain no ifs, ands, or buts.[7] The negation entailed is pure, simple, and categorical.

Even when one has succeeded in gaining such an ascertainment, one must maintain and cultivate it. Following Dharmakīrti's understanding of how two opposing perspectives counter each other, Tsongkhapa understands a dynamic relationship between ignorance and the view of emptiness wherein our innate assumption of intrinsic existence and our new understanding of emptiness constantly compete with each other for our approval. As the force of our ascertainment increases, it automatically diminishes the force of our innate grasping at intrinsic existence, and eventually our natural sense of reality no longer comes from an instinctual assumption that things exist objectively. In his *Great Treatise*, Tsongkhapa makes these points:

> Even if you have ascertained the view through study and contemplation, you must still continue to cultivate that ascertainment. To the extent that you cultivate the ascertainment, that certainty is seen to become stronger, more enduring, clearer, and more stable. The *Commentary on Reliable Cognition* says: "Ascertainment and the thought that distorts / have the nature of being the opponent and that which is opposed." Thus, as the opposing force and what is being opposed, to the extent that your ascertainment becomes stable and forceful, to that extent it undermines that which is its opposite. Here too you must optimize the stability of your ascertainment of the lack of intrinsic existence; this also needs to be done through contemplating numerous refutations and proofs.[8]

Ascertainment thus must be maintained through continuing practice.

---

7. For a differentiation between two forms of negation, see Tsongkhapa's *Essence of Eloquence,* translated in Thurman 1984, 376–81, and his *Ocean of Reasoning* (Tsongkhapa 2006, 50–54). What form of negation is entailed in the context of emptiness is the first of the seven issues addressed in Ju Mipham's *Torch of Certainty.*

8. Tsong kha pa, *Lam rim chen mo,* 700. For an alternative translation of this passage, see Tsongkhapa 2002, 341. The two remaining lines of the stanza from Dharmakīrti's *Commentary on Valid Cognition* read: "Know that ascertainment engages / with the absence of [the content] of the distorting thought."

How Ascertainment Is Transformed into Insight (vipaśyanā) through Meditation

Although ascertainment is first developed through analysis and contemplation, giving rise to what is called "finding the view," it is only through prolonged meditation that ascertainment is transformed into genuine insight into emptiness. Here, Tsongkhapa rejects the idea proposed by some that while analysis is necessary for initially gaining the view, once ascertainment has arisen, one then needs to set it aside and remain solely in a nondiscursive state, without any further analysis. This is, in fact, the second erroneous view on meditation on emptiness identified in the *Great Treatise*.[9]

This raises the broader issue of the nature of meditation itself, especially the question of whether genuine meditation should necessarily be nondiscursive, a question Tsongkhapa raised in his youth in his open letter entitled *Queries from a Pure Heart*.[10] There, as well as in his later work, the *Great Treatise*, Tsongkhapa presents a powerful case for not just the legitimacy but the indispensability of analytical meditation, which is by its very nature discursive. His case is premised on the proposition that, just as the method for cultivating tranquil abiding involves primarily a nondiscursive resting of the mind, the method for cultivating insight must entail inquiry and analysis. In other words, to attain insight into emptiness, it is essential to employ discriminative wisdom when meditating on emptiness. It is only when one successfully combines these two approaches—single-pointed resting and discursive analysis—that one will attain true insight, which is characterized by *single-pointed focus* and *ascertainment* endowed with certainty. On these two features of the meditative state, Tsongkhapa writes:

> Thus the mark of tranquil abiding is that your mind rests right where it is placed, not distracted from the object of meditation, while the mark of insight is that you realize the suchness of selflessness and eliminate erroneous views, such as the view of self, and your mind remains firm like a mountain that cannot

9. For Tsongkhapa's refutation of this view, see Tsongkhapa 2002, 337.

10. *Dri ba lhag bsam rab dkar.* See Jinpa 2019, 93.

be shaken by any opposing standpoint. In this way, distinguish between these two [forms of meditation].[11]

In his later summary of the stages of the path in the style of an experiential song, Tsongkhapa describes in a more poetic way these two distinctive features and the power of the mind when the two come together into a union:

> So saddling this wisdom decisively penetrating the true mode of
>   being
> astride the horse of unwavering tranquil abiding, and with
> the sharp weapon of reasoning of the Middle Way free of extremes,
> tear down all sites of objectification of the mind grasping at
>   extremes.[12]

While the two skills—single-pointing resting of the mind and probing analysis—need to be cultivated separately, Tsongkhapa envisions a dynamic and complex relationship between the two unfolding. He writes:

> You alternate between resting meditation—which stays with that conclusion without scattering—and analysis with discriminating wisdom. At that time, if stability decreases due to excessive analytic meditation, do more stabilizing meditation and restore stability. As stability increases under the influence of extensive stabilizing meditation, if you lose interest in analysis and thus fail to analyze, then your ascertainment of reality will not become firm and powerful. In the absence of a firm and powerful ascertainment of reality, you will not do the slightest damage to the countervailing superimpositions that conceive of the existence of two selves.[13]

In summarizing Tsongkhapa's points on emptiness meditation, as outlined in the *Great Treatise* and the *Middle-Length Treatise on the Stages*

---

11. Tsongkhapa 2004, 20; translation slightly modified.

12. Tsong kha pa, *Lam rim nyams mgur*, verse 36.

13. Tsongkhapa, *Lam rim chen mo*, 710. For an alternative translation, see Tsongkhapa 2002, 351.

of the Path, the fifteenth-century Geluk meditator Gomchen Ngawang Drakpa poetically describes what such a meditative state might feel like:

> At the end of analysis as you sustain the ascertainment,
> suddenly arisen, *that nothing exists of that purported object,*
> with no interruption of any extraneous thoughts,
> learn to gain a happy freedom from laxity and excitation.
> During resting meditation, when through three factors—
> mindfulness, meta-awareness, and prior intention—
> you attain equipoise free of laxity and excitation,
> without losing the mode of apprehension as you relax your effort,
> you will then attain the peak of faultless meditation.[14]

Tsongkhapa admits that, at least in the initial stage, analysis could inhibit the ability to rest the mind, while nondiscursive resting can weaken the force of ascertainment. Therefore the meditator needs a skillful balance of the two, where within perfect tranquil abiding, they maintain in each and every moment a vibrant and clear awareness of emptiness. Once they become accustomed to integrating the two in this dynamic manner, eventually there emerges a stage where probing analysis itself can strengthen the depth of focus and the abiding of the mind.[15] This is when a true union of tranquil abiding and insight has been attained in relation to emptiness.

Critics of Tsongkhapa sometimes fail to appreciate an important element in his understanding of the nature of analysis in the context of emptiness meditation. In brief, for Tsongkhapa, ascertainment constitutes the view of emptiness. However, analysis does not, as his critics tend to assume. This is to say, in the initial stages of gaining ascertainment and finding the view during which the practitioner's understanding of emptiness remains at best a form of inferential understanding, analysis is indeed crucial. However, analysis itself does not constitute gnosis at the more advanced stage of the direct perception of emptiness. Indeed, Tsongkhapa envisions a progressive attenuation of analysis with a progressive decreasing in the force required, such that when a union of tranquil abiding and insight into emptiness is attained, there is no longer any need for a conscious application of analysis.

---

14. Sgom chen Ngag dbang grags pa, *Lam gyi rim pa gsal 'debs su bya ba'i bskul ma,* 549.

15. Tsongkhapa 2002, 354.

In fact, at this point, the meditator feels as if the meditating mind itself has become fused with emptiness, with no sense of separation of subject and object, like pure water poured into pure water, as the texts often say. In a short guide on how to cultivate the view, for example, Tsongkhapa states:

> Then sustain the continuity of the ascertainment just arisen *that nothing exists as perceived and apprehended by this sense of "I am,"* and reinforce that strong ascertainment several times. Again, proceed like this: in subsequent [reinforcements of ascertainment], apply analysis with less force while sustaining ascertainment in a vibrant way. As to (a) the way to maintain mindfulness and apply meta-awareness such that, during the reasoning of the absence of identity and difference and the concluding ascertainment resulting from it, no extraneous thoughts interrupt the process, and (b) the way to prevent mental laxity and excitation, follow the explanation given in the context of tranquil abiding practice. And as you meditate in this way, you will feel as if the subject itself is subsumed by its object, emptiness, while the object arises as if it is an aspect of the subject.[16]

In brief, in the advanced stages of meditation, while there is no analysis in any formal sense, in the wisdom of emptiness, there is in fact both ascertainment and a mode of apprehension (*'dzin stang*), albeit of a pure absence or negation. In other words, there is still an awareness of emptiness, endowed with certainty. To stress this critical importance of ascertainment and certainty, Tsongkhapa uses a unique phrase in relation to the quality of one's view. The phrase is *phu thag chod pa*, which can be rendered as "conclusive certainty," with the Tibetan phrase invoking the imagery of someone who has conclusively identified the source of a stream. He speaks of "the view endowed with conclusive certainty with respect to the truth of the way things are," "the profound view endowed with conclusive certainty," "the view of emptiness endowed with conclusive certainty," "wisdom endowed with conclusive certainty with respect to the way things are," and so on.[17]

---

16. Tsong kha pa, *Dbu ma thal 'gyur ba'i lugs kyi lta khrid*, 522.

17. Respectively, *yin lugs kyi don la phu thag chod pa'i lta ba; zab mo'i lta ba phu thag chod pa;*

Furthermore, Tsongkhapa's presentation on the role of ascertainment in the cultivation of insight—especially the presentation in his *Great Treatise*—must be situated within its proper context: the beginner's approach to cultivating insight. In a later work, Tsongkhapa speaks of five distinct styles of meditation on emptiness: (1) when cultivating experiential understanding of the view in the beginner's stage; (2) when cultivating insight on emptiness based on a similitude of tranquil abiding; (3) when cultivating insight based on genuine tranquil abiding; (4) when realizing emptiness directly; and (5) when meditating on emptiness in the Vajrayāna completion stage—namely, the gnosis of innate bliss and emptiness.[18]

In relation to the fifth, meditation on emptiness in Vajrayāna, Tsongkhapa writes:

> Here is our own position. Even in the context of highest yoga tantra, you must cultivate the view of emptiness as presented in the Madhyamaka treatises. As for sustaining the view [in meditation], both the generation stage and the post-meditation period of the completion stage contain instances when you bring suchness to mind through analysis. However, when the completion-stage yogin who has attained the power to penetrate the vital points of the body meditates on emptiness during the period of equipoise, even though he certainly does meditate on the basis of maintaining the view, he does not engage in analysis in the fashion explained in other systems. Thus at this stage, as you let go

stong nyid kyi lta ba phu thag chod pa; and *yin lugs phu thag chod pa'i shes rab*. Ju Mipham also adopts the phrase "conclusive certainty" (*phu thag chod pa*) and speaks of "conclusive certainty with respect to absence of true existence" (*bden stong phu thag chod pa*), *Nges shes sgron me*, in Pettit 1999, 204; Pettit renders the line as "One must definitely realize the absence of true existence."

18. This *Short Piece on the View* (*Lta ba'i yig chung*) is number 18 in *Anthology of Brief Instructions on Guhyasamāja*. It consists of the words of the root lines (*lta ba rdo rje'i tshig*) as well as an accompanying exposition of each of the lines on the five styles. That this list is actually by Tsongkhapa is evidenced from Gyaltsab Jé's reference to it in his *Precious Garland: A Guide to the Profound View* (Rgyal tshab Rje, *Zab mo'i lta khrid*, 189), where he writes, "There are five ways in which the view could be sustained. What is presented here, however, is from the perspective of a beginner who has ascertained the view and has not forgotten it."

of analytical meditation, do not also let go of your meditation of resting single-pointedly on suchness on the basis of your view.[19]

Therefore, according to Tsongkhapa, even when the yogin needs to set aside analytic meditation on the advanced completion stage of Vajrayāna, he or she must still maintain awareness of emptiness while resting single-pointedly on the basis of the view ascertained previously. In other words, although there is no longer analysis, there is still a mode of apprehension—namely, the awareness of emptiness.

Furthermore, if the realization of emptiness at that point is nonconceptual direct experience, there is no ascertainment either, for the subject, gnosis, has become totally fused with the object, emptiness.[20] In any case, Tsongkhapa reminds us that trying to compare emptiness meditation by a beginner with that of a yogin on the Vajrayāna completion stage is like comparing the size of space covered by an open palm to the sky itself![21]

Concluding Points

For Tsongkhapa, ascertainment is key to the attainment of insight into emptiness, and ascertainment necessarily requires, at least in the initial stage, application of sustained analysis. Furthermore, ascertainment endowed with a mode of apprehension—that things are empty of intrinsic existence—serves to constitute the knowledge of emptiness at the beginner's stage. Given that emptiness remains a concealed fact, as opposed to an evident fact, for those at the beginner's stage, one's engagement with and knowledge of emptiness is mediated by its generic concept, with the knowl-

19. Tsong kha pa, *Lam rim 'bring*, 284. For an alternative translation, see Tsongkhapa 2021b, 410.

20. Ju Mipham seems to agree that the logical character may be captured by portrayal of emptiness as nonimplication—absolute negation of intrinsic existence—but, according to him, such an absence of intrinsic existence does not represent ultimate reality. For Mipham, ultimate reality is a fusion of emptiness and gnosis into an indivisible reality sometimes characterized as a coalescence of appearance and emptiness devoid of conceptual elaboration. As such, when gnosis directly realizing emptiness arises, it does so with no mode of apprehension whatsoever. Furthermore, because he assumes the mode of apprehension to necessarily entail the presence of ascertainment, he seems to mistakenly attribute to Tsongkhapa the idea that ascertainment is present even in an ārya's meditative equipoise. See Pettit 1999, especially 146–67.

21. Tsong kha pa, *Rim lnga gdan rdzogs*, 563.

edge gained remaining a form of inferential understanding. There simply is no possibility at the beginner's stage to engage with emptiness nonconceptually; the nonconceptual realization of emptiness remains the purview of ārya beings—that is, those who have attained the path of seeing.

Here it is critical to appreciate the distinction between a *nondiscursive* approach versus a *nonconceptual* approach, with the former possible even at the beginner's stage. Although the same Tibetan word, *mi rtog pa*, is used in both contexts, in the first context it refers to a form of resting the mind, devoid of engagement with thoughts such as "This is that and this is not that." In case of the latter, the term refers to being devoid of any thought or concept.[22]

In terms of development, first an *intellectual understanding of emptiness* (*stong nyid kyi go ba*) needs to be developed based on study—reading or listening to teachings. This understanding derived from study then needs to be enhanced through critical reflection and meditation practice so that it leads to gaining an *experiential understanding of the view* (*lta ba'i myong ba thon pa*), eventually leading to gaining the view in the form of inferential understanding. This inferential understanding effortlessly leads to what Tsongkhapa calls the *culmination of analysis of the view* (*lta ba'i dpyad pa rdzogs pa*), when, as instructed by Mañjuśrī, "there is no unease after arriving at a given conclusion."[23] In his *Three Principal Elements of the Path*, Tsongkhapa describes such a culmination of analysis in terms of a powerful convergence of the understanding of dependent origination and emptiness. He writes:

As long as the two understandings—
of *appearance*, undeceiving dependent origination,
and *emptiness*, the absence of all positions—remain separate,
then you have not realized the intent of the Sage.

However, if at some point, not in alternation but at once,

22. Tsongkhapa 2002, 338.

23. Mañjuśrī's oral communication with Tsongkhapa as reported in Mkhas grub, *Sheaves of Precious Jewels* (2019), 124. What exactly the relationship is between (a) inferential cognition of emptiness (*rjes dpag gis stong nyid rtogs pa*), (b) culmination of the analysis of the view (*lta ba'i dpyad pa rdzogs pa*), and (c) realization of subtle dependent origination (*rten 'brel phra bo rtogs pa*) is a matter of debate among Geluk commentators.

the instant you see that dependent origination is undeceiving,
this ascertainment entirely dismantles your grasping the object,
then your analysis of the view is complete.[24]

The progressive stages of engagement with emptiness have correspondingly progressive levels of ascertainment of the view. At the beginner's stage, meditation on emptiness primarily entails maintaining, strengthening, and refining the ascertainment of emptiness such that "to the extent that you cultivate ascertainment, that certainty is seen to become stronger, more enduring, clearer, and more stable."[25] Successful meditation on emptiness then is, on this level, a matter of sustaining the force of ascertainment, especially through a balanced but dynamic application of analysis and resting the mind during formal sitting (or meditative equipoise), followed by robust awareness of the illusion-like perspective that arises in the aftermath of the meditation session. The first is known as "yoga of space-like equipoise," while the second is called "yoga of illusion-like perception in the periods subsequent to equipoise." Tsongkhapa constantly reminds us that the illusion-like perspective will arise naturally in the aftermath of space-like meditation and thus requires no separate cultivation. This said, he does speak of two distinct types of post-equipoise illusion-like perception: one arising purely through the force of what has been experienced during the equipoise (*myong stobs kyis bsgom pa*) and another where the perception arises through the power of recollection (*dran stobs kyis bsgom pa*).[26]

The picture we get from the above treatment of ascertainment as defined by Tsongkhapa is the following. As our ascertainment progressively advances, with respect to its force, duration, clarity, and refinement, it challenges the perspective of its opposing force—our habitual assumption of intrinsic existence—eventually overwhelming it to the point where the latter no longer remains our natural or default perspective. Instead, our entire outlook comes to be shifted: our perception of the world, including our own existence, is tempered by an awareness of its lack of intrinsic exis-

---

24. Tsong kha pa, *Lam gtso rnam gsum*, 287. This rendering of *nges shes* as "ascertainment" in the third line (*nges shes yul gyi 'dzin stangs yun zhig na*) reflects the reading of, e.g., the Fifth Dalai Lama. Others, such as the Second Panchen Losang Yeshé, interpret *nges shes* in the sense of "certitude," making the line read "this entirely dismantles your grasping at certitude."

25. As cited from the *Lam rim chen mo* above in note 8.

26. Tsong kha pa, *Dbu ma thal 'gyur ba'i lugs kyi lta khrid*, 523.

tence, causing us to relate to things as "mere conventionalities" (*kun rdzob tsam*).[27]

This fundamental shift in outlook—or "mindset," in contemporary parlance—is not simply a shift in intellectual standpoint; it is a deep psychological and emotional transformation. In classical Buddhist language, ascertainment is what is *sought* at the stage of understanding derived from study, it is what is *cultivated* at the stage of understanding derived from contemplation, and finally it is *enhanced and refined* on the stage of understanding derived from meditation. Tsongkhapa memorably conveys this idea of the synergy between the trio—study, contemplation, and meditation—with the phrase "racing the horse on the course the horse was trained on."[28] Similarly, ascertainment is what constitutes the heart of the *view*, what has been ascertained in the view is what is brought to maturity through *meditation*, and finally it is the maturity of what is ascertained by the view that shapes our *conduct* in the world in a manner that is free of grasping, attachment, and dichotomizing dualism.

Once one has developed deep appreciation for how effective and enduring spiritual transformations can and do occur, especially through ascertainment, one may then be inspired by what Khedrup Jé, a key student of Tsongkhapa, declares in the following:

> If one who has understood all the essential points of our precious master's instructions and comprehended the overall structure of the path were to engage single-pointedly in meditative practice, unmoved by chatter and distractions, with even half the effort of masters like Milarepa and Götsangpa, undoubtedly they would attain tantric-level realizations akin to the great siddhas of India.[29]

---

27. See, for example, the discussion on how the things of everyday experience appear to ārya beings as "mere conventionalities," as explained by Candrakīrti, in Tsongkhapa 2021a, 244–46.

28. Tsong kha pa, *Lam rim chen mo*, 5, citing an analogy from Kamalaśīla's *Bhāvanākrama*.

29. Mkhas grub Rje, *Gsang ba 'dus pa'i yig chung nyer gcig sogs*, 224.

Tantra

5. Tsongkhapa's Masterful Exegesis of Cakrasaṃvara Tantra

David B. Gray

Introduction

Tsongkhapa (1357–1419) lived and wrote at a pivotal point in Tibetan Buddhist history. The "later transmission" (*phyi dar*) of the Dharma to Tibet, which began in the late tenth century with Rinchen Sangpo's (958–1055) journey to Kashmir in 975 CE,[1] was more or less complete by the fourteenth century. The end of this period of intercultural transmission was triggered by the collapse in the late twelfth century of the Pāla dynasty, which had long governed the Buddhist heartland in northeast India, followed by the conquest of Magadha by Muhammed ibn Bakhtyār Khaljī circa 1205 CE.[2] These events triggered a small surge in translation activity, as Buddhists from northern India fled to Nepal and Tibet to escape conflict and persecution in their homeland, leading to new teachers and teachings becoming available to Tibetan scholars. However, this process had largely come to a halt by Tsongkhapa's lifetime. Tsongkhapa and his contemporaries thus faced the challenge of assimilating this new material and organizing and making sense of the vast trove of tantric texts and traditions that were circulating in Tibet. He was also among the first generation to benefit from the compilation of the canon by Butön Rinchen Drup (1290–1364) and company. In addressing this challenge, Tsongkhapa made use of the wide range of resources available to him—namely, the exegetical strategies developed by his Indian and Tibetan forebears. He did so in a skillful way to advance Tibetan understanding of an obscure tantric corpus.

---

1. Regarding Rinchen Sangpo's journey to India, see Tucci 1988, 3–4.
2. See Davidson 2002b, 61, and Davidson 2005, 325.

The focus of this paper will be Tsongkhapa's approach to tantric exegesis illustrated by his masterful commentary on the *Cakrasaṃvara Tantra*, *Illumination of the Hidden Meaning* (*Sbas don kun gsal*). It is an extensive commentary on an important Indian Buddhist scripture of the *yoginītantra* class that is also known as the *Saṃvara Light* (*Laghusaṃvara*) and the *Discourse of Śrī Heruka* (*Śrīherukābhidhāna*). It was when Tsongkhapa was at the peak of his teaching career and nearing the end of his life that he gave the teachings on the *Cakrasaṃvara Tantra* that would be recorded as *Illumination of the Hidden Meaning*.[3] It could be considered his final and perhaps definitive statement on tantric exegesis. Tsongkhapa's significance in Tibetan religious history is exemplified by this work, which attempts to maintain fidelity to the Indian commentarial traditions while advancing his own uniquely Tibetan commentarial agenda.

Sources for This Work

In undertaking this work, Tsongkhapa took into consideration a wide range of sources, including the multiple Tibetan translations of the root tantra itself. Four translations were available to Tsongkhapa. These included Rinchen Sangpo's original translation made with the Kashmiri scholar Padmākaravarman, which is unfortunately—to my knowledge—now lost. They also included the three revised translations based on it, all of which are extant. The most important of these, naturally, is the translation preserved in all editions of the Kangyur, the revised translation undertaken by the Tibetan scholars Dro Lotsāwa Sherab Drak (ca. twelfth century), also known as Prajñākīrti, and Marpa Chökyi Wangchuk (ca. 1043–1138), who was also known as Marpa Dopa or Mardo. This is a generally good translation, although it is significantly different from the extant Sanskrit manuscripts due to extensive interpolations from explanatory tantras such as the *Discourse Appendix Tantra* (*Abhidhānottaratantra*). Another revised translation undertaken around the same time, circa the late eleventh century, was that of the Tibetan translator Malgyo Lotsāwa Lodrö Drakpa and the Kashmiri scholar Sumatikīrti, a disciple of Nāropa. This transla-

---

3. This event took place during the last year of his life, in 1418 or 1419. See Kaschewsky 1967, 329, and Jinpa 2019, 308–9.

tion was preserved extra-canonically by the Sakya tradition as well as in the Phukdrak Kangyur.

While Tsongkhapa frequently refers to alternate translations in the above works, his preferred translation was the final attempt at revising the text undertaken by Sumatikīrti and Mardo. It is a text that according to its colophon was actually revised twice, first in the eleventh century by the Indian scholar Sūryagupta and the Tibetan translator Gö Khukpa Lhetsé. Gö Lhetsé lived during the eleventh century and was a student of Atiśa and a teacher of Khön Könchok Gyalpo (1034–1102), founder of the Sakya tradition. This duo translated Kambala's *Treasury of Sādhanas* (*Sādhananidhi*) commentary into Tibetan and also revised Rinchen Sangpo's original translation of the *Cakrasaṃvara Tantra* on the basis of this work, which quotes the root text extensively. It was further revised by Sumatikīrti and Mardo, most likely during the late eleventh or early twelfth century.[4] This text has been extra-canonically preserved by the Geluk tradition, no doubt because Tsongkhapa favored it.

Tsongkhapa also referred to the explanatory tantras themselves and to the surviving Indian commentaries on them. In addition, he consulted all twelve of the Indian commentaries on the Cakrasaṃvara, with particular focus on Kambala's *Sādhananidhi* commentary, which accords nicely with his preferred translation of the root text. He also relied on the work of Tibetan scholars who preceded him. He mentions two Tibetan works by name: the *Pearl Garland* (*Mu tig phreng ba*) commentary by Sachen Kunga Nyingpo (1092–1158), and *Clarifying the General Meaning* (*Spyi rnam don gsal*), a root tantra commentary by Butön. Tsongkhapa quotes and refers to the former text only occasionally but relies more on Butön's commentary, which he repeatedly quotes and paraphrases and discusses openly, primarily when he disagrees with Butön.

I believe that Tsongkhapa also frequently quoted from or paraphrased a third Tibetan work, a root tantra commentary composed by Mardo, though he does not refer to it by name, and it appears to be lost.[5] As I

4. For a discussion of these translations, see Gray 2012, 237–47, 415–16, and 483–86; and Gray 2017, 5–7.

5. I have not been able to secure a copy of this text but have found references to it. I presume it is the text entitled *Mar do lo tsā ba chos kyi dbang phyug gi bde mchog rtsa rgyud bsdus don dang ṭik ka rgya pa* listed by Akhuching Sherab Gyatso (1803–75) in his catalogue of rare works preserved at Labrang Monastery in the middle of the nineteenth century. See Chandra 1963, 3:522.

have not had the good fortune to consult this work, I cannot confirm this, but I hope that a copy will turn up in the near future.

Lastly, Tsongkhapa also relied on the oral instructions of past gurus, as passed down through the practice lineages he received, and on the textual records of such instructions. The oral instructions are essential, but in Tsongkhapa's judgment, they are not sufficient for understanding the tantras. This is because the oral instructions depend on the explanatory tantras and tantric commentaries. Following his discussion of the fifty-first chapter's fourteen realities of the creation stage, he argues:

> The above presentation of fourteen realities is said in the oral instructions to be easily found; however, it is not easily found when the root and explanatory tantras are not well integrated, because the explanatory tantras are the standard that the root tantra's oral instructions are based on. However, their integration is not lacking in the explanations by the gurus who know the oral instructions of great saints like Lūipa, Kāṇhapa, and Ghaṇṭapa.[6]

In Tsongkhapa's view, tantric exegesis should rest on a sound understanding of the textual tradition in which the work is embedded. While oral instructions are essential for a correct understanding of the tantras in light of the tradition that has preserved and practiced them, receiving the oral transmission does not obviate the need to study the exegetical corpus.

Illumination, or Tsongkhapa's Intellectual Project

By the fourteenth century, the Tibetan canon of Buddhist scriptures was more or less complete, at least from the perspective of the New (*gsar ma*) traditions of Tibetan Buddhism.[7] Yet this canon contained a bewildering array of tantras and ritual texts, as well as Indian commentaries on the more important and influential of these works. Moreover, the relation

6. Gray 2019, 297. Note that translations from my earlier publications have sometimes been modified when reproduced in this article.

7. That is to say, the disclosure of new scriptures is ongoing in the Nyingma tradition. Though as Ronald Davidson has pointed out, new scriptures have occasionally appeared in the Gsar ma traditions as well. See Davidson 2002a.

between these works was not always clear. Indian and Tibetan scholars generally grouped tantric works into collections or "cycles" (*skor ba*), centering around a single root tantra (*mūlatantra, rtsa rgyud*). Other tantras would be included in these collections, relegated to subsidiary status vis-à-vis the root tantras as "explanatory tantras" (*vyākhyātantra, bshad rgyud*).

But the relationship between root and explanatory tantras was not always clear, and it was sometimes contentious. For example, while the *Abhidhānottara Tantra* was generally considered an explanatory tantra for the Cakrasaṃvara, evidence in the text contradicts this identification. For example, at the end of chapter 27 of the *Cakrasaṃvara Tantra* appear two verses (20–21) asserting its superiority to earlier tantras:

> That which is stated in the *Tattvasaṃgraha*—and is likewise stated in the *Saṃvara* and proclaimed in the *Guhya Tantra*, in the *Śrī Paramādya*, and in the *Mahābhairava*—bestows the powers of mantra repetition, observance, and so forth. Here the mantrin brings [those powers] forth in an instant through meditation alone.[8]

This verse points to some of the challenges in interpreting tantric texts, which are often deliberately vague. In this example, while titles such as *Tattvasaṃgraha* and *Śrī Paramādya* are easy to identify, *Guhya Tantra* is less clear, given the large number of tantric works with the word *guhya*, "secret," in their titles. And while the term *Saṃvara* here is generally identified with the *Sarvabuddhasamāyoga-ḍākinījālasaṃvara Tantra*, the parallel passage in the *Abhidhānottara Tantra* here reads "*Cakrasaṃvare*," implying that the *Abhidhānottara* is superior to the *Cakrasaṃvara*, since it grants all the powers achieved through ritual practice in other tantras through meditation alone. Needless to say, this passage problematizes the general identification of the *Abhidhānottara Tantra* as a Cakrasaṃvara explanatory tantra.[9]

8. See Gray 2007, 279–80, and Gray 2012, 160.

9. Tsongkhapa discusses the complex relationship between root and explanatory tantras at some length; see Gray 2017, 31–56. The *Abhidhānottara*'s claim of supremacy over the *Cakrasaṃvara* points to the competitive milieu in which these texts were composed, featuring rival factions that advocated distinct versions of texts. The root versus explanatory tantra rubric no doubt developed later, as advocates sought to make sense of these "cycles" of closely related scriptures.

While this may seem like a minor concern, it actually points to a very serious intellectual problem: What exactly is the standing of the *Cakrasaṃvara Tantra* relative to the large number of closely related works? Is it really a root tantra, the core work for a major tradition of scripture and practice? Or is it a relatively minor work, given its relatively short length (about seven hundred stanzas) compared to much longer related works such as the *Abhidhānottara*? If one answers yes to the latter question, the work would arguably be unworthy of serious consideration by Tibetans seeking to make sense of the large corpus of works transmitted from India.

Tsongkhapa thus begins his detailed commentary on the *Cakrasaṃvara Tantra* with an exploration of its provenance, exploring its legendary origin in a root scripture consisting of at least a hundred thousand stanzas and its relation to the works that may be considered explanatory tantras for it.[10] Establishing the relationship between the root and explanatory tantras is particularly important in the case of the *Cakrasaṃvara Tantra* because of its extreme concision and abstruseness. As Tsongkhapa noted, "since the numerous explanatory tantras of the enigmatic root tantra are autocommentaries of the root tantra, it is extremely important to properly integrate the root and explanatory tantras."[11]

The term *kun gsal*—the Tibetan translation of Sanskrit terms such as *prakāśa,* "illumination," in the title of Tsongkhapa's commentary (*Sbas don kun gsal*)—indicates his aim in this work: to make clear the unclear and shed light on this challenging scripture. To do this requires all the resources available in Tibet circa the early fifteenth century. To give a brief example, in commenting on the root tantra's abstruse account of drawing the maṇḍala in chapter 2, he observes, "The statement in the root tantra that one first draws by color and then by marking string is jumbled. The explanatory tantra resolves the confusion with its explanation of drawing."[12] Here he refers to the root text's account of the steps in the maṇḍala drawing process being out of order, first mentioning drawing the maṇḍala with charnel-ground ash and brick (that is, colored powders) in chapter 2, verse 3ab, and only later the laying out of the maṇḍala with a cord

10. For my full translation of these passages, see Gray 2017, 31–56.

11. Gray 2017, 56. The explanatory tantras can be considered autocommentaries since they, like the root tantra, are also deemed *buddhavacana,* authentic speech of the Awakened One.

12. Gray 2017, 145.

in chapter 2, verse 11. He proceeds to explain the ritual process by relying on the clearer presentation of the rite in the *Origin of Saṃvara* (*Saṃvarodaya*) explanatory tantra.

Tsongkhapa's approach to tantric exegesis is also level-headed and non-sectarian. Because dedicated practitioners may spend years practicing deity yoga, identifying themselves with the maṇḍala's deities, interpretive zeal is understandably a pitfall. For example, chapter 3, verse 23, was commonly read as a reference to the four classes of tantra. It reads: "Smiling, gazing, holding hands, coupling, and so forth: one should be initiated in that, the supreme of all tantras."[13] Sachen Kunga Nyingpo, clearly an advocate for the *Cakrasaṃvara Tantra*, reads this list not as a reference to the four classes of tantra but as a list of six classes, with the particle "and so forth," *ādikaṃ / sogs kyis*, indicating the "yoginī further unexcelled mother tantra" class. Tsongkhapa gently dismisses this exegetical exuberance: "Although someone claims that the expression 'and so forth' here indicates the further unexcelled mother *Saṃvara Tantra*, since the *Saṃvara Tantra* is also a tantra of coupling, there is nothing aside from that. Since it is said that an alternate meaning of the expression *ādikaṃ* is 'supreme,' it means that it is the supreme of the coupling tantras."[14] While he allows that the *Cakrasaṃvara Tantra* might be considered the supreme of the unexcelled yoga tantras, he dismisses the idea that it might constitute a "further unexcelled" class unto itself.

Tsongkhapa's level-headed rationality is leavened with a touch of dry humor. For example, chapter 3 closes with the following self-aggrandizing verse: "This king of maṇḍalas does not occur, nor will it occur, in the *Tattvasaṃgraha, Saṃvara, Guhyasamāja,* or *Vajrabhairava*."[15] He wryly notes here that "though it is indeed difficult to find this maṇḍala in those others, it is not superior to the maṇḍalas of those profound and vast tantras. Were it otherwise, then they would be superior to this tantra as well, since their maṇḍalas likewise do not occur in this tantra."[16]

He rejects such sectarian impulses because his approach is ecumenical; he does not wish to study tantras within the narrow confines of single oral

---

13. Gray 2007, 176.

14. Gray 2017, 172.

15. Gray 2007, 176–77.

16. Gray 2017, 173–74.

transmissions and instead seeks the larger scope of the Buddhist tantric tradition. He often sheds light on the text by referencing other tantras. Elsewhere in the text he quotes, with approval, Abhayākaragupta's comment that "one should be aware of what is said in other tantras," adding, "Those who know much advise this."[17] In other words, zealous focus on a single tradition does not provide a firm basis for elucidating the tantras; a well-rounded perspective is essential for this challenging task. Indeed, sometimes elements of advanced practice can only be fully understood with reference to other traditions. For example, at the conclusion of a discussion of completion-stage practice in chapter 51, Tsongkhapa observes, "In particular, integration via samādhi of the illusory body (*māyākāya*) is attained via entry of the illusory body into clear light. To know this fully, consult the *Glorious Guhyasamāja*."[18] The ability to make such a comment depends on mastery of multiple tantric traditions; Tsongkhapa possessed this vast understanding and deployed it well.

The Hidden Meaning

The aim of Tsongkhapa's exegetical work was the "hidden meaning" (*sbas don*), the ultimate import of the text concealed within it. For Tsongkhapa, this is definitely not the ritual practices that are the text's overt focus. Rather, the true secret, the hidden meaning, of the tantra is the "union of emptiness and bliss." By this he means that the realization of the great bliss on which the text is focused depends upon prior realization of emptiness.

Tsongkhapa's addition of emptiness into the equation was somewhat radical. For one thing, the term is not mentioned once in the tantra. Tsongkhapa ingeniously accounts for this as follows:

> Here the yoginī tantras teach primarily the inseparability of
> bliss and emptiness from the perspective of wisdom. The view
> of the reality of emptiness (*śūnyatātathā*) is taught in brief in
> the tantras, since Lord Nāgārjuna's thinking was that there was

17. Gray 2017, 156.
18. Gray 2019, 302.

nothing left to explain beyond what he had already established at length.[19]

Since Nāgārjuna had already stated everything that could be profitably said about emptiness, the tantras have nothing to add on this subject. Instead, they focus on bliss as the explicit topic. Emptiness thus remains the hidden, implicit import of the text. This interpretation almost certainly reflects Tsongkhapa's larger intellectual project, the proper interpretation of Madhyamaka philosophy.

What exactly does "the union of bliss and emptiness" (*bde stong zung 'jug*) mean here? Tsongkhapa makes clear that it pertains to the achievement of completion-stage practice. In his commentary on the concluding fifty-first chapter, Tsongkhapa argues that this depends on receiving and properly understanding the esoteric instructions on completion-stage practices. And this in turn requires an understanding of the underlying textual tradition. He quotes with approval the following verse passage in Kambala's commentary on the root text:

> One cultivates the gnosis of wisdom
> through hearing, reflecting, and meditating on
> the oral instructions passed one to another.
> They're the supreme coming from the supreme,
> the Buddha's eye, possessing the answer,
> that has the means to induce and apply
> the yoginīs' command. The position
> of the buddhas' awakening, mahāmudrā,
> perfects the meditation that's drawn from
> the unification of all buddhas,
> the network of the ḍākinīs.
> Regular contact with yoginīs,
> brings the fortune of unending meaning,
> ripening and purifying.
> It is the secret in all tantras
> derived from this scriptural tradition.
> The great secret of all buddhas exists

---

19. Gray 2017, 343.

as the three hundred thousand–[stanza text]
and is derived from the extensive tantra.[20]

At the end of his explanation of this passage, Tsongkhapa relates that this "hidden meaning" relates to a specific part of the completion stage: the stage of integration (*yuganaddha*). He comments:

> The text is not clear regarding the hidden [meaning], even though it is [hidden] to safeguard those tantras. They are hard to obtain because of this [secrecy]. The oral instructions that are thus hard to obtain in general pertain to the practice of Heruka [Cakrasaṃvara]'s two stages. In particular, they are the difficult-to-obtain method for achieving integration by means of the samādhi of the illusory body.[21]

Tantric exegesis is challenging, and Tsongkhapa, through his level-headed analysis of the tantric scriptures in light of their larger intellectual and practice contexts, set a high standard. His ultimate goal in works such as this was integration—of theory and practice and the exoteric and esoteric dimensions of Buddhist practice. Moreover, he strove to undertake tantric exegesis across the boundaries of traditions, using insights from one tradition to better understand another. Doing so did not make him a maverick but rather a master scholar. He understood how tantric traditions developed diachronically and impacted one another. Whether it was the influential Guhyasamāja five levels of the completion stage or the yoginītantra systems of body maṇḍala and *caṇḍālī* (*gtum mo*) contemplation, he cultivated a wisdom that transcended sectarian constraints. He was a scholar-practitioner extraordinaire, which is why he is still so revered six hundred years after passing into the awakened state.

20. Gray 2019, 289. "Kambala" here refers to the origin myths of the extant *Laghusaṃvara Tantra*, which relate its derivation from an extensive urtext a hundred thousand stanzas or more in length. See Tsongkhapa's summary of this at Gray 2017, 33–34.
21. Gray 2019, 291.

6. A Lamp to Illuminate the Five Stages: Tsongkhapa's Reformatory Work on the Guhyasamāja Tantra

Gavin Kilty

The master Tsongkhapa was of immense benefit to the Dharma in general, and in particular, it was he who spread the Guhyasamāja in this land.[1]

TSONGKHAPA SAW THE *Guhyasamāja Tantra* tradition in Tibet as in a state of decline, and he took on the responsibility of reforming it. He spoke of "the darkness of unknowing and misunderstanding surrounding its five stages"[2] and said, "The (Guhyasamāja) teachings in general, and specifically the Ārya tradition, have long been severely weakened."[3] In the colophon of his Guhyasamāja commentary *Lamp to Illuminate the Five Stages* he concluded, "I composed this work with a pure motivation for the severely weakened Guhyasamāja Ārya tradition to be restored and remain strong for a long time."[4]

It was in such a reformist spirit that he composed this important work on the Guhyasamāja. Having had the good fortune to translate *A Lamp to Illuminate the Five Stages*[5] into English, I will examine some of the extensively researched conclusions he arrived at that exemplify his reformatory efforts, which have served as the benchmark for future practitioners of

---

1. 'Gos Lo tsā ba, *Deb ther sngon po*, 1:444.

2. Tsongkhapa 2013, 564.

3. Tsongkhapa 2013, 564.

4. Tsongkhapa 2013, 564.

5. *Rim lnga rab tu gsal ba'i sgron me*, translated in Tsongkhapa 2013. The five stages of body and speech isolation, mind isolation, illusory body, clear light, and union make up the completion stage of the Guhyasamāja tantra, which is the main subject matter of the book.

Guhyasamāja. His analysis not only clarifies the essential meanings of the tantra but rebuts some commonly held positions of his time.

The Guhyasamāja Tantra

The *Guhyasamāja Tantra* holds a special place in the Buddhist tantric tradition. It is referred to as the root of all other classes of tantra and as the King of Tantras. Of the four classes of tantra, it belongs to highest yoga tantra, which means that it contains special methods not found in the three lower classes for attaining the two enlightened bodies. This is because the lower classes of action (*kriyā*), performance (*caryā*), and yoga tantra do not contain methods for bringing the winds into the central channel.

The Sanskrit term *guhyasamāja* means "a gathering of secrets." Tsongkhapa says that according to one tradition, this refers to a gathering or bringing together of the secrets of the body, speech, and mind of the enlightened state. According to another tradition, it means a place where the meanings of all other tantras are gathered. "Secrets" does not mean something deliberately withheld but something so difficult to comprehend that its meaning is not apparent.

The tantra itself is extant in the original Sanskrit and was translated into Tibetan during the second wave of translations in the tenth century, although there may have been an earlier translation.[6] It consists of seventeen chapters, with an eighteenth chapter classified as a separate work known as the *Later Tantra* (*Uttaratantra*, not to be confused with the well-known treatise of Maitreya by that title). The chapters describe the various practices and rituals of the generation and completion stages. Depending on the tradition, the main deity of the Guhyasamāja generation stage is either Akṣobhyavajra or Mañjuvajra, and the number of maṇḍala deities is either thirty-two or nineteen. It is said that the *Guhyasamāja Tantra* was taught by the Buddha in his lifetime. The Buddha is present throughout the whole tantra, teaching and revealing its secrets to the large assembly.

The root tantra has five or six explanatory tantras, and Tsongkhapa insists that the *Later Tantra* should also be considered an explanatory tan-

---

6. According to the *Blue Annals*, "The teachers belonging to the Nyingma school declared the Guhyasamāja to be the most important text among the eighteen classes of their tantras" ('Gos Lo tsā ba, *Deb ther sngon po*, 359).

tra. Even the explanations in these explanatory tantras need elucidating, and so there arose a corpus of commentaries by Indian masters. Tsongkhapa holds the *Vajra Garland Tantra* (*Vajramālātantra*) to be the best explanatory tantra:

> In the translator's colophon of the *Vajra Garland* it says, "No explanatory tantra better than this has appeared before." This is still the case.[7]

It is also because of its importance that many commentaries on the *Guhyasamāja Tantra* appeared in India. This led to multiple commentarial traditions. The two main ones were the Ārya tradition and the Jñānapāda tradition, each named after its initiator: "Ārya" refers to Nāgārjuna and "Jñānapāda" to Buddhaśrījñāna. Nāgārjuna heard the *Guhyasamāja* from the siddha Saraha, but apparently the latter did not compose any specific works on this tantra and therefore is not credited as the tradition's founder.[8] Instead, Nāgārjuna's *Five Stages* (*Pañcakrama*) became the authority for the Ārya tradition of interpretation.

Buddhaśrījñāna received his teachings on the *Guhyasamāja Tantra* in a vision directly from Mañjuśrī, after which he composed several influential works on the tantra. Tsongkhapa says that Buddhaśrījñāna in his main work, *Oral Teachings of Mañjuśrī* (*Dvikramatattvabhāvanāmukhāma*), concentrates on the *Later Tantra*, which explains the tantra using the six-branch yoga rather than the five stages. Both masters' works on the *Guhyasamāja Tantra* spawned many subcommentaries. Of the two traditions, Tsongkhapa clearly favors the Ārya tradition, and his *Lamp to Illuminate the Five Stages* focuses on it.

It is because of the great accomplishment of the translation into Tibetan of the root tantra, explanatory tantras, and works from the two main com-

---

7. Tsongkhapa 2013, 53.

8. The mahāsiddha Saraha is dated to around the eighth century, and Nāgārjuna is traditionally dated to the second or third century CE. However, many early Tibetan masters, as well as some Indian masters, claim that Nāgārjuna lived for six hundred years, which would make him contemporary with Saraha. Modern scholars assert that the early Mādhyamika Nāgārjuna was a different person to the later tantric practitioner who composed works on the five stages. Consequent to the earlier assertion, some Tibetans claim that Candrakīrti was a direct disciple of Nāgārjuna. Tsongkhapa is of this opinion, and he states that the great Indian master Atiśa thought likewise. See Tsongkhapa 2013, 67.

mentarial traditions that Tsongkhapa and many other Tibetan masters
were able to study and investigate the Indian teachings on the Guhyasamāja generation stage and five-stage completion stage.

The Transmission of Guhyasamāja into Tibet

According to Tsongkhapa, seven Guhyasamāja teaching lineages appeared
in Tibet by way of the great Tibetan translator Marpa Chökyi Lodrö
(1012–97), who traveled more than once to India and Nepal to collect
teachings. He received teachings and transmissions on both the Ārya and
Jñānapāda traditions of Guhyasamāja from seven masters, although his
main teacher in India was the pandit Nāropa. Subsequently, the widespread Marpa Guhyasamāja tradition in Tibet relied on the works and
teachings of Nāropa, especially his *Clear Compilation of the Five Stages*
(*Pañcakramasaṃgrahaprakāśa*).

The eleventh-century Tibetan translator Gö Khukpa Lhetsé traveled
to India twelve times, where he studied the Ārya tradition of the Guhyasamāja literature from nine Indian teachers. He brought back to Tibet
not only textual explanations of the classic texts but also the collections of
core instructions that had developed around the classic texts. Tsongkhapa
makes it clear that he holds the lineage of Gö in high regard:

> While many *Guhyasamāja Tantra* teachings belonging to the
> Ārya tradition may have come from India to Tibet, it is evident
> that the teaching tradition of Gö Rinpoché is supreme.[9]

There was also an oral-tradition lineage of the five stages that was transmitted by the Indian master Jñānākara to the Tibetan master Naktso
Tsultrim Gyalwa (1011–64). Tsongkhapa mentions that there were other
Guhyasamāja traditions in Tibet in the early days, started by one or two
Tibetan translators, but that they did not last. The *Blue Annals* states that
the Jñānapāda Guhyasamāja tradition was introduced into Tibet by the
great translator Lochen Rinchen Sangpo and subsequently by the Indian
pandits Smṛti and Śūnyaśrī.

According to the *Blue Annals* and the Sakya master Amé Shab's *His-*

---

9. Tsongkhapa 2013, 76.

tory of the Guhyasamāja,[10] the Marpa tradition and the Gö tradition were transmitted eventually to the great scholar Butön Rinchen Drup (1290–1364). Also, the *Blue Annals* states that many masters of the Marpa Guhyasamāja tradition studied the Guhyasamāja of the Gö tradition. Tsongkhapa received the Marpa Guhyasamāja tradition from Khyungpo Lhepa Shönu Sönam, who had received it from Butön Rinpoché. He received the Gö tradition from Khyungpo Lhepa and from Jetsun Rendawa, one of his main teachers.

The Importance of the Guhyasamāja Tantra

The importance Tsongkhapa gave to the Guhyasamāja can be seen from the number of works he composed on this topic. Even after composing his groundbreaking work on the tenets of tantra in general, *Great Exposition of Secret Mantra*, he set out to write several works covering the path of Guhyasamāja. These cover more than three volumes of his eighteen-volume collected works. These compositions ranged from annotations to commentaries on the initiation procedure, explanatory tantras, Indian compositions, and the generation and completion stages of the Guhyasamāja path. Of these, the most important and comprehensive is *A Lamp to Illuminate the Five Stages*.

Tsongkhapa devotes a whole section of this work to praise of Guhyasamāja. He quotes the *Root Tantra*, where it states that every secret of the body, speech, and mind of every tathāgata is contained within this tantra. He explains this to mean that every essential secret point of the Vajrayāna is contained within this tantra. He cites other tantras and commentaries that speak of its greatness and says that just to read, study, or even encounter this tantra is of immense benefit. He quotes Buddhaśrījñāna's *Oral Teachings of Mañjuśrī*, which states that as long as the *Guhyasamāja Tantra* remains, the teachings of the Buddha will remain, and if it disappears, the teachings will disappear, and, citing the *Guhyasiddhi*, he says "it is the amulet that holds the Buddhadharma."[11]

---

10. Amé Shab Ngawang Kunga Sönam (1597–1659) is usually referred to as Jamgön Amé Shab. His history of the Guhyasamāja is entitled *Precious Treasury of Wondrous Excellent Explanations: A History of the Glorious Guhyasamāja* (*Dpal gsang ba 'dus pa'i dam pa'i chos byung ba'i tshul legs bshad ngo mtshar rin po che'i bang mdzod*).

11. Tsongkhapa 2013, 56–57.

His personal connection to the Guhyasamāja can be understood in
the colophon, where he states he had received special signs of permission to compose this work, and he signs the work as "a yogi of glorious
Guhyasamāja."

At the end of his life, having taught the Four Commentaries Combined,[12]
he asked who would be able to preserve and disseminate these teachings.
Finally, Sherab Sengé (1383–1445) stood up, prostrated, and said, "I will
do it." He, in turn, passed the lineage to Dulnakpa Palden Sangpo (1402–
73), who taught Guhyasamāja extensively. Sherab Sengé founded the Segyü
Monastery and the Lower Tantric College in 1433, and his student Kunga
Döndrup founded the Upper Tantric College in 1474, which eventually
moved to Ramoché Temple in Lhasa.

The Reformatory Nature of Lamp to Illuminate the Five Stages

So concerned was Tsongkhapa about "the darkness of unknowing and misunderstanding surrounding the five stages" that he devotes the first part of
the book to a detailed and thorough investigation of all Indic Guhyasamāja
literature, including research into the tantra itself, its explanatory tantras,
and the commentarial traditions. Moreover, as every essential point of the
Vajra Vehicle is within the *Guhyasamāja Tantra*, Tsongkhapa's investigations and conclusions can be regarded as applying to the highest yoga tantra tradition as a whole.

What is evident from this work is the way Tsongkhapa balances the
authority of tradition and scripture with the authority of reason and conclusions induced by analysis. He has a deep faith in the root and explanatory tantras but does not shy away from seeming contradictions appearing
in these texts and does not hesitate to investigate how they can be resolved.
At every turn he consults the commentaries to compare and contrast until
he comes to a satisfactory conclusion. He does not hesitate to refute any
that do not stand up to reason. His faith never leads him to just put his
hands together and say, "Who are we to challenge such sacred texts?"

For example, the *Later Tantra*—the *Guhyasamāja Tantra*'s eighteenth

---

12. The four commentaries are the *Illuminating Lamp* (*Pradīpodyotana*) by Candrakīrti and
three subcommentaries by Tsongkhapa: a work consisting of notes on difficult points (*Mchan
gyi yang 'grel*), a general commentary called *Precious Sprout* (*Mtha' gcod rin po che'i myu gu*), and
an outline summary (*Sa bcad bsdus don*).

chapter—explains the completion stage according to the six-branch yoga and not according to the five stages, as the first seventeen chapters do. These two ways of practicing the completion stage appear to contradict. However, Tsongkhapa does not just leave that unresolved or conclude that the eighteenth chapter was added much later by somebody who wanted it to coincide with the six-branch yoga of the Kālacakra that entered India in the eleventh century. Instead, he embarks on a long investigation of how each of the five stages can be incorporated into the six yogas.

He attempts to elucidate every topic and point that is obscure in the tantra by examining all the commentaries and traditions; he is not, as the Tibetan saying goes, "like an old man eating meat," who only chews the soft parts. Among other topics, he discusses the difference between the *Root Tantra* and the *Later Tantra*, what constitutes a root tantra as opposed to a later tantra, and the number of explanatory tantras, going into great detail on each explanatory tantra, noting which part of the root tantra they elucidate. In his discussion on the commentarial traditions, he describes the advent of the Jñānapāda tradition from Buddhaśrījñāna and his *Oral Teachings of Mañjuśrī*, asserting that since this work explains only the last four of the six yogas taught in the *Later Tantra*, the first two yogas must belong to the generation stage in this tradition.

Tsongkhapa devotes a great deal of time to the Ārya tradition. He examines works on the generation stage by Nāgārjuna, weeding out those that are merely ascribed to him. Of Nāgārjuna's works on the completion stage, he concentrates on the well-known *Five Stages*, examining whether all five stages described in this work were actually written by Nāgārjuna. He looks at Guhyasamāja works of Āryadeva, Nāgabodhi, Śākyamitra, and Candrakīrti and casts doubt on the authenticity of a few. He also makes the assertion, backed up with reasons and scripture, that Candrakīrti was a direct disciple of Nāgārjuna.[13]

He critiques later Guhyasamāja commentaries that follow the Ārya tradition, including those ascribed to Nāropa and translated by Marpa, one of which he dismisses as being falsely ascribed. He also looks at the Guhyasamāja works of at least twelve other Indian commentators to ascertain their validity.

13. Tsongkhapa 2013, 67.

Prerequisites for Entering Tantra

As a preliminary to entering the Guhyasamāja completion stage and generally to the path of tantra itself, Tsongkhapa makes it clear that training in the common paths is essential. Moreover, citing the *Vajrapāṇi Initiation Tantra* (*Vajrapāṇyabhiṣekhatantra*) and Aśvaghoṣa's *Fifty Verses on the Guru* (*Gurupañcāśikā*), he says, "Those not completely trained in bodhicitta are not suitable for initiation,"[14] and recommends the teachings of Atiśa as a way of training in bodhicitta. He does not say that those who aspire to bodhicitta or who are partially trained in bodhicitta are suitable for initiation but only those who are completely trained:

> If you do not train well in the stages of the paths common to both vehicles as explained above, you will not cut the attachment to this life, and no firm desire to practice Dharma will arise. Sincere faith will not develop, and consequently you will not give yourself completely to the objects of refuge. You will not find a true conviction in cause and effect, and any guarding and protecting of whatever vows you may have becomes coarse and superficial. There will be no genuine turning away from the attachment to saṃsāra, and "striving for freedom" simply becomes an academic understanding. An uncontrived bodhicitta built on love and compassion will not grow, and you will be a Mahayanist in name only. There will be no strong desire to practice the activities of the bodhisattvas in general, and consequently there will be no genuine generation of the bodhisattva vows. There will be no pure understanding of mental quiescence and special insight in general, and therefore you will become prone to error on even the smallest samādhi and will not find any right conviction concerning the view of no-self. Therefore, if you wish not to go this way, you should train in the path common to both Mahāyāna vehicles.[15]

He cites masters from both the Gö and Marpa Guhyasamāja traditions

14. Tsongkhapa 2013, 78.
15. Tsongkhapa 2013, 80.

who back up this point, concluding that "among the earlier masters who practiced the Guhyasamāja, none did not follow this tradition of the graded path."[16] Tsongkhapa's stress on this point seems to indicate that there were those during his time who headed straight into the practice of tantra without these essential prerequisites.

He is saying something similar when talking about the necessity of keeping the vows and pledges taken at the initiation:

> If you have gained conviction that the pure initiations and the practices surrounding the pledges are preliminaries to being guided through the two stages, then practices such as guru yoga, the hundred-syllable mantra, and maṇḍala offerings designated as preliminary practices will be incidental practices. If you have conviction only in these latter practices, it means that you have no understanding of the former, and you should make efforts to understand them.[17]

Tsongkhapa here indicates that practicing the preliminaries of guru yoga, maṇḍala offerings, and so on means little if one is not also adhering purely to the vows and pledges taken at the time of initiation.

The Generation Stage

Just as there are prerequisites for entering tantra, the generation stage is a prerequisite for entering the completion stage:

> A person who wishes for the supreme attainment is not someone who does not meditate on the generation stage but instead is someone who enters the completion stage after having first trained well on the generation stage.[18]

He backs this up with a citation from Nāgārjuna's *Five Stages*, which compares the two stages to a ladder and says that even the best, jewel-

16. Tsongkhapa 2013, 81.
17. Tsongkhapa 2013, 83.
18. Tsongkhapa 2013, 84.

like disciples must once have been beginners. Therefore there must be a beginning stage; an all-at-once approach (*cig char 'jug pa*), where the completion stage is practiced from the outset, has no authority in the tantras.

This too seems aimed at practices prevalent in his time. He goes on to say that there were powerful beings in the past who over many previous lives trained on the lower paths and were now able to begin from the higher paths, but to use that as a justification for all-at-once approach is laughable. He praises the generation stage and cites a tantra that compares it to a boat necessary for crossing that can be discarded only after arriving at the far side of the river.

He says that many texts, such as those by Saraha, in their sections on the meditation upon innate wisdom, refute the need for the elaborations of the generation stage and that this has led to the assertion that the tradition of Saraha follows an all-at-once approach while the tradition of Nāgārjuna follows a gradual approach. Tsongkhapa stresses that this is a misunderstanding. Any presentation stating that the gradual approach is for those of low or intermediate intelligence and the all-at-once approach is for those of high intelligence, he says, contradicts all tantra and soundly sourced scripture.

The Guhyasamāja generation stage consists of the four branches of approach (*bsnyen*), close accomplishment (*nyer grub*), accomplishment (*sgrub pa*), and great accomplishment (*sgrub chen*). Tsongkhapa says that by understanding how much meditation there is to be done in these four branches to ripen the mindstream for the insights of the completion stage, it becomes very clear how important it is to begin with the generation stage's meditations.

He points out that the order of practice of the generation stage is found in Āryadeva's *Lamp for Integrating the Practices* (*Caryāmelāpakapradīpa*) and spends some time analyzing the meaning of the term *single-thought meditation* (*dran pa gcig*) mentioned there, concluding that it means thinking of the deities together as one, or thinking of yourself and the deities together as one, and not thinking of the deities one time or thinking of just one deity. He notes that the generation stage possesses many excellent qualities:

> For example, within it lie profound auspicious features that correspond to future production of the insights of the completion

stage. The mindstream becomes blessed by the conquerors and their noble children, and in all lives you are cared for by the great deities. You are never separated from remembering the Buddha. You easily complete the accumulation of merit through the practices of offering and praise. You are never harmed by hindrances. You will be able in this life to attain many siddhis—those of pacification and so on.[19]

Emptiness

Tsongkhapa identifies the syllables *e* and *vaṃ* as the principal components of the completion stage and spells out their significance extensively, but he says that the definitive meaning of *evaṃ* is "inseparable bliss and emptiness." He says that the view of emptiness, which is referred to as *ultimate bodhicitta*, should be that of the Madhyamaka:

> For those within secret mantra to develop the ultimate bodhicitta through the force of meditation, they must initially seek the view of no-self in accordance with what is taught in the texts on Madhyamaka.[20]

He backs this up with citations from Nāgārjuna's *Commentary on Bodhicitta (Bodhicittavivaraṇa)*, in which *bodhicitta* refers to the second chapter of the *Guhyasamāja Tantra*. Citing numerous tantras, he establishes that the view of emptiness taught in tantra is that of the Perfection Vehicle. This is to counter the assertions of some[21] that the view of emptiness in tantra is incompatible with that of the Perfection Vehicle, an assertion they back up with this citation from a Kālacakra text:

19. Tsongkhapa 2013, 90.

20. Tsongkhapa 2013, 99.

21. Probably referring to the Jonang tradition, whose views were far removed from mainstream Madhyamaka and who specialized in the practice of Kālacakra tantra. For them, the emptiness taught in Kālacakra texts is not the emptiness of the Perfection Vehicle.

The emptiness of examining the aggregates is, like the plantain tree, without essence. Emptiness endowed with supreme characteristics[22] is not like that.[23]

Tsongkhapa refutes this with quotations from Puṇḍarīka's seminal *Stainless Light* (*Vimalaprabhā*) commentary on the Kālacakra. He concludes:

> Of the four tenet systems, the emptiness of bliss and emptiness united taught on the basis of the best and jewel-like disciple of highest yoga mantra is that of the Prāsaṅgika Madhyamaka.[24]

But, he adds, "in tantric commentaries there is a tradition of explaining united bliss and emptiness on the basis of the Cittamātra position."[25]

Bliss

Tsongkhapa goes to great lengths identifying this special meaning of *bliss*, distinguishing it from types of bliss found in various samādhis and Perfection Vehicle practices before identifying it as "the bliss of the melting bodhicitta brought on by the blazing *caṇḍālī*[26] ignited by the force of the winds entering the central channel from the practice of penetrating the vital points of the channel cakras in the body."[27] This teaching on innate bliss is an exclusive feature not found in other vehicles and lower tantras, and therefore the bliss felt when, say, experiencing emptiness is not the innate bliss and emptiness of highest yoga tantra.

---

22. *Rnam pa kun gyi mchog ldan pa'i stong pa nyid.* In the *Kālacakra Tantra, emptiness* sometimes refers to an emptiness, or empty form, endowed with various features rather than the mere negation of true existence. The supreme empty form is Viśvamātā, the consort of male deity Kālacakra.

23. Tsongkhapa 2013, 100.

24. Tsongkhapa 2013, 103.

25. Tsongkhapa 2013, 104. This refers to an emptiness of the apprehending consciousness and apprehended object as separate entities.

26. That is, *gtum mo*, mystical inner heat.

27. Tsongkhapa 2013, 105.

Emptiness and Bliss United

The uniting of bliss and emptiness is described as:

> The subject consciousness is developed into the entity of innate bliss and unerringly perceiving its object of emptiness. At the time of the development of actual innate bliss, object and subject become of one taste, like milk poured into water, and even the subtlest dualistic appearance is removed.[28]

The mind is one of innate bliss, which in terms of possessing the power to ascertain emptiness is unlike any other consciousness. Therefore, although the object is the same, the method of using bliss in this vehicle surpasses the Perfection Vehicle. Without developing the mind of innate bliss, the vital principle of the supreme path of mantra is missing. In summary:

> The phrase "bliss and emptiness inseparable" is as widespread as the wind, but knowing great bliss distinct from the types of bliss, ultimate emptiness distinct from the types of emptiness, and the way these two are united is very rare. With this in mind, Saraha says:

> > In house after house they talk about it,
> > but there is no complete knowledge
> > of the principles of great bliss.[29]

Tsongkhapa talks of a second meaning of *evaṃ*, which is the inseparability of the two truths. Here *conventional truth* refers to the pure illusory body and *ultimate truth* to the actual clear light. These are also referred to as "method and wisdom." The two combined are the fifth stage, union. Tsongkhapa stresses that the causes for the illusory body are the subtle winds, and that the third stage—the illusory body—must be adorned with the marks and features of a fully enlightened being because that becomes the similar-type-cause for the form body of a buddha. He says that on the Perfection

28. Tsongkhapa 2013, 108.
29. Tsongkhapa 2013, 113.

Vehicle and the Tantra Vehicle, the coarse body does not just spontaneously transform into the enlightened form body but that a similar-type cause is necessary in both, and in highest yoga tantra that cause is the illusory body. In the completion stage, after entering into emptiness, the yogi has to arise in the form of a deity that is not created by mere imagination. Such a form will arise at that time if it is known how to accomplish the illusory body.

Penetrating Vital Points

The bliss consciousness generated by the winds entering the central channel is the best consciousness for perceiving the emptiness that will destroy the subtlest holding to true existence and remove all obscurations. This bliss is brought about by penetrating the vital points of the body, which is accomplished by way of a consort or by meditation on the inner channels, winds, and drops.

The Consort

Union with a *karmamudrā*—a flesh-and-blood consort—brings the winds from the left and right channels into the central channel. The *caṇḍālī* blazes, causing the bodhicitta to melt. This is known as external *prāṇāyāma*. Whatever arises from reliance upon a *karmamudrā*, the same can arise from the reliance upon a visualized wisdom consort (*jñānamudrā*).

Meditation on Channels and So On

Tsongkhapa lists the different starting places—such as the heart, navel, and secret cakra—for this practice according to the different tantras and goes on to explain the basic principle of vital-point penetration:

> Because mind and wind work in tandem, holding the mind in these places—even though it is not actual wind meditation—is the reason why they are methods for bringing the two winds into the central channel.[30]

30. Tsongkhapa 2013, 127.

The five stages of the completion stage, in the way they create the three bodies, correspond to the stages of birth, death, and the intermediate state, or *bardo*, just as in the generation stage because "the intention of highest yoga tantra is to correlate the creation of the supporting and supported maṇḍalas of the generation stage to the stages of creation and destruction of the container world and its contained sentient beings."[31] Therefore this leads to death, bardo, and birth in the basic state being labeled as the three bodies and to basic-state events such as sleep, dreams, and so on being labeled by way of the five stages. To sum up:

> Therefore the whole process follows the five stages of the basic state. You meditate on the indestructible drop at the heart. Focusing on the heart you perform vajra repetition on the arising, entering, and abiding winds. On its completion the winds are turned away from moving in and out of the body and gradually dissolve into the heart. From this arise the four kinds of emptiness, after which a very subtle illusory body is formed solely from the winds and mind that abide within the coarse body. After the development of the actual clear light, this illusory body is the body of union. After the development of the illustrative clear light, this is the impure illusory body. The *sambhogakāya* cannot be seen by all eyes. Only when it is contained within a body of coarse aggregates does it become an object for fleshly eyes. Then that is the *nirmāṇakāya*.[32]

Core Instructions

> The ultimate source of the core instructions on the five stages is the *Guhyasamāja Root Tantra*. In that tantra, however, the completion stage of the five stages is sealed and is not evident. To remove the seal, the explanatory tantras were taught. Nevertheless, without an explanation from a qualified master who explains the complete meaning of the tantra by joining root with explanatory tantra, it is said that even the jewel-like disciple will

31. Tsongkhapa 2013, 128.
32. Tsongkhapa 2013, 133.

not fully understand the tantra. Hence, rely on the instructions of the guru.[33]

Tsongkhapa argues that it is not the case that core instructions (*man ngag*) were not written down. Tsongkhapa goes through the core instructions of the Marpa tradition to illustrate that point. In the Ārya tradition, *core instructions* must refer back to the works of Nāgārjuna and his disciples. His Holiness the Dalai Lama often says that generally all core instructions must be grounded in the classical texts.

The First Stage

The first of the five stages is *body and speech isolation*, and speech isolation involves vajra repetition (*vajrajāpa*) and *prāṇāyāma*. With the attainment of body isolation, which involves the divine view of one's bodily constituents, the practitioner engages in speech isolation, and by abiding in vajra repetition, *focus on the mind* (*sems la dmigs pa*) is attained, which leads to *mind isolation*, the second stage. The *illusory body*, the third stage, is purified by the ultimate reality of *clear light* (the fourth stage), and from within that state is achieved *nondual union*, the final stage.

Tsongkhapa refutes certain reasons for the order of the five stages as posited by some of the Marpa tradition, and even some from the Indic tradition, including that of the renowned Abhayākaragupta. Some Indian scholars place body isolation in the generation stage. Some say that the generation stage is one of the five stages. Others combine body isolation with vajra repetition to become one stage of speech isolation. Tsongkhapa's position is that the practice of body isolation is spread over both stages, determined by whether the winds have entered the central channel. He elucidates various types of body isolation: those of the hundred sacred families separated into the five aggregates division, the four elements division, the six sense powers division, and the five objects division. He explains how individual withdrawal (*pratyāhāra*) and absorption (*dhyāna*), the first two yogas of the six-branch yoga, are incorporated into body isolation.

Tsongkhapa discusses the sequencing of body isolation and speech isolation, refutes assertions that speech isolation is generation stage, teaches

----

33. Tsongkhapa 2013, 137.

a whole section on the nature of the winds, the nature of the mantras, how speech isolation becomes "skillful manipulation of the breath" (*prāṇāyāma*), and the way to practice speech isolation:

> The necessity of accomplishing body isolation with the body vajra as the play of great bliss before speech isolation is that speech isolation is the exclusive mantra recitation of the completion stage, and if this vajra body does not exist in the deity meditation of the reciting practitioner, the potential of the recitation will not be fully realized.[34]

Winds

In the section on winds, he discusses the faults of not knowing and the advantages of knowing the reality of the winds, the divisions of the winds, the explanation of each division, how the winds move, and how they perform their functions. The reason for knowing the winds is that the mantras of vajra repetition engage with the various winds. Also, completion-stage meditations of penetrative focusing on the body's vital points involve the workings of the winds. He examines the ten, fifty-four, and 108 winds and discusses how they relate to each other, where they exist in the body, how they are obstructed by the channel knots, the elements and goddesses they correspond to, their colors, and their relationship to the mind. There is an extensive section on which nostril they flow through in correspondence with the *Kālacakra Tantra*, the shifts that correspond to the movement of the zodiac constellations through the sky, and how the winds move from one channel petal to another.

He explains that the statement in tantric texts that winds are the cause of saṃsāra means that they are cooperative causes of the eighty indicative or intrinsic conceptual minds that arise and dissolve with birth and death:

> The *Vajra Garland* states that the wind as the chariot of the consciousness is mixed with the imprints of consciousness, and when objects are engaged, this will create the intrinsic conceptual

---

34. Tsongkhapa 2013, 214.

minds. Through the contamination by the imprints, you wander in saṃsāra, and there is no saṃsāra other than that.[35]

Also:

> If you understand the uncommon view of the process of engaging in saṃsāra through the force of the winds, you will see the need to halt the karmic winds that move the conceptual minds, and a search for instructions on penetrative focusing on the body as the method to halt these winds will begin.[36]

Mantras

Like the section on winds, there is an extensive discussion of mantras, specifically the three-syllable mantra (*oṃ āḥ hūṃ*) used in vajra repetition, and how all other mantras are contained in these three syllables. Also, there is an explanation of how the letter *a* is the root of all winds and abides at the indestructible point in the heart:

> The indestructible is the root of all the winds in the form of inner vowels and consonants, and seeing how those winds gathered into that indestructible drop will actualize the clear light is the exclusive way to understand the nature of the mantras in vajra repetition.[37]

He explains how speech isolation becomes the branch of *prāṇāyāma* from the six-branch yoga taught in the *Later Tantra*, and he explains in great detail the three *prāṇāyāma* meditations on the three drops at the secret place, heart, and nose (a.k.a. the three "tips") and compares and analyzes all available commentaries on this topic. The natural or innate tone of the winds entering, abiding, and rising is applied to the three syllables. This tone is inseparably joined with the tone of the mantras.

Therefore recitation possessing the nature of the three syllables of the

35. Tsongkhapa 2013, 249.
36. Tsongkhapa 2013, 252.
37. Tsongkhapa 2013, 265.

three vajras inseparably combined with the tones of the three winds is called *vajra repetition*. This practice loosens the knots at the heart. He concludes:

> There are many practices of vajra repetition in the instruction texts, but a complete explanation of vajra repetition like that found in the Guhyasamāja literature is not present in other tantras or treatises. A good explanation from the Guhyasamāja tradition is rare. Therefore this extensive explanation of vajra repetition has been for the purpose of conclusively ascertaining this wind yoga as taught by the Ārya master and his disciples, who did not teach other wind yogas.[38]

The Final Four Stages

Tsongkhapa explains the reasons for knowing the reality of the mind, which is the essence of *mind isolation* (*cittaviveka*). He concentrates on the three appearances that naturally appear at death, describing each of them and each of the eighty intrinsic conceptual minds that subside at this time. He also describes different traditions of generating mind isolation by way of the three appearances.

The basis for any deity body in body isolation and in the generation stage is the coarse body of atoms and not the winds, and there is no deity in speech isolation. However, here the basis of the *illusory body* (*māyākāya*) is the life-sustaining wind (*prāṇa*). He clearly teaches the way to attain illusory body from the mind and wind of the three empty states, as explained in the core instructions and the Ārya tradition. He examines and finds the literary sources for these core teachings. He also explains the nine mixings[39] of the Marpa tradition.

For the actual *clear light* (*prabasvara*) that is a direct realization of the very subtle reality by innate bliss consciousness, it is necessary to have previously generated the illusory body.

---

38. Tsongkhapa 2013, 328.

39. *Bsre ba.* These involve applying sleep, death, and meditative experience to each of the three enlightened bodies, making nine in total.

The illusory body enters clear light and then arises in the form of the *union* (*yuganaddha*) of the two truths.

How the Path of Tantra Must Occur on the Sūtra Path

Having explained how the five paths and ten levels fit into the five stages, he asserts and explains how the Buddha attained enlightenment as a tenth-level bodhisattva by receiving initiation and relying upon the tantric path during the night of his enlightenment. This is in reply to the qualm:

> Before he displayed deeds of the austerities and so on by the river as described in the *Great Play Sūtra* (*Lalitavistarasūtra*), Śākyamuni was already a buddha. In that case, what does it mean here to say that he became a buddha by the path of mantra at the conclusion of the path of the Perfection Vehicle?[40]

Desire

In tantra it is taught that enlightenment will be attained by engaging the five types of sense objects. How does the path of desire not contradict the teaching that attachment to the objects of the five senses is a poison to be abandoned? Tsongkhapa answers by saying that the desire used in tantra is unadulterated desire. It is not desire that has been transformed into something else, nor is it non-desire labeled as desire. On the contrary, the practitioner has the power to engage desire to actualize the path. He backs this up with a number of citations:

1. The afflictions become the conditions for the afflictions for those with apprehending views, such as śrāvakas, because they do not understand the nature of afflictions. If the nature of the afflictions is understood, they become a cause for enlightenment.[41]
2. Just as the manure of a city benefits the sugarcane fields and so on, the manure of the bodhisattva's afflictions is beneficial for becoming a buddha.

40. Tsongkhapa 2013, 468.
41. Tsongkhapa 2013, 513.

3. That which binds the stupid will liberate the wise.
4. Bliss is gained by bliss.[42]

He concludes:

> Having no attachment to objects of desire does not contradict
> seeking out objects of desire such as food and clothing. Merely
> making use of sense objects that may be attractive, unattractive,
> or neutral and merely seeking out sense objects that arise in the
> mental consciousness do not become afflictions.[43]

Also, with tantras that engage anger, he stresses that when acting wrath-
fully, the motivation must be one of compassion.

Summary

With this extensive work built on equally extensive research, the points
and stages of the Guhyasamāja completion stage are clarified, all misconceptions are pointed out, and all doubts resolved. This is a reformer at work.
In his colophon he says:

> I familiarized myself for a long time in enthusiastic application
> to show the ways that disciples are guided by the stages of the
> complete corpus of each of these paths, ornamented by relevant
> transmitted instructions; to promote the ascertainment of emp-
> tiness, and having ascertained it, the way to meditate upon it;
> to reveal the ways that each Guhyasamāja tradition has been
> explained; and to present all the genuine Indian works of the
> Ārya tradition that have been translated into Tibetan, together
> with their transmitted instructions. With this, I compared the
> root tantra and the explanatory tantras, and with much prayer
> and request I received special signs of permission to compose this
> work. Then, with a pure motivation for the severely weakened

42. The last three citations are all found at Tsongkhapa 2013, 514.
43. Tsongkhapa 2013, 515.

Guhyasamāja Ārya tradition to be restored and remain strong for a long time, I composed this work.[44]

44. Tsongkhapa 2013, 563.

7. The Shadow of Heshang: Tsongkhapa on Chan, Dzokchen, and Mahāmudrā Meditation

Roger R. Jackson[1]

We have taken from the defeated
What they had to leave us—a symbol:
A symbol perfected in death.
—T. S. Eliot, "Little Gidding"

Introduction

Tsongkhapa, or Jé Rinpoché, as he is frequently called, often presented himself, and has been presented by Geluk tradition, as a scholar who, above all, read carefully and interpreted properly the Indian Buddhist classics that formed the core of the Sūtra Vehicle curriculum at the great Tibetan monasteries, including key texts on Vinaya and Abhidharma, the Madhyamaka treatises of Nāgārjuna and his successors, the Yogācāra-inflected Maitreya/Asaṅga corpus, the epistemological writings of Dignāga and Dharmakīrti, and many more works besides. In presenting himself in such a way, Jé Rinpoché implicitly or explicitly set himself apart from his Tibetan predecessors, whom he felt had failed to investigate the Indian texts with sufficient care and hence had fallen prey to grave errors with regard to view, meditation, and conduct. Tsongkhapa was a man of his time and culture and was educated by lamas from every major Tibetan tradition—Kadam, Kagyü, Sakya, Nyingma, and even Jonang—and while he gratefully acknowledged all that he learned from them, he attributed some of his most penetrating

---

1. Many thanks to John Newman, who read an earlier version of this paper and made a number of helpful terminological and historical observations, from which I have benefited greatly.

insights, especially regarding Madhyamaka, to the guidance he received in visions from the wisdom buddha Mañjughoṣa. From Jé Rinpoché's perspective, such guidance enabled him to uncover the true purport of difficult passages in the Indian classics. However, as Thupten Jinpa notes:

> [F]or the contemporary reader, this kind of invocation [of] mystic guidance . . . is often a device signaling a fundamental shift away from an existing tradition. In other words, it allows the claimant to put forth his or her original and often revolutionary ideas without jeopardizing the need for faithfulness to a tradition.[2]

Innovation was, of course, an intellectual sin no Tibetan traditionalist sought to commit, so however we (or his Tibetan critics) might regard Tsongkhapa, he saw himself not as an original thinker but as a scholar who had recovered the true authorial intent of his Indian predecessors.

Thus, in his discussions of tranquil abiding meditation (*śamatha, zhi gnas*) in the *Great Treatise on the Stages of the Path* (*Lam rim chen mo*) and other texts, Tsongkhapa typically insisted that he was just explicating the system laid down by Asaṅga in his *Śrāvaka Levels* (*Śrāvakabhūmi*), with additional support from various sūtras, notably the *King of Samādhis* (*Samādhirāja*) and *Unraveling the Intent* (*Saṃdhinirmocana*), and the treatises of Vasubandhu, Śāntideva, Kamalaśīla, Atiśa, and others. His extraordinarily detailed expositions of insight meditation (*vipaśyanā, lhag mthong*) are primarily rooted in the works of Nāgārjuna and Candrakīrti, with supporting material drawn from many of the same sources as his analysis of tranquil abiding. However Indic Jé Rinpoché's presentation of meditation and the view may appear, he wrote on these topics not only by consulting writings by the South Asian masters but also by keeping in mind the perspectives of his Tibetan predecessors, either as inspiration or foil.

Here, keeping our lens focused primarily on the realm of contemplative practice, we will inquire into Tsongkhapa's treatment of three systems of view, meditation, and conduct that were important in Tibet in the centuries preceding him but appear to be peripheral to the system he outlined in the *Great Treatise* and other works of his "mature" period: Chinese Chan

---

2. Jinpa 2002, 17.

Buddhism and two significant Tibetan traditions: Nyingma *atiyoga*, better known as the "great perfection," *dzokchen* (*rdzogs pa chen po*); and the Kagyü "great seal," *mahāmudrā* (*phyag rgya chen po*).[3] In our necessarily brief analysis, we will set each one within its larger Asian and Tibetan context, then note some of the ways in which Tsongkhapa seems to have regarded each. In doing so, we may perhaps enhance our understanding of Jé Rinpoché's approach to meditation by delineating the "negative space" provided by the Tibetan traditions that surrounded it.

Tsongkhapa on Chan

It is, of course, quite wrong to say that Tsongkhapa knew anything of Chinese Chan, since very few Tibetans of his era (or, for that matter, previous eras, going back many centuries) were conversant with Chinese culture, literature, or religious practices, even where Buddhism was concerned. What Jé Rinpoché *did* know was the spectral image of a Chinese monk a half-millennium dead—Heshang Moheyan, known in Tibetan as Hva shang Mahāyāna. Heshang, whose precise sectarian affiliation within Chan is uncertain,[4] was a popular figure at the court of the second "Dharma king," Trisong Detsen (742–97), and became a major player in the so-called Samyé Debate, or Council of Lhasa, called by the king in the early 790s to resolve questions about the course that Buddhism, still quite new in Tibet, would take on the plateau. Would it be mainly Chinese in flavor, or Indian? How should the wisdom literature of Mahāyāna be read? What is the most spiritually efficacious type of meditation? Where should ethics be located on the Buddhist path? These were some of the points of contention. In a style emblematic of the developing Chinese Chan tradition, Heshang—who was apparently supported by a number of Indian and Tibetan masters partial to dzokchen—adopted a subitist or all-at-once (*cig car ba*) approach to the path, in which the attainment of wisdom was possible only through a sudden and total break with conventional ways of thinking and acting, that meditation required the complete suspension of conceptual thought, and that ethics should be the outcome rather than the basis of insight

---

3. For a thoughtful analysis of Tsongkhapa's views of tranquil abiding over against those of mahāmudrā and dzokchen, see Wallace 1998, 225–48.

4. van Schaik 2015, 131–32.

into reality. Heshang's teachings were opposed by numerous Indian and Tibetan masters, most notably the Indian paṇḍita Kamalaśīla (740–95), who argued in favor of a gradual (*rim gyis pa*) approach to the Buddhist path, in which ethics is foundational, tranquil abiding is practiced on the basis of ethics, and wisdom is attained through decisive philosophical analysis, which then is deepened into direct realization by conjoining insight with tranquil abiding.

Much is uncertain about the circumstances, procedures, and outcome of the debate. We do have texts written by the main participants— Kamalaśīla's three *Stages of Meditation* (*Bhāvanākrama*) texts, various treatises attributed to Heshang,[5] and a slightly later text on early Tibetan practice systems, the *Lamp for the Eye of Meditation* (*Bsam gtan mig sgron*), credited to Nub Sangyé Yeshé[6]—but these writings only generally allude to the issues at stake and never mention the debate explicitly. Indeed, we have no reliable contemporaneous account of the events, merely a variety of documents, produced a century or more after the fact, that differ on key points. The most prominent are the Tibetan *Testimony of Ba* (*Dba bzhed*), which affirms the victory of the gradualists and the king's subsequent banishment of the Chinese monks and their tradition,[7] and the Chinese *Ratification of the True Principles of Mahāyāna Sudden Awakening* (*Dun wu da cheng zheng li jue* 頓悟大乘正理決), by Wangxi, which depicts Heshang as the victor and has the king declaring that his doctrine would prevail thereafter in Tibet.[8] The *Testament* and the *Ratification* do concur that at the conclusion of the debate the king upheld "the doctrine of Nāgārjuna," but they disagree on which side this was.

These uncertainties notwithstanding, two things are clear. First, in the wake of the debate, India increasingly became the main source from which Tibetans drew their version of Buddhism, and correspondingly, the influence of Chinese Buddhism in general and Chan in particular began a slow but steady decline on the plateau, such that Heshang's actual teach-

---

5. For Kamalaśīla, see, e.g., Beyer 1974, 99–115, Tucci 1986, 465–592, Kamalaśīla 1988, and Kellner 2020. For Heshang, see especially Gomez 1983, Gomez 1987, and van Schaik 2015.

6. Meinert 2003.

7. Translated in Kapstein 2013, 142–50. A later, oft-cited account that runs along similar lines is that of Butön Rinchen Drup (1290–1364), translated in Obermiller 1986, 191–96.

8. Demiéville 1952; a similar view is found in the twelfth-century *Five-Part Edict* (*Bka' thang sde lnga*), on which see Tucci 1986, 391–412.

ings were long forgotten by the time Tsongkhapa arrived on the scene. Second, and more significantly, Heshang himself lived on in the Tibetan imagination, both as a comically pathetic figure in popular mythological dance-dramas and, for scholars, as representative of a fruitless approach to Buddhist thought and practice, one that maintained that knowledge of reality could only be achieved through a sudden, trans-rational leap, saw meditation as blank-minded catalepsy, and utterly disregarded ethics. In time, as Chan itself faded from Tibetans' collective memory, the caricature of Heshang persisted and was increasingly used by Tibetan masters as a cudgel to attack not Chinese Buddhists but their compatriots.

The most famous, if not the earliest, such instance is found in the writings of Sakya Paṇḍita Kunga Gyaltsen (or Sapaṇ, 1182–1251), who criticized Kagyü mahāmudrā traditions such as the white panacea (*dkar po gcig thub*) and single intention (*dgongs gcig*), in large part on the grounds that the great-seal approach to Buddhism in general and its meditation techniques in particular were simply the Heshang position in disguise— and indeed, like dzokchen, more likely of Chinese than Indian origin.[9] Although early Kagyü masters like Gampopa Sönam Rinchen (1079– 1153) did, in fact, draw on Chinese sources,[10] later Kagyüpas (and others, including Gelukpas) defended their great-seal traditions from Sapaṇ's attack, arguing that their sources were solidly Indic and their subitist perspective easily misunderstood if taken out of a larger context in which "immediate" practices are appropriate only for the most gifted individuals, with the less talented majority required to follow a gradual path.[11] Although their tradition was historically interwoven with Chan, Nyingmapas too defended their tradition as primarily Indic in origin, and dzokchen as quite different from—and superior to—Chinese subitism.[12] In any case, over time most Kagyüpas and even many Nyingmapas came to accept the caricature of Heshang promulgated by the *Testament of Ba,* Sapaṇ, and Butön Rinchen Drup (1290–1364), so that the stereotypical image of

---

9. Seyfort Ruegg 1989, D. Jackson 1994, and Sakya Pandita 2002.

10. D. Jackson 1994, 20–24.

11. See, e.g., Broido 1987 and Dakpo Tashi Namgyal 2019, 129–35.

12. Meinert 2003, 185 and 192–93; cf. Karmay 1988, 105. See also Dudjom 1991, 896 and 899— although Rinpoche's comments on pages 905 and 906 seem more positively disposed toward Heshang.

the Chinese master that was inherited by Tsongkhapa—perhaps from his Sakyapa master Rendawa Shönu Lodrö (1349–1412)[13]—was already quite fixed in the Tibetan Buddhist imagination.

Tsongkhapa's references to Heshang are scattered throughout his collected works. Here we will focus on just two sources: his open letter to the "great meditators of Tibet," *Queries from a Sincere Heart* (*Dri ba lhag bsam rab dkar*), and his *Great Treatise on the Stages of the Path.*

Queries,[14] which was probably written around 1390–91, is framed as a series of rhetorical questions on Buddhist view, meditation, and practice posed to unnamed contemplatives—although it is widely accepted in later tradition that the target of Tsongkhapa's implicit critique is a group of Kagyüpas with whom he may have undertaken a mahāmudrā retreat while in his early thirties. We will return to *Queries* in our discussion of Tsongkhapa vis-à-vis the great seal, noting here only his references to Heshang. These come almost exclusively in a section midway through the text, where Jé Rinpoché interrogates his imagined interlocutors as to the proper way of meditating on emptiness according to Nāgārjuna's system. He focuses in particular on the contemplative technique of nonattention (*amanasikāra, yid la mi byed pa*)—that is, not engaging the mind with any object, a practice often associated with the Indian siddha Maitrīpa,[15] himself a key source of Kagyü mahāmudrā ideas and practices.[16]

Tsongkhapa specifically questions the way in which nonattention might affect two basic types of meditation: placement or resting meditation (*'jog sgom*), which leads to tranquil abiding, and investigative or analytical meditation (*dpyad sgom*), which leads to insight. If placement meditation involves nonattention, he asks, then in what sense is one "placing" the mind on some specific object, and if one is not focused on *some* object, what hope is there of attaining tranquil abiding, samādhi, or meditative equipoise (*mnyam gzhag, samāpatti*)? If investigative meditation involves nonattention, then in what sense can one be said to "investigate" the nature of reality, and if one does not analyze the nature of reality—as Nāgārjuna and his successors did—what hope is there of realizing emptiness and

---

13. See Jinpa 2019, 93–94.

14. Jinpa 2019, chap. 4; cf. R. Jackson 2019, 156–59.

15. See, e.g., Higgins 2013 and Mathes 2015.

16. Tsong kha pa, *Dri ba lhag bsam rab dkar*, 116–18; cf. Jinpa 2019, 92–95.

attaining liberation? In each case, Tsongkhapa associates nonattention with the Heshang approach, adding that one important consequence of such a teaching is an implicit abrogation of ethics and other conventional path practices, which are, in his view, the foundation of proper meditation, whether of the placement or investigative variety. As a countermeasure, Tsongkhapa recommends reading Kamalaśīla's three *Bhāvanākrama* texts, which Kamalaśīla is believed to have been written as a follow-up to his encounter with Heshang at the Samyé Debate. Through their invidious comparisons, these "sincere queries" illustrate two key elements of Tsongkhapa's thought: his insistence that all cognitive states require an intentional object and his claim that a direct yogic realization of emptiness must be preceded by conceptual analysis.

In the *Great Treatise on the Stages of the Path*, completed in 1402, Tsongkhapa mentions Heshang several times in his sections on tranquil abiding and insight, which comprise more than a third of the text. Most of the references occur in discussions of insight, particularly when it comes to the question of whether conceptual analysis is a prerequisite for a direct realization of emptiness. For instance, after quoting a passage from the *Unraveling the Intent Sūtra* specifying that insight requires "full differentiation, thorough examination, thorough analysis," Jé Rinpoché reports that Heshang, having read this statement, "exclaimed, 'I don't know how this can be a sūtra!' and kicked it."[17] Later, he identifies as Heshang's the view of those who "hold that all thought consists of grasping to true existence and discard it altogether," adding that those who meditate on emptiness in such a way "do not reach an errorless view of selflessness" and recommends, yet again, Kamalaśīla's three *Stages of Meditation* texts as an antidote.[18] Kamalaśīla also is cited with approval for his quotation of a passage in the *King of Samādhis Sūtra* to the effect that analytical discernment of the lack of self in phenomena and cultivation of analysis in meditation will lead to nirvāṇa, which is quite the opposite of Heshang's approach. "You must," says Tsongkhapa, "have certain knowledge of this."[19]

Other *Great Treatise* references to Heshang run along similar lines. The Chinese master's claim to attain the "featureless" (*mtshan med, animitta*)

---

17. Tsongkhapa 2002, 16, and Tsong kha pa, *Lam rim chen mo*, 424.

18. Tsongkhapa 2002, 90, and Tsong kha pa, *Lam rim chen mo*, 493.

19. Tsongkhapa 2002, 108, and Tsong kha pa, *Lam rim chen mo*, 506.

by refuting "all conceptuality of any sort" is seen as a pernicious error, for it reverses the natural relation between featurelessness and emptiness, assuming that the former can lead to the latter, whereas in fact featurelessness (that is, nonconceptuality) is a *result* of emptiness meditation, which must proceed conceptually and only at its conclusion issues in a nonconceptual realization.[20] The same point is reinforced later, when Tsongkhapa shows how a passage from the *Cloud of Jewels Sūtra* (*Ratnameghasūtra*) indicates the necessity of using analysis during meditation on emptiness, and notes, pointedly, "this shows the impossibility of what Heshang claimed—that by merely withdrawing your mind and eliminating bringing anything to mind, you can enter into a featureless or nonconceptual state without first using rational analysis to search analytically."[21] Note that the phrase "eliminating bringing anything to mind" (*yid la byed pa yongs su spong ba*) is synonymous with nonattention (*yid la mi byed pa*), a meditative practice with both Chan and Kagyü overtones that troubles Tsongkhapa as surely in the *Great Treatise* as it did in *Queries from a Sincere Heart*.

Another result of the rejection of conceptual thought is its vitiation of ethics: those who reflect that in emptiness there is no notion of virtuous conduct—or of anything else—come to regard such conduct as only relevant to those who have not gained true insight rather than as something that must be observed at every stage of the path.[22] More broadly, in his section on how to meditate so as to achieve insight, Tsongkhapa first refutes inadequate approaches, the first of which involves:

> holding the mind in a state that lacks any thought. . . . Setting the mind in that way brings it into accordance with the way that things exist. For, with no object existing at all in the face of emptiness, the mind does not apprehend anything.[23]

After citing various texts that argue that such an approach forsakes the Mahāyāna, Tsongkhapa tells Tibetans who are partial to it that, even if they differentiate themselves from Heshang on the basis of their practice of

---

20. Tsongkhapa 2002, 194, and Tsong kha pa, *Lam rim chen mo*, 574–75.

21. Tsongkhapa 2002, 343, and Tsong kha pa, *Lam rim chen mo*, 702.

22. Tsongkhapa 2002, 260, and Tsong kha pa, *Lam rim chen mo*, 630.

23. Tsongkhapa 2002, 331, and Tsong kha pa, *Lam rim chen mo*, 690.

generosity and other perfections, "you and Heshang are alike in meditating on the definitive view."[24] Finally, in addressing his opponents, Tsongkhapa reverts to the sort of logical argument supposedly used by Kamalaśīla during the Samyé Debate:

> If you, like Heshang, claim that all thoughts whatsoever bind you in cyclic existence, then you must accept that you are bound in cyclic existence by all thoughts such as: "I have received personal instructions on the nonconceptual; I will meditate on this."[25]

In short, Tsongkhapa's take on Chan Buddhism has virtually nothing to do with Chan as a historical movement in either China or Tibet. He never refers to the tradition other than as the tradition of Heshang, and the Heshang he invokes is simply a representative of an approach to meditation and the view (perhaps best captured in the term *nonattention*) that he finds prominent among Tibetans of his own era, and refutes through scriptural citation, reasoning, and the rhetorical expedient of hanging around their necks a placard proclaiming their implicit affinity with the long-discredited Chan master who was Kamalaśīla's foil at the Samyé Debate.

Tsongkhapa on Dzokchen

If the version of Chan Buddhism to which Tsongkhapa reacted was stereotypical in the extreme and unmitigated by any knowledge of actual Chan texts or practices (which he might have encountered had he accepted the Ming emperor's invitation to visit China), there were Tibetan practitioners of dzokchen and mahāmudrā with whom Jé Rinpoché was acquainted, so his perspectives on these systems were based on his own experience and learning.

In the centuries preceding Tsongkhapa, dzokchen came increasingly to be accepted as the crux of the view, meditation, and conduct of the

---

24. Tsongkhapa 2002, 333, and Tsong kha pa, *Lam rim chen mo,* 693.

25. Tsongkhapa 2002, 346, and Tsong kha pa, *Lam rim chen mo,* 705–706. For Tibetan presentations of Kamalaśīla's argument, see Kapstein 2013, 147–48, and Obermiller 1986, 193–94. For an astute analysis of Kamalaśīla's views on the place of rational analysis in meditative practice, which anticipate Tsongkhapa's in many respects, see Kellner 2020.

Nyingma tradition, forming the heart of the highest of the nine vehicles, atiyoga.[26] The Nyingma[27] traces its origins to the early, imperial period of Buddhism's dissemination in Tibet (ca. 650–850), especially to the visits and activities of such masters from north and northwest India as Śrī Siṃha, Vimalamitra, Vairocana, and above all, Padmasambhava, as well as to translations of a set of "old" (*rnying ma*) tantras brought to the plateau by those masters. Apart from these translations, the best evidence we have of the early Nyingma is in the caches of documents discovered in the early twentieth century in the Dunhuang caves of northwest China, which show, among other things, that there was considerable interchange between Nyingma and Chan during the imperial period. There also are certain resonances between the Nyingma and the early Tibetan Bön religion, and it is not impossible that the tradition brought from India to Tibet was influenced by Kashmir Śaivism, to which it bears certain general similarities.

Some Nyingma tantras were rejected as spurious by members of the latter-day (post–1000 CE) Tibetan renaissance or New Translation schools, such as the Kadam, Kagyü, and Sakya, which focused on a newer set of tantras that had appeared in India after the end of Tibet's imperial period. Most notable in this regard was Butön, who omitted many Nyingma tantras from his influential edition of the Kangyur on the grounds that their Indic provenance could not be vouchsafed. And as we have seen, some members of the newer orders, such as Sapaṇ, sometimes dismissed dzokchen as a Chinese tradition. It was partially in response to the rise of these new orders that the Nyingma began to assume a corporate identity of its own, in part through fealty to the old tantras, in part through the revelation, by various masters, of treasure texts (*gter ma*) supposedly hidden by Padmasambhava during his sojourn in Tibet for later recovery from the ground, from pillars, or from the minds of the treasure revealers (*gter ston*) themselves.[28] Like the Nyingma tantras, treasure texts were regarded with suspicion by members of the newer orders, but they helped Tibetans who looked back to the "golden age" of the empire to cohere into a single, if complex, tradition. Much of what Padmasambhava communicated in the treasure

26. The "lower" eight are the śrāvaka, pratyekabuddha, bodhisattva, kriyātantra, caryātantra, yogatantra, mahāyoga, and anuyoga.

27. See, e.g., Karmay 1988 and Dudjom 1991.

28. See, e.g., Thondup 1986.

texts had to do with dzokchen, which was codified and systematized by a series of great masters, most notably Rongzom Chökyi Sangpo (1012–88) and Longchen Rabjampa (1308–64).

Rongzompa[29] was noted as a great philosopher, a champion of the tantras over the "standard" Mahāyāna literature of Indian Buddhism (which he nonetheless mastered and commented on), and the recipient of a variety of dzokchen lineages, most notably those for the mind class (*sems sde*) of teachings, which emphasize the natural luminosity of the mind and are associated with such eighth-century masters as Vairocana and Vimalamitra. A second class of teachings, the space class (*klong sde*), focuses on the spaciousness or openness of the mind in its natural state. Longchenpa[30] was the greatest single scholar and proponent of dzokchen in the pre-Tsongkhapa era. His treatment of the tradition set the standard for later masters and still is considered definitive in most respects. Although well versed in the mind and space classes of texts, he paid special attention to the third—and from his perspective the subtlest—set of traditions, the esoteric-instruction class (*man ngag sde*), which provided a set of radical practices said to lead directly to buddhahood. Having studied at recently founded non-Nyingma monasteries, Longchenpa was knowledgeable about the New Translation schools' ideas and practices, and he wrote in such a way that members of those traditions could see the relevance of dzokchen and that Nyingmapas could understand how their teachings could fit with newer systems of thought.

As Longchenpa articulated it,[31] dzokchen theory focused above all on mind itself (*sems nyid*), which was seen as a primordially pure (*ka dag*), empty (*stong pa*), and luminous (*gsal ba*) gnosis (*ye shes*) or awareness (*rig pa*), which is not only the nature of each individual mind but the very source and substance of the cosmos itself, consisting of essence (*ngo bo*), nature (*rang bzhin*), and compassionate energy (*thugs rje*, or *rtsal*). Beginninglessly pure mind itself is captured symbolically in the figure of the primordial buddha Samantabhadra (luminosity) and his consort, Samantabhadrī (emptiness). Although we and all beings—indeed, all things—are thus originally pure, we fail to recognize this fact and hence wander in saṃsāra,

29. See, e.g., Almogi 2009 and Köppl 2008.
30. See, e.g., Thondup 2014 and Longchenpa 2017–18.
31. E.g., in Longchen Rabjampa 2014 and Longchenpa 2017–18.

bound by delusion and defilement. To reclaim our primordial purity and awareness, we must understand the true nature of mind. If we are spiritually adept, we may do so by leaps and bounds, or even (as described in Chan traditions) instantaneously, but for most people, the path is gradual, beginning with a seminal recognition of our true nature, then moving on to consideration of such stages-of-the-path topics as the rarity and preciousness of a human rebirth, the inexorability of impermanence and death, the operations of karma, the realms of saṃsāra and their disadvantages, the bodhisattva path, the basic practices leading to tranquil abiding and insight, and so on. Dzokchen may be approached more directly through engaging in tantric preliminary practices (*sngon 'gro*), which include a hundred thousand repetitions of rituals geared to (1) taking refuge and engendering bodhicitta, (2) purifying transgressions, (3) offering up oneself and all precious things, and (4) obtaining the blessings of one's guru and their lineage. Once these are complete, we can enter the first of the two main stages of esoteric-instruction class dzokchen: cutting through (*khreg chod*). This involves contemplating and realizing the primordial purity, emptiness, and luminosity of the mind. Once cutting through has been mastered, it is possible to move on the final stage, transcendence (*thod rgal*), which entails a set of yogic practices for functioning insightfully and powerfully within the world, seen from a visionary standpoint as the spontaneous accomplishment (*lhun grub*) of reality. Through the practice of transcendence, buddhahood may be achieved in this very life.

Discerning Tsongkhapa's attitude toward dzokchen is no easy matter. The great perfection and other Nyingma practices were part of the milieu in which he grew to spiritual maturity in the late fourteenth century, and his biographers make it clear that he enjoyed a close spiritual bond in the mid 1390s with a Tibetan master regarded by later Nyingmapas as one of their own, the figure variously referred to as Lekyi Dorjé (Karmavajra), Lhodrak Drupchen (the mahāsiddha from Lhodrak), or Namkha Gyaltsen (1326–1401).[32] The mid 1390s were when Tsongkhapa and a number of his disciples undertook lengthy retreats in the southern Tibetan region of Ölkha. It was at this time that Jé Rinpoché would gain full visionary

---

32. Jinpa 2019, 140–50. Jinpa questions the degree to which Lekyi Dorjé was steeped in dzokchen, suggesting that although he may have hailed from a Nyingma family and received Nyingma-inflected instructions from Vajrapāṇi, the preponderance of biographical and textual evidence indicates that his main training and outlook were Kadam.

access to Mañjughoṣa and succeed, after many struggles, in resolving his doubts about the meaning of Madhyamaka, opening the way for a twenty-two-year burst of activity in the Lhasa area that saw him undertake extensive teaching, writing, and public works—activity that ceased only with his death in 1419. In a break from their retreat, Tsongkhapa and his disciples spent a number of months in the summer of 1395 at Lekyi Dorjé's hermitage in Lhodrak, where Jé Rinpoché and Lekyi Dorjé developed a strong kinship. Lekyi Dorjé transmitted to Tsongkhapa a number of Kadam traditions that Jé Rinpoché had not yet received, including that of the stages of the path, and also conferred upon him the initiation of Great-Wheel Vajrapāṇi, a deity with whom Lekyi Dorjé enjoyed a special relationship. The Lhodrak master expected great things from Tsongkhapa, who was not yet forty, and used his well-developed prophetic abilities to guide some of Jé Rinpoché's decisions, advising him against a journey to India he was strongly considering at the time, urging him to compose a hymn to Maitreya, and predicting that if he traveled next to Tsari, the sacred mountain of Cakrasaṃvara, it would lead to a full understanding of emptiness facilitated by the writings of an "Indian master." After Tsongkhapa's sojourn in Lhodrak, he and Lekyi Dorjé kept up a friendly correspondence, which included the exchange of gifts, for several years.

For our purposes, the most significant event during Tsongkhapa's stay in Lhodrak was his instigation of a visionary conversation between Lekyi Dorjé and Vajrapāṇi, in which the bodhisattva answered the lama's questions on a range of topics, including the nature of luminosity; pitfalls to avoid in view, meditation, and conduct; the place of bodhicitta on the tantric path; the role of a consort in tantric practice; the "purity" of the dzokchen view; and the destiny of Buddhism in Tibet in general and of Tsongkhapa in particular. It is unclear whether Lekyi Dorjé reported Vajrapāṇi's instructions to Tsongkhapa at the time, though likely he did, and in any case he wrote out a transcript of the conversation and several years later sent it to Jé Rinpoché, who gratefully acknowledged receipt. Eventually, under the title *Garland of Supreme Medicinal Nectar* (*Bdud rtsi'i sman mchog phreng ba*),[33] it was incorporated into the first volume of Tsongkhapa's collected works and was included as well in Lekyi Dorjé's collected works. The text's importance for understanding Tsongkhapa's

---

33. It is translated in full in Thurman 1982, 213–30.

views on various meditative traditions lies in the fact that it is one of the few—perhaps the only—text in Jé Rinpoché's corpus that invokes dzokchen terminology in any detail or directly addresses the validity of the tradition.

The portions of the *Garland* most steeped in dzokchen come near the beginning and end of the text. At the outset,[34] after Vajrapāṇi has consented to answer Lekyi Dorjé's questions—stating that he will do so by conveying "the intention of Father Samantabhadra and the heart advice of Mother Samantabhadrī"—he adds that in order to achieve the "supreme medicine," one must "seek out the luminosity that is mind itself" (*sems nyid 'od gsal*). When Lekyi Dorjé asks about the essence of luminosity, Vajrapāṇi explains, using classic dzokchen terminology, that it is divisible into essence, nature, and compassionate energy. He goes on to detail each of these three modes and to explain the pitfalls (*gol sa*) involved in trying to understand each. The *essence* of luminosity is "originally clear emptiness wherein nothing is . . . established," "introspectively known reality . . . free from the adulteration of present artificial consciousness."[35] The major pitfall in wrongly understanding emptiness is that one may fall into nihilism, abandoning ethics and other path practices, and end up in the vajra hell. The *nature* of luminosity is "a clarity in which the body and gnosis [possess] the natural radiance of empty awareness." The pitfall in wrongly understanding clarity is that one may fall into an eternalism that absolutizes the experience of clarity, mistaking it for awakening and forgetting that clarity must always be understood within the context of emptiness; those who err in this way will be reborn in the form realm. The *compassion* of luminosity arises "as the intrinsic brilliance of clear empty awareness."[36] The pitfall in wrongly understanding compassion is that one mistakes that intrinsic brilliance for external variety and falls into constructive thought and worldly attachments, which result, after death, in continued rebirth in saṃsāra.

The middle portion of the *Garland*, around half the text, is taken up with Vajrapāṇi's detailed advice on how to avoid pitfalls with regard to view, meditation, conduct, and result.[37] The exposition in this section is

34. Tsong kha pa, *Bdud rtsi'i sman mchog phreng ba*, 196–98.

35. Thurman 1982, 214, and Tsong kha pa, *Bdud rtsi'i sman mchog phreng ba*, 196.

36. Thurman 1982, 215, and Tsong kha pa, *Bdud rtsi'i sman mchog phreng ba*, 197.

37. *Bdud rtsi'i sman mchog phreng ba*, 198–204; trans. Thurman 1982, 216–24.

less dzokchen-inflected than the earlier teaching, mostly providing important but rather more "standard" advice as to how to carry out one's practice without fear of straying from the proper perspective and path. In addressing pitfalls of the view, Vajrapāṇi pays considerable attention to the nihilistic stance that there is no good or evil and that one should be content with inactivity, and to an approach to meditation that rests content in the stupefaction brought on by attachment to nonconceptuality (*mi rtog pa*), which merely perpetuates one's sojourn in the upper reaches of saṃsāra. Although Heshang is not invoked explicitly in these passages, his approach to both view and meditation seems to lurk in the background.

In the last section of the *Garland,* Lekyi Dorjé resumes his interrogation, asking questions, as noted, on a range of topics. Only two exchanges need detain us. First, in answer to a query about the fate of Buddhism in Tibet, Vajrapāṇi issues dire warnings of incipient war, famine, plague, and exile, but he assures Lekyi Dorjé that such events may be forestalled or mitigated if teachers are compassionate and learned and students are devoted to their gurus and intent on achieving the perfection of wisdom on the basis of tranquil abiding. "The most excellent technique" for this, he states, "is the six yogas [of Kālacakra] and the great perfection, the extraordinary instruction of the tantra."[38] Lekyi Dorjé next asks Vajrapāṇi whether dzokchen is a "pure view" (*lta ba rnam dag*), to which the bodhisattva replies: "Dzokchen is indeed an elevated view, but/and with regard to the view, the exposition by masters Nāgārjuna and Candrakīrti is undeluded."[39] I have deliberately translated the Tibetan particle *mod* as an ambiguous "but/and," for if the particle is read as a concessive "but," the passage seems to be saying that dzokchen is excellent but not as excellent as the approach of Nāgārjuna and Candrakīrti, while if *mod* is read conjunctively, the passage appears to be equating dzokchen with the view of the great Indian Mādhyamikas.[40] Lekyi Dorjé himself seems to have opted for the latter, conjunctive reading, for in his afterword to the *Garland* he specifies that the tradition propounded by Vajrapāṇi is in harmony with the three

38. Thurman 1982, 227–28, and Tsong kha pa, *Bdud rtsi'i sman mchog phreng ba,* 207–8.

39. Tsong kha pa, *Bdud rtsi'i sman mchog phreng ba,* 208–9: *rdzogs pa chen po yang lta ba rnam dag yin mod/ lta ba'i phyogs la slob dpon klu sgrub dang zla grags kyis bkral ba 'di 'khrul med yin.* Cf. trans. in Thurman 1982, 228.

40. Jinpa (2019, 146–47) reads it as a concessive, while Thurman (1982, 228) reads it conjunctively. The *Bod rgya tshig mdzod chen mo* (2:2122b) seems to point to *mod* as a concessive.

great viewpoints—mahāmudrā, great Madhyamaka,[41] and dzokchen—that transmit the insights of the Indian tantric adepts to various sets of disciples. He goes on to specify that the *Garland* is the special teaching intended for Tsongkhapa, and that—apparent ambiguities and contradictions aside—Vajrapāṇi clearly intended to equate dzokchen with the system of Nāgārjuna and Candrakīrti, seeing the former as a way of clarifying the view, meditation, and conduct expounded in the latter.

All this begs the question of Tsongkhapa's actual view of the great perfection. Thupten Jinpa notes that the Nyingma were not a major presence in central Tibet during Tsongkhapa's time, so although Jé Rinpoché certainly was aware of the tradition, he may have lacked the textual resources or the personal contacts to study it in depth.[42] Indeed, as noted, the *Garland of Supreme Medicinal Nectar* is unusual, if not unique, within Tsongkhapa's oeuvre for its inclusion of dzokchen terminology and perspectives. Furthermore, although included in Jé Rinpoché's collected works, it is not, properly speaking, a work composed by him, for the compiler of the text is Lekyi Dorjé, and its most authoritative voice belongs to Vajrapāṇi. We can be quite sure that Tsongkhapa heard and later read the advice imparted by the bodhisattva, and we know that he expressed appreciation for it, but how significant it was to his spiritual development and what he actually thought of dzokchen is difficult to discern, for we lack credible independent evidence.[43]

Later Nyingmapa scholars, such as the great eastern Tibetan masters Getsé Mahāpaṇḍita Gyurmé Tsewang Chokdrup (1761–1829) and Shabkar Tsokdruk Rangdröl (1751–1851), argued on the basis of the *Garland* itself, the correspondence surrounding the text, and opinions attributed to two of Tsongkhapa's disciples, Tokden Jampal Gyatso (1356–1428) and Gungru Gyaltsen Sangpo (1383–1450), that the teachings imparted in the

---

41. It is unclear whether this refers the "great Madhyamaka of other-emptiness" (*gzhan stong*) of the Jonang school or simply the Madhyamaka of Nāgārjuna and Candrakīrti, though the latter seems likelier.

42. Jinpa 2019, 148. Jinpa notes, too, that there is no evidence that Tsongkhapa knew the writings of Longchenpa.

43. There are unconfirmed reports that Tsongkhapa once told his disciple Joden Sönam Lhundrup that he considered dzokchen pure but that it had been "adulterated by later ignoramuses," and that another disciple, Neringpa, saw in Tsongkhapa's study a text he had written on dzokchen, but we have no "paper trail" to prove either of these claims; see Jinpa 2019, 458n651.

Garland were decisive in Tsongkhapa's spiritual breakthrough and that he was, in his heart of hearts, a dzokchen practitioner, perhaps even a manifestation of Padmasambhava. This theme has been repeated, with occasional variations, by a number of modern Nyingma masters, including Dudjom Rinpoché (1903–87) and Khenchen Jikmé Phuntsok (1933–2004).[44]

Such a claim is not borne out by the Geluk biographical literature devoted to Tsongkhapa, which while acknowledging Lekyi Dorje's role in Jé Rinpoché's life, does not see him as a major figure on the order of Rendawa or Umapa Pawo Dorjé (ca. fourteenth–fifteenth centuries). The latter, in particular, is seen by Gelukpas as a far more significant visionary than Lekyi Dorjé, for it was Umapa's intercession with Mañjughoṣa on Jé Rinpoché's behalf that led eventually to Jé Rinpoché's own direct encounters with the wisdom bodhisattva and to his subsequent full comprehension of the meaning of emptiness. By the same token, many of the opinions on Tsongkhapa's view of dzokchen attributed by Nyingma scholars to Jé Rinpoché himself or his disciples are not well sourced, hence must be regarded with suspicion.[45] In the end, unfortunately, we must concur with Jinpa's observation that "there is simply no adequate textual evidence on the basis of which to make any determination of Tsongkhapa's actual views on Dzokchen."[46]

Tsongkhapa on Mahāmudrā

Of the three contemplative traditions under review here, Tsongkhapa undoubtedly knew mahāmudrā the best, for it was at the heart of view, meditation, and practice in the Kagyü traditions that—along with the Sakya and Kadam—predominated in central Tibet when Jé Rinpoché arrived there in the early 1370s. We will say more about his exposure to Kagyü shortly.

If Chan was brought to Tibet from the east and dzokchen primarily from the west, mahāmudrā came from the south, especially from north-central and northeast India, the source of many of the texts, ideas, and practices that helped form the New Translation schools from the eleventh

44. On this, see R. Jackson 2020, 81–97.

45. R. Jackson 2020, 97–108.

46. Jinpa 2019, 458n651.

century onward. *Mudrā*, a Sanskrit term usually translated as "seal," carries multiple meanings in Indic culture: it refers to a royal imprimatur, a symbolic hand gesture displayed in dance or ritual contexts, or, in tantric settings, a female sexual partner or a blissful state of gnosis.[47] The term *mahāmudrā*, "great seal," is largely confined to Buddhist literature,[48] where it first appears in tantric texts in the seventh or eighth century. In such foundational works as the *Basic Ordinance of Mañjuśrī* (*Mañjuśrīmūlakalpa*) and the *Litany of Names of Mañjuśrī* (*Mañjuśrīnāmasaṅgīti*), it refers both to a "five-peaked" ritual hand gesture that "seals" particular contemplative states and to the practice of a particular buddha family (that of Amoghasiddhi) in which constructive thought ceases and one enters the supreme realization of the dharma realm (*dharmadhātu*).[49] In such eighth-century yoga tantras as the *Compendium of the Principles of All Tathāgatas* (*Sarvatathāgatatattvasaṃgraha*)—texts that were influential both in East Asia and in the early Tibetan court—*mahāmudrā* still may refer to a hand gesture (the "vajra fist") but primarily denotes one of a set of four seals that "lock in" meditative practices; the *great seal* refers primarily to a procedure for confirming the meditator's clear visualization of themselves as a buddha deity. The yoga tantras also contain the first, scattered references to mahāmudrā as a consort for tantric sexual practices.[50]

This theme was expanded considerably in the still later mahāyoga tantras, of which the *Guhyasamāja* is exemplary, and the even later yoginī tantras, such as the *Cakrasaṃvara*, *Hevajra*, and *Catuḥpīṭha*.[51] In this highly esoteric and often transgressive literature, references abound to females as "the great seal" through whom the yogin, via sexual union, may achieve the blissful gnosis of buddhahood. And so, by extension, *mahāmudrā* comes also to refer to that awakened state in which emptiness, luminosity, and bliss are completely interfused: buddhahood itself as the great-seal attainment (*mahāmudrāsiddhi*).[52]

---

47. See, e.g., Gray 2011 and R. Jackson 2019, 18–23.

48. See, e.g., Gray 2011 and R. Jackson 2019, 23–64.

49. R. Jackson 2019, 31–32.

50. Gray 2011 and R. Jackson 2019, 32–33.

51. In the scheme accepted by most Tibetan New Translation schools, these two categories are folded into the single category of unexcelled yoga tantra (*bla na med pa'i rnal 'byor rgyud*), as "father" and "mother" tantras, respectively.

52. Gray 2011 and R. Jackson 2019, 34–39.

These later tantric systems were practiced, propounded, and popularized by the charismatic and countercultural Indian mahāsiddhas, or "great adepts," who often lived unconventional lives at the margins of society and expressed their realizations in spontaneous songs of spiritual joy composed in the vernacular.[53] Such late-first and early-second millennium masters as Saraha, Kṛṣṇācārya (or Kāṇha), Virūpa, Tilopa, and Nāropa celebrated their social and spiritual freedom in verse forms like *dohā*s (couplets), *caryāgīti* (performance songs), and *vajragīti* (diamond songs), singing of their rapturous experience of the great seal, the connate (*sahaja*), or great bliss (*mahāsukha*). Although the mahāsiddhas were primarily tantric practitioners, in some of their works the reference field of *mahāmudrā* begins to expand beyond the esoteric so that it increasingly is seen as synonymous with such Sūtra Vehicle notions as emptiness, mind only, buddha nature, and dharmakāya. In this way, the great seal could be read back into Buddhist texts in which the term never appeared, because it had come to connote the ultimate—however that was described. The mahāsiddhas also advocated certain meditative techniques, many of which involved dropping all conceptual thought so as to enter directly into an experience of the mind's empty, luminous, and blissful nature. Among the best known of these was that mentioned above: the "nonattention" (*amanasikāra*) practice associated with Maitrīpa and his followers, who were instrumental in the transmission of mahāmudrā traditions to Tibet.

Thus, by the beginning of the Tibetan renaissance in the eleventh century, mahāmudrā had taken on multiple connotations in Indian Buddhism. Certainly, the tantric literature that was adopted as authoritative by the nascent New Translation schools was suffused with great-seal discourse, so it is unsurprising that the term found its way into the ideas and practices of the newly developing orders.[54] Indeed, mahāmudrā is a concept of greater or lesser import in all the schools that arose during the later spread of the teaching in Tibet. The Kadam masters, despite their reputation for asceticism and their emphasis on the compassion-centered mind-training (*blo sbyong*) practices, did transmit, and sometimes commented upon, teachings by Saraha and other mahāsiddhas. The Sakyapas developed their own distinctive path-and-fruit (*lam 'bras*) contemplative

---

53. R. Jackson 2019, chap. 2.
54. R. Jackson 2019, chap. 3.

tradition but certainly were aware of the great seal, which, following the lead of Sakya Paṇḍita, they restricted solely to tantric contexts, as a practice and realization requiring prior initiation. The Pacification (*zhi byed*), Severance (*gcod*), Shangpa Kagyü, and Jonang traditions all incorporated mahāmudrā prominently into their systematic thought, and even the Nyingma, at the hands of Longchenpa, found a place for it within their scheme of Buddhist vehicles in the penultimate tantric tradition, anuyoga, which corresponds to the yoginī tantras, where as we have seen, mahāmudrā was a vital notion.

The tradition in which the great seal assumed the greatest prominence was the Marpa Kagyü,[55] a complex of schools and subschools that trace their origin to the lay translator Marpa Chökyi Lodrö (1012–97), who is reputed to have made numerous trips to India to obtain texts and transmissions, most notably from Nāropa and Maitrīpa, each of whom is said to have taught him mahāmudrā ideas and practices.[56] Marpa passed on these traditions to his own Tibetan disciples, the best known being the great poet-yogin Milarepa (1040–1123), whose songs contain countless references to the great seal—primarily, though not solely, in terms of the highly advanced tantric practices summarized in the six Dharmas of Nāropa.[57] Milarepa, in turn, transmitted mahāmudrā ideas and practices to his two principal students, Rechungpa Dorjé Drak (1083–1161) and Gampopa Sönam Rinchen (1079–1153). Rechungpa became the fountainhead of a small but vital "ear-whispered lineage" (*snyan brgyud*) within the Kagyü that preserved tantric great-seal teachings. Gampopa, who had been a Kadampa monk before meeting Milarepa, wrote a great deal on mahāmudrā.[58] He was the first Tibetan to suggest that, quite apart from the tantric great seal emphasized by the Indian adepts and Marpa and Milarepa, there was a Perfection Vehicle mahāmudrā, which did not require initiation and might be received simply through a lama's blessing,

55. R. Jackson 2019, chaps. 4–5.

56. See, e.g., Nālandā Translation Committee 1982. However, citing Tibetan renaissance sources, Ronald Davidson (2005, 143–48) questions the degree to which Marpa actually studied with Nāropa.

57. See, e.g., Tsangnyön Heruka 2016.

58. See, e.g., Kragh 1998.

accompanied by pointing-out instructions (*ngo sprod*) on the nature of mind. It was this notion of mahāmudrā that was criticized by Sapaṇ.[59]

Gampopa also was the great institution builder of the Marpa Kagyü: his disciples and grand-disciples founded the various great schools and sub-schools of the tradition, most notably the Karma Kamtsang of the Karmapa hierarchs, the Phakmodrupa, the Drigungpa, and the Drukpa. These masters and their successors did much to systematize mahāmudrā theory and practice, exploring the implications of the empty and luminous nature of mind; expounding on sudden and gradual approaches to the great seal; integrating mahāmudrā practices with tantric and nontantric path systems, including the procedures of tranquil abiding and insight meditation on the Sūtrayāna side and the six Dharmas of Nāropa on the Mantrayāna side; discussing the implications of the experiences (*nyams*) of bliss, clarity, and nonconceptuality that often accompany great-seal meditation; detailing the meaning of the four great-seal yogas: one-pointedness (*rtse gcig*), nonelaboration (*spros bral*), the single taste (*ro gcig*), and nonmeditation (*sgom med*); and relating the theory and practice of mahāmudrā to the dharmakāya and other facets of classic Mahāyāna buddha-theory.[60] Because Kagyü lamas attracted patronage from noble families in central Tibet, they and their mahāmudrā traditions were a major part of the religious landscape in which Tsongkhapa lived his life.

Tsongkhapa's contacts with Kagyü teachers were frequent and significant, especially in the first half of his life. At age four, he received a blessing from the Fourth Karmapa, Rölpai Dorjé (1340–83), and although his main teacher in Amdo was a Kadampa, Chöjé Döndrup Rinchen (1309–85), when he arrived in central Tibet in 1373, he went first not to the great Kadam center of Nyethang but to the Drigung Kagyü monastery of Thil, where the presiding master, Chenga Chökyi Gyalpo (1335–1407), conferred upon him teachings on a range of practices, including the Drigung fivefold mahāmudrā[61] and the six Dharmas of Nāropa.[62] And, while his subsequent studies of the Indian classics were most often overseen by Sakyapa

59. See, e.g., D. Jackson 1993.

60. See, e.g., Roberts 2011.

61. The five elements of this gradualist system are generation of the awakening mind (*bodhicitta*), yidam practice, guru yoga, mahāmudrā proper, and dedication of merit.

62. Jinpa 2019, 32.

masters, notably Rendawa, whom he met in 1376, Tsongkhapa's travels brought him into contact with other Marpa Kagyü teachers, including representatives of the Phakmodrupa and Drukpa lineages, as well as masters of the Shangpa tradition.[63] It is worth noting that he received the transmissions of such important tantric systems as Guhyasamāja and Cakrasaṃvara initially from Kagyü masters.

Given his exposure to Kagyü great-seal contemplative traditions and his readings in the Indian Buddhist tantras, it is safe to assume that Tsongkhapa was quite familiar with mahāmudrā theories and practices of both Indic and Tibetan provenance, and the Kagyü historian Pawo Tsuklak Trengwa (1504–64/66) may well be correct in contending that Jé Rinpoché participated in at least one mahāmudrā group retreat with Kagyü acquaintances, probably in the late 1380s. It was this retreat experience, according to Pawo, that resulted in Tsongkhapa's composing his open letter to the "great meditators of Tibet," *Queries from a Sincere Heart,* which we mined earlier for its references to Heshang.[64] As in most of his writings, Tsongkhapa is oblique in *Queries* as to the actual target of his critique, but there are a number of mentions there of mahāmudrā, and the attitudes toward view, meditation, and conduct questioned in the text are close enough to well-known Kagyü positions to make it likely that he was indeed addressing a primarily Kagyüpa audience. Certainly, later writers read the text in that way: the Gelukpa scholar Desi Sangyé Gyatso (1653–1705) specifies that *Queries* is mainly a critique of "neo-Drukpa" attitudes, and for their part, numerous Kagyü (or Kagyü-sympathetic) scholars wrote refutations of the text.[65]

Tellingly, perhaps, Tsongkhapa begins *Queries* by citing Sakya Paṇḍita—famous for his criticism of Kagyü mahāmudrā—to the effect that although many Tibetans are intent on meditation, few know how to practice it properly, and he goes on to quote Nāgārjuna's admonition (*Fundamental Verses on the Middle Way* 24.11) that those who do not know how to think about emptiness—taking it either nihilistically or as an absolute in its own

63. R. Jackson 2019, 149. Tsongkhapa's guide in visionary encounters with Mañjughoṣa during the 1390s, Umapa, is reputed to have studied with the Drukpa master Barawa Gyaltsen Palsang (1310–91).

64. Jinpa 2019, 88.

65. R. Jackson 2019, 157.

right—are doomed to spiritual failure.[66] He goes on to question his audience on the degree to which their approach to view and meditation may undermine their concern for proper conduct. Such basic practices as taking refuge, generating the awakening mind, confessing moral transgressions, reflecting on the deficiencies of saṃsāra, and identifying proper objects of meditation and analysis ought to be easy, says Tsongkhapa, and are in any case basic to Buddhist practice, yet his contemporaries, he notes, seem to find them very difficult indeed.[67]

In the main part of *Queries,* Jé Rinpoché goes on to pose a series of questions about meditation and proper view. We cannot explore these in detail here[68] but will note that among the key points he makes are the following:

◊ Various features of meditation, including mindfulness, alertness, clarity, and nonconceptuality, must be understood as pertaining not so much to subjective states of mind as to the ways the mind engages with its object, and the mind must *always* be engaged with an object—that is, it must be "intentional."

◊ Because of this, the notion—identified here with Heshang but common in Kagyü circles—that the key to meditation on emptiness is the practice of nonattention, or mental inactivity (*yid la mi byed pa*), is incorrect in terms of both tranquil abiding and insight meditation. For tranquil abiding, like all mental acts, requires some sort of object, and realization of emptiness, which is the aim of insight meditation, cannot be attained simply through emptying the mind of concepts but, as in the tradition of Nāgārjuna, requires conceptual analysis.

◊ Nāgārjuna's way of explaining the view of emptiness requires that we interpret his fourfold negation[69] not as leading to nihilism, skepticism, agnosticism, or "mystical obscurantism"[70] but as

---

66. Tsong kha pa, *Dri ba lhag bsam rab dkar*, 108; translated in Jinpa 2019, 89–90.

67. Tsong kha pa, *Dri ba lhag bsam rab dkar*, 114.

68. For a summary, see Jinpa 2019, 91–101. The points below are drawn from Tsong kha pa, *Dri ba lhag bsam rab dkar*, 114–26.

69. The denial that any concept or entity may be found under analysis to exist, not exist, both exist and not exist, and neither exist nor not exist.

70. Jinpa 2019, 96.

indicating that Madhyamaka logic refutes the *intrinsic* existence (*rang bzhin gyis grub pa*) or *true* existence (*bden par grub pa*) of entities and concepts, not the entities and concepts themselves.

◊ Kagyü "guidance on the nature of mind" (*sems 'khrid*)—which instructs one, for instance, to search the mind for its color, shape, or other properties, or to look directly at the mind of the present moment and then in the next moment recognize mind's emptiness—actually keeps one within the realm of the merely conventional nature of mind, hence cannot be a proper way to meditate on emptiness, which requires transcending convention through a laser-like search for intrinsic existence and *only* intrinsic existence in the object of meditation—be it the mind or something else.

◊ The range of perspectives on view and meditation in Tibet result in antinomies that seem difficult to resolve. For instance, some assert that all thought should be stopped, while others claim it may, if intensified, lead to liberation. Some assert that conceptualization is ignorance, while others see it as the dharmakāya. Some assert that the practice of nonattention is buddhahood and all mental engagement is saṃsāra, while others say that observing concepts directly leads to liberation. Some assert that meditation on emptiness involves darkening the mind so that buddha qualities shine forth and one attains the dharmakāya, while others say that this is solely a realization of emptiness and not the attainment of buddhahood. Some assert that the ultimate perceived in meditation must be an extrinsic emptiness (*gzhan stong*), while others argue that it can only be intrinsic emptiness (*rang stong*). Each member of these and other such pairs, Tsongkhapa notes, contradicts its counterpart, leaving us unsure how to think about the tradition as a whole.

◊ Many Tibetan contemplatives abandon study and critical reflection in favor of the experiences of bliss, clarity, and nonconceptuality ensuing from tranquil abiding, while others are so addicted to study that they neglect to meditate; only by combining both may one complete the path as described by the great Indian masters.

◊ Most crucially, perhaps, the actual practice of mahāmudrā, which is meditation on ultimate reality or the definitive meaning (*nges don*), is, quite simply, meditation on emptiness (*stong nyid sgom pa*), the approach to insight meditation taught in the system of Nāgārjuna—a system that, in Tsongkhapa's view, definitely requires conceptual analysis.

Apart from a few observations along similar lines in writings he sent to Rendawa,[71] this is all that Tsongkhapa had to say about the Kagyü forms of mahāmudrā practiced in his own day.

When we shift from Tsongkhapa's reactions to his contemporaries' approach to mahāmudrā to the sense of the great seal he derived from reading the Indian Buddhist classics, we notice that Jé Rinpoché's works on Madhyamaka do not, so far as I am aware, ever mention the term. However, it turns up frequently in his tantric writings, both in his *Great Exposition of Secret Mantra* and in his commentaries on several specific systems of Vajrayāna theory and practice. This is not surprising, given mahāmudrā's primarily tantric context and usages in India. This is not the place to survey these references in detail,[72] but we may generally observe that in the *Great Exposition of Secret Mantra, mahāmudrā* in the context of yoga tantra refers, as we would expect, to a hand gesture and the accompanying visualization of oneself as possessing a deity's body,[73] while in the context of unexcelled yoga tantra, the usages are more diverse: it is, among other things, the gnosis of luminosity, a synonym for the understanding of emptiness entailed by the fourth empowerment, the great bliss of the immovable perfection of wisdom, the formed or imaginal emptiness (*śunya[tā] bimba, stong [pa nyid kyi] gzugs [rnyan]*) described in the Kālacakra tradition, a mirror-like image free from any obscuration, and the final attainment on the tantric path.[74]

In Tsongkhapa's *Guhyasamāja Tantra* commentaries, the *great seal* sometimes refers to the practitioner's visualization of themselves as assuming a divine body, and at least once is described as a yoga in which one engages with emptiness,[75] but most often it is simply the buddhahood ensuing from

71. R. Jackson 2019, 155; for Rendawa's views on these matters, see Jinpa 2019, 93–94.

72. See R. Jackson 2019, 150–53.

73. Tsong kha pa, *Sngags rim chen mo*, 135ff.; translated in Dalai Lama et al. 2005, 73ff.

74. For references, see R. Jackson 2019, 150–51nn514–23.

75. In his *Lamp to Illuminate the Five Stages (Rim lnga gsal sgron)*, translated in Tsongkhapa 2013. For references, see R. Jackson 2019, 151nn525–27.

practice of the tantric path. In his commentaries on the Cakrasaṃvara system, Jé Rinpoché describes mahāmudrā as, among other things, a consort for sexual yoga practices;[76] the inseparable bliss-emptiness awareness arising from the experience of great bliss that is induced by bringing vital winds into the central channel;[77] as immovable bliss;[78] and as a "lightning-like" (*klog ltar*) nonanalytical, luminous awareness that leads to the production of the connate.[79] Finally, in his treatises on the six Dharmas of Nāropa, he refers to mahāmudrā as the realization of the empty nature of mind as taught by Maitrīpa, Marpa, and Milarepa, who themselves were in accord with the Madhyamaka approach of Nāgārjuna and Candrakīrti;[80] as the connate gnosis, or realization, produced by bringing the vital winds into the central channel and inducing the four joys;[81] and as an experience within which one can "seal" the emptiness of all appearing objects with a mind pervaded by great bliss.[82]

In a manner reminiscent of later Nyingmapas' construction of "Tsongkhapa the dzokchenpa," subsequent Geluk tradition insists that, quite apart from the implicit critiques of Kagyü mahāmudrā in *Queries from a Sincere Heart* and the many references to the great seal in his tantric writings, Jé Rinpoché actually had a mahāmudrā tradition of his own, which he received—along with other teachings and an "emanated scripture" (*sprul pa'i glegs bam*) containing all the teachings—in a visionary encounter with Mañjughoṣa, sometime in the 1390s.[83] He passed on the great seal and other teachings, along with the emanated scripture, to a single disciple, Tokden Jampal Gyatso, thereby initiating what now is known as the Ganden Ear-Whispered Transmission (*dga' ldan snyan brgyud*).[84]

---

76. Tsong kha pa, *Sbas don lta ba'i mig 'byed*, 175–77. The term employed here is *phyag rgya chen mo* rather than the more common *phyag rgya chen po*.

77. Tsong kha pa, *Sbas don lta ba'i mig 'byed*, 161.

78. Tsong kha pa, *Sgrub le'i phyag rgya bzhi'i zin bris*, 471 and 474.

79. Tsong kha pa, *Sgrub le'i phyag rgya bzhi'i zin bris*, 482. For a key to references to mahāmudrā in another of Tsongkhapa's Cakrasaṃvara treatises, see his *Illumination of the Hidden Meaning* (*Sbas don kun gsal*), translated in Gray 2017, 448, and Gray 2019, 402.

80. Tsong kha pa, *Yid ches gsum ldan*, 292–97; translated in Mullin 1997, 126–31.

81. Tsong kha pa, *Yid ches gsum ldan*, 303; translated in Mullin 1997, 139.

82. Tsong kha pa, *Nā ro'i chos drug kyi dmigs skor*, 379; translated in Mullin 1996, 117.

83. R. Jackson 2019, 141–47.

84. It also is known as the Geden Oral Tradition (*dge 'dan bka' srol*) and the Ensa Ear-Whispered

The transmission was restricted to a small number of disciples until around 1600, when Panchen Lama Losang Chökyi Gyaltsen (1570–1662) wrote an account of the transmission masters and composed a versified root text for the mahāmudrā practice, *Highway of the Conquerors* (*Rgyal ba'i gzhung lam*)—which at times uses terminology traceable to Kagyü literature—along with a lengthy prose commentary on the verses, which cites both Indic and Tibetan mahāmudrā sources with great frequency.[85] From then on, Geluk mahāmudrā was more or less in the public domain; it would undergo changes over the centuries, but it remains an oft-discussed tradition to this day.[86]

As the Paṇchen describes it, the mahāmudrā practice transmitted to Tsongkhapa by Mañjughoṣa is broadly divisible into Sūtra Vehicle and Mantra Vehicle approaches. The mantra approach refers to the clear-light realization of the empty nature of mind that is induced in the completion stage of unexcelled yoga tantra by the introduction of the vital winds into the central channel of the subtle body. Sūtra mahāmudrā (to which the Paṇchen devotes most of his attention) requires prior reflection on topics from the stages-of-the-path literature and, ideally, a hundred thousand repetitions of such tantric preliminaries as prostration, purification, maṇḍala offerings, and guru yoga. The actual session described by the Paṇchen begins with refuge and bodhicitta prayers and is instigated by guru yoga—specifically the guru's dissolution into the practitioner's heart, so that their mind and the guru's mind are fused. The practitioner then pursues tranquil abiding, focusing on the mind's clear and cognizant nature, settling into a space-like state of awareness. When tranquil abiding has been achieved, it is harnessed to the analytical search for an intrinsically existing meditator or mind; when these are not found, the practitioner settles into not-finding and enters a space-like experiential recognition of the empty nature of mind. During meditation, this awareness is returned to again and again; afterward, all phenomena are regarded as illusion-like: that is, as empty, their apparent intrinsic reality a mere false appearance.

As with Nyingma claims about Tsongkhapa's secret identity as a dzok-

Transmission (*Dben sa snyan brgyud*). The former includes an alternative name for the Geluk; the latter refers to the area of Tsang inhabited many of the early practitioners of the tradition.

85. R. Jackson 2019, chap. 9 and 457–558.

86. R. Jackson 2020.

chenpa, Geluk assertions about Tsongkhapa's receipt, practice, and promulgation of a mahāmudrā tradition cannot be verified on the basis of textual evidence.[87] Early biographies of Tsongkhapa, including secret biographies dealing with his visionary life, do not mention his receipt or possession of his own sūtra-based great-seal teaching,[88] nor do Jé Rinpoché's collected works provide any such evidence. Indeed, later Gelukpa writers freely acknowledge that Tsongkhapa, feeling that the time was not right to reveal it publicly, chose not to write down his own version of the great seal. The great historian of the Ganden Ear-Whispered Transmission, Kachen Yeshé Gyaltsen (1713–93), takes passing comments made by Jé Rinpoché to the effect that he holds a special teaching on the view but will not disseminate it as confirmation that he would not commit his mahāmudrā tradition to writing and as implicit proof that he possessed such a teaching.[89] The word *mahāmudrā* does not, however, appear in these passages, so we cannot be certain that Jé Rinpoché is actually referring to the teaching that the Paṇchen would publicize two centuries later.

If, in fact, Tsongkhapa possessed such a teaching, the only way we can begin to reconstruct it is to draw out clues from his writings. In that regard, two observations are in order.

First, there are passages in Jé Rinpoché's Sūtra Vehicle writings that seem—if sometimes faintly—to anticipate the Paṇchen's description of sūtra mahāmudrā. For instance, in the tranquil abiding sections of both his *Great* and *Middle-Length* stages-of-the-path treatises, following on a passage from Asaṅga's *Śrāvaka Levels*, Tsongkhapa describes the "phase of complete pacification" (*nye bar zhi ba*), in which nonattention actually is appropriate—not in the sense that the mind intends no object but in the sense that it pays no attention to internal or external "signs," concepts subside, and "there is a sense as if the mind has become indivisible with space."[90] With regard to insight meditation, Jé Rinpoché insists in *Queries* that mahāmudrā is simply meditation on emptiness as taught by

---

87. R. Jackson 2019, 159–64.

88. A secret biography of Jé by Jamyang Tashi Palden (1379–1449) describes Jé Rinpoché's experience of the "luminosity of mahāmudrā," but this is very much in a tantric context; see Thurman 1982, 52, and R. Jackson 2019, 139–40.

89. R. Jackson 2019, 161–62.

90. Tsong kha pa, *Lam rim 'bring*, 217–19, translated in Tsongkhapa 2021b, 324–26; cf. Tsong kha pa, *Lam rim chen mo*, 491–92, translated in Tsongkhapa 2002, 88–90.

Nāgārjuna and his successors, and observes more specifically, in a treatise on the six Dharmas of Nāropa, that the great seal is a realization of the emptiness of mind as taught by the early Kagyü masters. All these claims tally with the sūtra mahāmudrā practice of later Geluk tradition.

Second, in his tantric writings, Tsongkhapa repeatedly describes mahāmudrā as the unexcelled yoga tantra completion-stage realization of the empty, luminous nature of mind—the connate gnosis of conjoined emptiness and bliss—that follows upon introducing the vital winds into the central channel of the subtle body, a description that tallies precisely with the definition of Mantra Vehicle mahāmudrā provided by the Panchen.

None of this assures us that Tsongkhapa actually possessed a great-seal practice as claimed by later tradition, but it does demonstrate that the elements out of which that system was constructed may be found in his writings. Further assurance may only be obtained "beyond words and letters," in our acceptance of the integrity of unwritten oral traditions—never an easy matter for modern scholars.

Conclusion

In brief, Tsongkhapa clearly was aware of the three contemplative traditions considered here: Chan, dzokchen, and mahāmudrā. The degree to which he actually knew these traditions, however, varied widely, as did the explicitness of his attitude toward each.

Chan, by the fourteenth century, was virtually unknown in central Tibet as a living tradition, and persisted mostly in the single, symbolic image of Heshang Mahayana. For his part, Tsongkhapa used Heshang as a trope to point out deficiencies in the view and meditation propounded by Kagyü mahāmudrā practitioners of his acquaintance. These contemplatives are fairly clearly his target in *Queries from a Sincere Heart* and rather less so in the *Great Treatise on the Stages of the Path*.

Dzokchen was very much a part of the Tibetan religious landscape during Tsongkhapa's time, and we have strong evidence that Tsongkhapa knew something of the Nyingma approach to view, meditation, and conduct, and *may* have approved of it—though the evidence for this approval is scant and ambiguous. Furthermore, because neither Jé Rinpoché's own writings nor the extensive Geluk biographical tradition devoted to him has anything much to say about his perspective on dzokchen, later Nyingma claims to the effect that the great perfection was actually crucial to his spiritual awakening in the 1390s and remained his innermost practice for the rest of his life seem ill supported by textual evidence, hence dubious as historical claims.

Mahāmudrā was undoubtedly the tradition among the three discussed here that Tsongkhapa knew best. Even if we question later Geluk assertions that Jé Rinpoché received a distinctive great-seal meditation practice in a visionary encounter with Mañjughoṣa and taught it privately to one or more close disciples, we know from his tantric writings that he understood mahāmudrā's multiple usages in Indian Buddhist tantric literature and, from his disciple-biographers, that he spent considerable time at Kagyü monasteries, where he received teachings on a number of different mahāmudrā systems. It seems, too, that he may have undertaken a great-seal retreat with Kagyü contemplatives in the late 1380s—an experience that prompted the composition of *Queries from a Sincere Heart*, with its pointed questions as to whether the view, meditation, and conduct promoted by his contemporaries was truly in accord with the approach of Nāgārjuna, Asaṅga, and other great Indian masters—or even coherent on its own terms.

If there is a common denominator to Tsongkhapa's perspective on Chan, dzokchen, and mahāmudrā view, meditation, and practice, it is probably to be found in his suspicion—expressed throughout the length and breadth of his writings—that any approach to the Buddhist path that interprets emptiness in nihilistic or absolutistic terms, reduces meditation to blissful nonattention, and devalues the foundational role of ethics is intellectually indefensible, spiritually fruitless, and karmically disastrous. And if the single figure in which such a distortion of the Dharma is perfectly embodied is Heshang Moheyan, we may say at the very least that the shadow cast across the centuries by that Chinese master fell heavily upon Tsongkhapa, not because it tempted him (though perhaps at some point it did) but because he saw it infecting the ideas and practices of his fellow Tibetans, whose approach to Buddhism—at once derivative and distinctive—he dedicated his life to clarifying, purifying, and finally transmuting.

Moving Minds

8. Jé Tsongkhapa's Contribution to Buddhist Hermeneutics

Geshé Ngawang Samten[1]

Jé Tsongkhapa's *Essence of Eloquence* (*Legs bshad snying po*) made a significant impact on the development of Mahāyāna studies in Tibet. It led to the emergence, as a distinct field of scholarship, of the study of hermeneutics, or *drang nges*—literally, "distinguishing the provisional from the definitive." But the notion of levels of scriptural and doctrinal interpretation predates Tsongkhapa. In fact, it has its origin in the Mahāyāna sūtras themselves, especially in the notion of the Buddha's skillful means (*upāya*).

The *Questions of Rāṣṭrapāla Sūtra* (*Rāṣṭrapālaparipṛcchāsūtra*) states:

> Not understanding emptiness, peace, and non-production, beings wander. With hundreds of skillful means, principles, and reasonings, you compassionately cause them to understand this.[2]

To reveal the intent of statements from the Mahāyāna sūtras such as this one, Master Kamalaśīla writes in his second *Stages of Meditation* (*Bhāvanākrama*):

> All the Buddha's words are well spoken. They are dedicated explicitly or implicitly to illuminating reality. One who realizes

---

1. I thank my esteemed friend Geshe Thupten Jinpa-la and David Gray for editing my paper for publication.

2. *Śūnyāśca śānta anutpādanaya avijānad eva jagadudbhramati / teṣām upāyanayayuktiśatair avatārayasi api kṛpālutayā //* (Vaidya 1961, 154).

reality is freed from the entire web of views, just as darkness is dispelled by light. Tranquil abiding (*śamatha*) alone cannot induce pure wisdom, nor can it eliminate the darkness of obscuration. Meditating correctly with the gradually progressing wisdom of reality, one attains the perfect wisdom. Only with wisdom can one realize reality, and only wisdom can eliminate obscuration.[3]

These statements show how crucial it is to understand the ultimate reality of phenomena; liberation from saṃsāra is impossible without it. Buddha's teachings on the twelve links of dependent origination, with contemplation on both the forward and reverse sequences, clearly show that the root of any karma that keeps sentient beings bound to saṃsāra is ignorance, and this ignorance is nothing but the ignorance of apprehending a self (*ātmagrāha*). As such, cultivating the wisdom that understands selflessness (*anātman* or *nairātmya*) is the only way to be liberated from saṃsāra.

Deconstruction of Reification

The hallmark of Buddhist philosophy, as understood within classical Indian thought, is selflessness. It is the foundational philosophical view of all the Buddhist schools. According to Mahāyāna thinkers, however, the Buddha deconstructed reification of the self on several levels for different audiences. Since not everyone can comprehend the subtlest philosophical view that deconstructs the subtlest reification, the Buddha, as a skillful teacher, taught in graduated stages for audiences of different dispositions and capacities. At the coarsest level, the self is explained as a permanent, unitary, and independent principle—the eternal self as postulated by the Vedic proponents of Ātman. Beyond this level, the teaching on selflessness negates the self that is an autonomous, self-sufficient agent who somehow "owns" the aggregates. On the subtlest level, the self negated is any objective existence defined by way of an intrinsic nature.

3. *Bcom ldan 'das kyi bka' thams cad ni legs par gsungs pa ste/ mngon sum mam brgyud pas de kho na mngon par gsal bar byed pa dang / de kho na la gzhol ba nyid do / de kho nyid shes na snang ba byung bas mun pa bsal ba bzhin du lta ba' dra ba thams cad dang bral bar 'gyur ro// zhi gnas tsam gyis ni ye shes dag par mi 'gyur zhing sgrib pa' mun pa yang sel bar mi 'gyur gyi/ shes rab kyis ni de kho na legs par bsgoms na ye she rnam par dag par 'gyur/ shes rab kho nas de kho nan yid rtogs par 'gyur/ she rab kho nas sgrib pa yang dag par spong bar 'gyur te/* (Namdol 1985, 109).

Such progressive levels of deconstruction of reification run throughout Buddhist philosophy. The Buddha's teaching on impermanence—captured in his statement "All conditioned things are impermanent"—deconstructs the temporal persistence of conditioned phenomena, a view that was challenged by all other schools of thought in India at that time. A deep realization of the impermanence of all composite phenomena strongly impacts our experience of ourselves and the world around us. But the realization of impermanence is at its root the realization that things possess no enduring entity—that is, no self. This is but one example of how the Buddha's insights, and Buddhist philosophy as a whole, are grounded in the wisdom of selflessness.

To really appreciate the deconstruction of self in Buddhism systematically, we need to look at the way that the understanding of reality—the way things truly are—is explained in the various Buddhist schools. The non-Mahāyāna schools, when identifying the final import of the doctrine of selflessness, confine their deconstruction of self to the person (*pudgala*)—the agent (*kartṛ/kāraka*) of action (*karman*).[4] The two Mahāyāna schools, Yogācāra and Madhyamaka, extend the Buddhist deconstruction of self to include both persons and factors of existence (*dharma*), such as the five aggregates. Hence they speak of both selflessness of persons (*pudgalanairātmya*) and selflessness of phenomena (*dharmanairātmya*).

---

4. Generally, the two Śrāvaka schools, Vaibhāṣika and Sautrāntika, can be said to deconstruct the reification of persons but not the reification of phenomena. Interestingly, however, while it does not maintain the selflessness of phenomena, the Sautrāntika school does enter the realm of deconstructing non-personal entities. We see how Dignāga and Dharmakīrti, who are considered Sautrāntika, refute the non-Buddhist Mīmāṃsaka, Vaiśeṣika, and Naiyāyika assertions that universals (*sāmānya*) are real entities substantially different from particulars (*viśeṣa*) and their assertions of the reality of abstract entities such as relation and difference, which are mental constructs. These masters categorically refute the objective reality of universals and other mental constructs. See, for example, Dharmakīrti's *Pramāṇavārttika* 3.140 (*sarve bhavah svabhaven . . . vyavrttibhaginah*) and 3.185 (*svabhavavadabhavasya . . . vyavacchedvacakah*) in Shastri 1994. Therefore, according to this school, such abstract objects fall under the rubric of conventional truth (*saṃvṛtisatya*), as they are true from the perspective of an obscured mind. Such a mind is obscured by conceptual thought (*kalpanā*), which obstructs direct cognition of real objects. Real objects, in the Sautrāntika view, are those that exist through their defining characteristics (*svalakṣaṇa*); they are true because they appear to an ultimately true mind, one that is free of obscuration and is therefore not in error about the nature of the objects appearing to it.

Mahāyāna Hermeneutics

One distinctive feature of Mahāyāna Buddhism is its acceptance of a large body of diverse sūtras, especially the Perfection of Wisdom scriptures, as authentic words of the Buddha (*buddhavacana*). Embracing such a wide range of scripture in a way that avoids apparent contradiction necessitated some methodological innovations. One of these is the distinction between provisional (*neyārtha*) statements of the Buddha and definitive (*nītārtha*) ones. Broadly speaking, a statement of the Buddha is *provisional* if it cannot be accepted literally and requires interpretation. The Buddha is said to have given such teachings "provisionally" to help fulfill a specific immediate need. In contrast, a statement or teaching is *definitive* if it reflects the final truth about the nature of reality and thus requires no interpretation.

Though their interpretations of the Buddha's statements are broadly similar, the two Mahāyāna schools, Yogācāra and Madhyamaka, differ on key points. First they have different criteria for defining a statement as provisional or definitive, and thus their notions of what constitutes the definitive meaning—that is, ultimate truth—differ. Second, the way they assign provisional and definitive status to the sūtras belonging to each of the three turnings of the wheel of Dharma differ. Finally, they differ on which specific sūtras they rely on to ground their hermeneutic principles.

For example, the founding figures of Yogācāra, Asaṅga and Vasubandhu, draw extensively on the *Unraveling the Intent Sūtra* (*Saṃdhinirmocana Sūtra*) for their hermeneutical approach to the teachings of the three turnings.[5] In contrast, the Madhyamaka school of Nāgārjuna and Candrakīrti chooses principally sūtras like the *Teachings of Akṣayamati* (*Akṣayamatinirdeśa*) as the basis for its hermeneutic of the three turnings. The choice of such primary scriptures matters a lot. For if the determining sūtra itself cannot be accepted as definitive, it simply cannot serve as the basis to ascertain the provisional or definitive status of other scriptures. Only a sūtra that does not depend on another sūtra for its interpretation, and where the meaning of the sūtra is explicit, can be regarded as definitive.

---

5. This is evident from such works as Asaṅga's *Summary of Mahāyāna* (*Mahāyānasaṃgraha*) and *Bodhisattva Levels* (*Bodhisattvabhūmi*) and from Vasubandhu's *Twenty Verses* (*Viṃśikā*) and *Thirty Verses* (*Triṃśikā*). A list of seminal Yogācāra works must also include Maitreya's *Ornament of the Mahāyāna Sūtras* (*Mahāyānasūtrālaṃkāra*) and *Differentiation of the Middle and the Extremes* (*Madhyāntavibhāga*).

Perhaps the most obvious difference in the two Mahāyāna schools' choice of sūtras to ground their hermeneutics is the way this impacts their interpretation of the Buddha's teaching on selflessness, especially the selflessness of phenomena. By prioritizing the *Unraveling the Intent Sūtra* to interpret the Buddha's teaching on emptiness (*śūnyatā*) or essencelessness (*niḥsvabhāvatā*), especially as revealed in the Perfection of Wisdom scriptures, Yogācāra emphasizes the theory of the three natures. In this model, the ultimate nature—referred to also as the *consummate (pariniṣpanna)* nature—is defined in terms of the negation of the imputed (*parikalpita*) nature in relation to the dependent (*paratantra*) nature. Furthermore, they say the Buddha's statement that all phenomena lack essence, or "entityness," must be understood in three ways: the imputed is essenceless in that it lacks defining characteristics (*svalakṣaṇa-niḥsvabhāva*), the dependent is causally essenceless (*uttapatti-niḥsvabhāva*), and the consummate is ultimately essenceless (*parmārthataḥ-niḥsvabhāva*). In contrast, the Madhyamaka school understands the Buddha's teaching on emptiness in the Perfection of Wisdom sūtras as uniform across the board for all phenomena, with no need for contextual interpretation.

What this brief review of the two Mahāyāna schools reveals is the crucial importance of hermeneutics in the development of their philosophical stances, especially their understanding of the ultimate nature of reality. Any deeper understanding of the contributions of the two Mahāyāna schools requires appreciating their sophisticated philosophical arguments, their distinct hermeneutic principles, and their specific choice of sūtras on which these principles are based.

Jé Tsongkhapa's Essence of Eloquence

Jé Tsongkhapa's *Essence of Eloquence*, whose subtitle reads *Distinguishing the Provisional and Definitive Meanings of the Conqueror's Scriptures*, is without doubt a landmark treatise and a significant contribution to Buddhist hermeneutical literature. The work provides a systematic account of how Yogācāra and Madhyamaka developed their distinct interpretations of the Mahayana sūtras and how their approaches underpin their distinct philosophical views on the ultimate nature of reality. In choosing hermeneutics as the key methodological principle to elucidate these philosophical views, the *Essence of Eloquence* differs significantly from typical doxographical (*grub mtha'*) texts, which present the views of the various Indian schools in a more straightforward manner. Although the hermeneutic approach to hierarchic ordering of the teachings of the three turnings was already known in Tibet before Tsongkhapa's time, his *Essence* brought a new level of depth and clarity and, more importantly, elucidated in a compelling way the relationship between hermeneutic practice and the establishment of philosophical views.

Space prevents me from exploring Tsongkhapa's *Essence* in detail, so I will choose two specific examples—one from the Yogācāra section and the other from his comments on Madhyamaka—to show how Tsongkhapa's hermeneutic method reveals philosophical nuances that often go unrecognized. The first draws out the fuller implications of the three-nature theory presented in the *Unraveling the Intent Sūtra* that is so foundational to Yogācāra philosophy.

At the core of the three-nature theory is the formulation that the consummate nature equals the absence of the imputed nature in the dependent nature, or—more concisely—the *consummate* equals the *dependent* minus the *imputed*. In examining what this means, Tsongkhapa makes an important observation. He notes that the Yogācāra rejection of conditioned things such as form being the object of words and concepts by virtue of their defining characteristics cannot be the same as the Sautrāntika rejection of abstract entities (*prajñapti*) as real. Saying that form and so on are not the objects of words by virtue of their defining characteristics, Tsongkhapa argues, is not the same as saying they are not direct objects of expression. If they were the same, then Yogācāra three-nature theory would not move beyond Sautrāntika. That the dependent—conditioned things— are not the direct objects of language and thought is already established by the Sautrāntika, for whom only universals (*sāmānya*) can be direct objects of thought and language and not particulars.

Furthermore, it would follow that negating nonreal entities like universals would not get at the emptiness of phenomena, and meditating on such a negation would not eliminate the obscuration to omniscience. Thus it would contradict the *Unraveling the Intent Sūtra*, which states that the emptiness of the dependent (*paratantra*) with respect to the imputed (*parikalpita*) established by virtue of its defining characteristics is the consummate (*pariniṣpanna*). It would also contradict the *Bodhisattva Levels* statement that emptiness is the object whose contemplation eliminates the obscuration to omniscience. In brief, Tsongkhapa is pointing out that there must be more to Yogācāra theory than the Sautrāntika insight that only universals can be the objects of thought and language.

A key aspect of Tsongkhapa's analysis here is the distinction he draws between the *basis of application* (*'jug gzhi*) and the *object of application* (*'jug yul*) of language. Both Sautrāntika and Yogācāra reject the notion that conditioned things are *objects* of the application of words by virtue of their own defining characteristics; that is to say, both understand that there is no intrinsic relationship between words and conditioned things as their referents. Yogācāra goes even further, however, asserting that conditioned things such as form do not exist even as the *bases* of application of words by virtue of their defining characteristics. Relating this distinction to concepts as opposed to words, the gist of the further elaboration is that the Yogācāra statement that forms and so on are not the basis for conceptual thoughts by virtue of their defining characteristics refers not only to the category of bases of conceptual generalities (*rtog pa'i zhen gzhi'i rang ldog*) but also to the particular instances (*gzhi ldog*)—forms and so on, which arise as sensory perceptions through the ripening of latent potentialities (*bag chags brtan byung gi dbang shes*), or karma.

One important upshot of Tsongkhapa's analysis of the three-nature theory is his recognition of two distinct formulations of the Yogācāra theory of the ultimate nature of reality. One is that of Asaṅga, who, following *Unraveling the Intent*, presents the theory primarily from the standpoint of how language and thought engage with reality. The second, found primarily in Vasubandhu's and Dharmakīrti's writings, presents the theory from the perspective of how conditioned things are perceived by direct perception. Their similarity is that both approaches lead to the realization of the nonduality of subject and object. Briefly, this example on Yogācāra three-nature theory demonstrates how, in Tsongkhapa's reading, a careful hermeneutic approach can shed important light on substantive philosophical aspects of a school.

The second passage from Tsongkhapa's *Essence* I wish to highlight in this paper is from the section on Madhyamaka. Once again, through careful hermeneutical analysis, Tsongkhapa is able to note important differences in philosophical positions, this time between the two main strands of Madhyamaka, Svātantrika and Prāsaṅgika, which are represented, respectively, by Bhāviveka and Candrakīrti. All major Tibetan interpreters of

Madhyamaka acknowledge the crucial methodological difference between the two in the context of establishing emptiness—Svātantrika's use of the autonomous syllogism (*svatantra*) and Prāsaṅgika's choice of *reductio* consequences (*prasaṅga*). What distinguishes Tsongkhapa's approach is his identification of a substantive philosophical difference between the two schools—their acceptance or rejection of an intrinsic characteristic (*svalakṣaṇa*) on the conventional level.

Once again, hermeneutics plays a crucial role in Tsongkhapa's analysis. One important source for Tsongkhapa on this is a passage from Bhāviveka's *Light of Wisdom* (*Prajñāpradīpa*), where the Svātantrika master maintains that to reject the dependent entity as existing through an intrinsic characteristic constitutes a form of nihilism denying its existence altogether. The passage reads:

> Here, if it is suggested that the essence of all imputed (*parikal-pita*), which consists of verbal and mental expressions such as "form," does not exist at all, that would repudiate fact since it repudiates verbal and mental expressions.[6]

In exploring the import of the above passage, Jé Tsongkhapa writes in his *Essence of Eloquence*:

> If "all imputed" (*parikalpita*) as stated in "all imputed does not have the essence of its intrinsic characteristic" refers to concepts and words, then since these are classified among the aggregates, this repudiates dependent phenomena (*paratantra*), saying they do not have the essence of an intrinsic characteristic. According to [Bhāviveka's] statement, dependent phenomena do have the essence of their intrinsic characteristic. The *Unraveling the Intent Sūtra* explains essencelessness (*niḥsvabhāvatā*) as not existing through its intrinsic characteristics, and these masters take the sūtra to be definitive. Therefore it is clear that they assert the dependent to have the essence of its intrinsic characteristics.[7]

6. Tsong kha pa, *Legs bshad snying po*, 370–71; for alternative translation, see Thurman 1984, 266.

7. Tsong kha pa, *Legs bshad snying po*, 371; cf. Thurman 1984, 266.

In a subsequent passage, Tsongkhapa writes:

> His [Bhāviveka's] explanation with respect to the meaning of the existence and nonexistence of intrinsic characteristics mentioned in *Unraveling the Intent* is the clearest source indicating that this master believes in the conventional existence of the things by virtue of their intrinsic characteristic.[8]

Having identified a source in Bhāviveka for his acceptance of dependent phenomena as existing by virtue of intrinsic characteristics, Tsongkhapa then proceeds to show how Candrakīrti explicitly rejects such a notion. An important source for Tsongkhapa here is three crucial stanzas from Candrakīrti's *Entering the Middle Way* (6.34–36), where Tsongkhapa understands Bhāviveka's views to be an important object of critique. According to Tsongkhapa, Candrakīrti and other Prāsaṅgika Mādhyamikas do not accept that objects have even an iota of existence on their own; rather, they assert that every phenomenon exists merely by being designated by thought and language. In this view, it is only a total rejection of objective existence that allows all transactions at the level of conventional truth to be possible and coherent.

Taking this rejection of intrinsic characteristic even on the conventional level as the defining feature of Candrakīrti's Prāsaṅgika Madhyamaka, Tsongkhapa understands the Prāsaṅgika subschool to have unique standpoints with respect to a wide range of issues. As examples, Tsongkhapa in his *Essence of Eloquence* declares these unique tenets of Prāsaṅgika:

◊ A unique realization of selflessness and identification of gross and subtle self-grasping (*ātmagrāha*), which distinguishes them from Vaibhāṣika and Sautrāntika

◊ A unique acceptance of the external object and rejection of reflexive awareness (*svasaṃveda*) and storehouse consciousness (*ālayavijñāna*), which distinguishes them from Yogācāra

◊ A unique rejection of the independent syllogism, which distinguishes them from Svātantrika[9]

---

8. Tsong kha pa, *Legs bshad snying po*, 371; cf. Thurman 1984, 267.

9. Tsong kha pa, *Legs bshad snying po*, 405–6: *Bdag med rtogs pa dang bdag 'dzin phra rags sogs*

Here too, as in the Yogācāra example, we see how hermeneutics, one's choice of interpretative stance and defining texts, plays a crucial role in drawing out important philosophical differences among Madhyamaka thinkers.

Conclusion

I began my paper by noting that the revelation of the truth of selflessness in Buddhist thought requires a deconstruction of concepts such as permanence, self, and so on. Furthermore, we discussed how the four classical schools of Buddhism—Vaibhāṣika, Sautrāntika, Yogācāra, and Madhyamaka—can be viewed in terms of progressive subtleties in this deconstruction. In this context, Tsongkhapa demonstrates how Prāsaṅgika's unique philosophy, grounded in a rejection of intrinsic existence even on the conventional level, leaves no room for even an iota of reification. In this way, Tsongkhapa shows how Prāsaṅgika represents the highest philosophical view, the culmination of a process of deconstruction traceable all the way back to the Buddha. Such a standpoint is a true middle way, where not only do emptiness and dependent origination coexist without contradiction, but emptiness and dependent origination are incoherent without each other. This is a point stressed by Nāgārjuna himself when he states in *Fundamental Verses on the Middle Way*:

> For those to whom emptiness makes sense,
> everything makes sense.
> For those to whom emptiness does not make sense,
> nothing makes sense.[10]

Nāgārjuna summarizes the entire objective of his philosophical enterprise in chapter 18 of the same work:

---

kyi thun mong ma yin pa'i khyad par dang/ phyi don 'jog cing kun gzhi dang rang rig khas mi len pa'i thun mong ma yin pa'i khyad par dang/ rang rgyud khas mi len pa'i thun mong ma yin pa'i khyad par bshad pa'o//. Cf. Thurman 1984, 306–21.

10. *Mūlamadhyamakakārikā* 24.14: *sarvaṃ ca yujyate tasya śunyatā yasya yujyate / sarvaṃ na yujyate tasya śūnyaṃ yasya na yujyate*; Vaidya 1960.

Through the elimination of karma and affliction there is nirvāṇa.
Karma and affliction come from conceptual thought.
These come from mental fabrication.
Fabrication ceases through emptiness.[11]

Here we can see why the correct view of emptiness is necessary: to cease conceptual fabrication (*prapañca*), and how only a thorough deconstruction of all reified constructs (*vikalpa*) can lead one to nirvāṇa. Such a process requires internalizing the insight into emptiness through meditative cultivation over a prolonged period of practice. Tsongkhapa, through his skillful application of hermeneutics, brings us into the very heart of this Middle Way.

11. *Mūlamadhyamakakārikā* 18.5. *karmakleśakṣayān mokṣaḥ karmakleśa vikalpataḥ / te prapañcāt prapañcas tu śūnyatāyāṃ nirudhyate*; Vaidya 1960.

9. Tsongkhapa's Hermeneutics of the Perfection of Wisdom

Gareth Sparham

H ERMENEUTICS IS A word derived from Hermes, the Greek god who carries messages from the gods to those on earth. The foremost god, as it were, for those who repose faith in the Three Jewels—the Buddha, Dharma, and Saṅgha—is the Dharma, and among the diverse scriptural Dharmas, the foremost is the Perfection of Wisdom (*Prajñāpāramitā*). In the context of the works of Tsongkhapa Losang Drakpa (1357–1419), therefore, a *hermeneutic* is principally a vehicle for explaining the meaning of the Perfection of Wisdom to ordinary beings.

Tsongkhapa, at the beginning of his early Perfection of Wisdom commentary *Golden Rosary of Good Explanation* (*Legs bshad gser phreng*), finished in about 1392, lists four hermeneutics or vehicles of explanation accepted by earlier Tibetans. He calls the hermeneutics "trailblazers" (*shing rta srol 'byed*) that convey the meaning of the Perfection of Wisdom to ordinary beings. These are the explanations of Nāgārjuna, Maitreya, Dignāga, and the Nöjom Khenpo ("the *Destroyer of Harms* scholar"). Having summarized their explanations, Tsongkhapa then says his own view is that there are only two truly trailblazing explanations, those of Maitreya and Nāgārjuna.

The Perfection of Wisdom scriptures say that all phenomena are empty of an intrinsic nature (*sarvadharmāḥ svabhāvaśūnyāḥ*). This gives rise to two major traditions of interpretation: one (the Middle Way) that employs the conventional and ultimate terminology associated with Nāgārjuna, and one (the Mind Only) that employs the imputed, dependent, and consummate terminology associated with Maitreya. Even in his early years, when writing the *Golden Rosary*, Tsongkhapa has this in mind when he

says he accepts only the two trailblazing explanations of Maitreya and
Nāgārjuna.

The Nöjom Khenpo

Tsongkhapa rejects the idea that Dignāga and the Nöjom Khenpo provide separate vehicles of explanation; the former, he says, because he follows Maitreya and the latter because he follows Nāgārjuna. In the context
of Tsongkhapa's contribution to hermeneutics, his rejection of the Nöjom
Khenpo has particular significance. We begin with an account of what is
known about the *Destroyer of Harms* and the scholar who wrote it/them.

To date, Hōdō Nakamura and I have discussed him in greatest detail.[1]
To summarize those findings, *Destroyer of Harms* (*Gnod 'joms*) is the name
of two Perfection of Wisdom treatises in the Tengyur. The most important of them for Tsongkhapa is an Indian treatise extant as a complete
work only in Tibetan translation, where it has the subtitle *Long Explanation of the Noble Hundred Thousand, Twenty-Five Thousand, and Eighteen
Thousand Perfection of Wisdom*.[2] This title is nearly identical to the title
of a work listed in the Lhenkarma, one of the oldest catalogues of works
translated into Tibetan,[3] the only difference being the single word *'phags
pa* added as an honorific in the later canons.

There is no known, surviving Sanskrit manuscript of this treatise, there
are no references in any book in Sanskrit presently extant to a treatise with
this title, and there is no Sanskrit title given either at the beginning of the
Tibetan translation or in the colophon. The present editions of the Tibetan
Tengyur only say the Indian preceptor (*upādhyāya*) Surendrabodhi and
editor-translator monk Yeshé Dé finalized the translation for publication.

The Sanskrit title has been reconstructed from the Tibetan as *Ārya-
śatasāhasrikāpañcaviṃsatisāhasrikāṣṭādaśasāhasrikāprajñāpāramitā-
bṛhaṭṭīkā*. Its short form, *Bṛhaṭṭīkā* (Bṭ3), is the most widely used title
in Western scholarly works. That it was written in Sanskrit by an Indian

---

1. See Sparham 2001 and Nakamura 2010–11.

2. *'Phags pa shes rab kyi pha rol tu phyin pa 'bum dang nyi khri lnga sgong pa dang khri brgyad
stong pa rgya cher bshad pa.* Dergé Tengyur 3808, Perfection of Wisdom vol. *pha*: 1b–292b;
Pedurma 55:645–1326.

3. It is numbered 515 in the *Lhan kar ma*; Herrmann-Pfandt 2008, 293.

author has been recently conclusively established from short sections of a Sanskrit manuscript of Abhayākaragupta's (fl. ca.1100) *Ornament of the Sage's Intent* (*Munimatālaṃkāra*), edited and published by Kazuo Kano and Xuezhu Li (2014, 130–31 [15–16] et passim), where Abhayākaragupta cites, or at least copies out verbatim, passages from Bṭ3.

A second treatise named *Destroyer of Harms* is a longer commentary that comes immediately before Bṭ3 with a similar title, *Long Explanation of the Hundred Thousand*, reconstructed in Sanskrit as the *Śatasāhasrikāprajñāpāramitābṛhaṭṭīkā* (Bṭ1).[4] These two treatises can be confused because they share the same names, *Bṛhaṭṭīkā* (*Long Explanation*) and *Gnod 'joms* (*Destroyer of Harms*), and because they share the same opening verse of homage and have many similar passages. Tsongkhapa's names for Bṭ3 are *Yum gsum gnod 'joms* (*Three Mother Destroyer of Harms*) and *Gnod 'joms che ba* (*Long Destroyer of Harm*). The latter distinguishes it from Bṭ1, which he titles *'Bum gyi gnod 'joms* (*Hundred Thousand Destroyer of Harms*) or *Gnod 'joms chung ba* (*Shorter Destroyer of Harms*), even though it is in fact a much longer treatise.

The Tibetan and Indian Perfection of Wisdom commentarial traditions have had a lot to say about the different names given to these two treatises and their different authors. Haribhadra (eighth century) refers in a slightly disparaging way to a *Commentary on the Scripture* (*Paddhati, Gzhung 'grel*) by Vasubandhu. He says Vasubandhu writes with only an understanding of the Mind Only view, not the Middle Way view. This same *Commentary on the Scripture*, where the scripture in question is specifically identified as the *Twenty-Five Thousand*, is cited by Abhayākaragupta and Jagaddalanivāsin (fl. ca. 1165). Influenced by these Indian references to a *Commentary on the Scripture* and the early Tibetan catalogues, Ar Jangchup Yeshé (ca. 1100), Chim Namkha Drak (1209–85), Jamsar Sherab Öser (fl. ca. thirteenth century), and Bodong Tsöndrü Dorjé (fl. ca. twelfth–thirteenth centuries?) set forth their opinions about Bṭ1 and Bṭ3. They are followed by the Narthang scholar Chomden Rikpai Raldri (1227–1305), or Rikral, who had access to a large number of manuscripts. In his *Historical Evolution of the Works of Maitreya* and his *Flower Ornament*, a summary explanation of the *Hundred Thousand*, he differentiates between Bṭ3 and Bṭ1 as "by the

---

4. *Shes rab kyi pha rol tu phyin pa 'bum pa rgya cher 'grel pa.* Dergé Tengyur 3807, Perfection of Wisdom vols. *na* and *pa.*

master Vasubandhu and the master Daṃṣṭrāsena."[5] In his *Early Survey of Buddhist Literature*, as part of a general survey, at the outset he does not attribute an author to Bṭ1 but clearly attributes Bṭ3 to Vasubandhu. Later in the same work, he says the *Commentary on the Scripture* is "attributed by some Tibetans to an Indian" and Bṭ1 is by "Trisong Detsen."[6]

Dölpopa Sherab Gyaltsen (1292–1361) unequivocally rejects Rikral and says with confidence in his *Sūtra-Based Commentary* that both the Bṭ1 and Bṭ3 are by Vasubandhu, and not just any Vasubandhu but "the direct student of Jina Maitreya, the great trailblazer Middle Way master Vasubandhu" and "the author of the commentary on Maitreya's *Ornament of the Mahāyāna Sūtras* (*Mahāyānasūtrālaṃkāra*)."[7] In this way, he unequivocally rejects the slightly disparaging earlier characterization of him by Haribhadra.

Butön Rinchen Drup (1290–1364) investigates the question of authorship in detail and tentatively attributes Bṭ1 to Daṃṣṭrāsena and Bṭ3, more confidently, to Vasubandhu.[8] Nyaön Kunga Pal, a student of both Butön and Dölpopa, says Bṭ3 is by Daṃṣṭrāsena and Bṭ1 by the Tibetan king Trisong Detsen, the position taken by Tsongkhapa at the beginning of his *Golden Rosary*. Tsongkhapa emphasizes that Vasubandhu did not write Bṭ3—he says it is probably by "Daṃṣṭrāsena from Kaśmīra" (*kha che mche ba'i sde*)—and says Bṭ1 has serious errors and therefore it is unlikely its author is an Indian scholar.

Shākya Chokden (1428–1507), writing in 1454 in his *Garland of Waves of Views* some thirty-five years after Tsongkhapa's death, says, "Most earlier Tibetan spiritual friends say there are four trailblazers into the Perfection of Wisdom" and lists the *Destroyer of Harms* (Bṭ1 and Bṭ3) as the third of these four ways. Then he either cites or paraphrases Butön Rinpoché as saying:

---

5. Kano and Nakamura 2009, 131–32. That is, in his *Byams pa dang 'brel ba'i chos kyi byung tshul* and *Shes rab kyi pha rol tu phyin pa stong phra brgya pa rgyan gyi me tog*.

6. *Bstan pa rgyas pa rgyan gyi nyi 'od*, in Schaeffer and van der Kuijp 2009, 154, 258, and 263.

7. Dol po pa, *'Grel pa mdo lugs ma*, 2–3: *rgyal ba byams pa'i dngos slob shing rta chen po slob dpon dbu ma pa dbying gnyen gyi zhal snga nas kyang / 'bum pa dang / nyi khri lnga stong pa dang / khri brgyad stong pa ste / yum rgyas 'bring bsdus pa gsum gyi gzhung 'grel gnod 'joms*; 20: *mdo sde rgyan gyi 'grel par slob dpon dbu ma pa chen po dbying gnyen*.

8. Bu ston, *Chos 'byung chen mo*, 156a7.

It is written in the Phangthang Kamé catalogue that Trisong Detsen composed this *Explanation of the Hundred Thousand* [=Bṭ1] in a bundle of seventy-eight fascicles, but in both the Chingphu and Phodrang Thongthangden catalogues it is said to be Indian, so it was composed by Padé. It is written that this one known as the *Three Mother Destroyer of Harms* [=Bṭ3] in a bundle of twenty-seven fascicles has been composed by Pawo, but it is the *Commentary on the Scripture* composed by Vasubandhu because the citations from the *Commentary on the Scripture* in [Abhayākaragupta's] *Ornament of the Sage's Intent* (*Munimatālaṃkāra*) are exactly as they are in this [Bṭ3], and because he [Vasubandhu] makes an opening promise to compose with "I want to compose a commentary on that scripture in which the harms have been overcome."[9]

Shākya Chokden does not use the names Chewai Dé (*mche ba'i sde*) or Daṃṣṭrāsena. It may be because those exact names are not in the two catalogues he is consulting. Whether Padé (*dpa' sde*) is an alias for Trisong Detsen or another Tibetan king, or for Daṃṣṭrāsena is uncertain, as is the identity of the person called Pawo (*dpa' bo*). Brunnhölzl has briefly commented on the problems raised by these names.[10]

9. Shākya Mchog ldan, *Bzhed tshul rba rlabs kyi phreng ba*, 167–68: *spyir bshad pa dang / byed brag bstan bcos 'di ji ltar bkrol ba'i tshul gnyis las / dang po la / bod lnga rabs kyi dge ba'i bshes gnyen phal mo che ni / dngos bstan stong nyid kyi rim pa gsal bar ston pa dbu ma rigs pa'i tshogs / sbas don mngon rtogs kyi rim pa gsal bar ston pa mngon par rtogs pa'i rgyan / sgo gsum rnam grangs bcu gcig gi sgo nas yum gyi don ston pa gnod 'joms / yang gtso bo'i don sum cu rtsa gnyis su brgyad stong pa'i don bsdus nas ston pa brgyad stong don bsdus te / shing rta'i srol 'byed chen po bzhi yin zer to // chos rje thams cad mkhyen pas ni / bzhi yin zhes smra ba ni mi 'thad de / snga ma gnyis las srol 'byed gzhan min pa'i phyir zhes gsung / gsung 'di la brten nas gung ṭīg tu / 'grel byed gzhan gnyis kyang de gnyis kyi rjes su 'brang ba'i phyir / zhes bris pa ni rtsing po ste / snga ma gnyis kyis dbu mar bkrol la / phyi ma gnyis kyis sems tsam du bkrol ba'i phyir ro // 'di la bu ston rin po che na re / stong phrag brgyad pa'i bshad pa bam po bdun cu rtsa brgyad pa 'di / 'phang thang ka me dkar [emend chug to] chag tu khri srong lde btsan gyis byas par bris mod / 'ching phu'i dkar chag dang / pho brang stong thang ldan dkar gyi dkar chag dang gnyis su / rgya gar mar bshad pas dpa' sdes mdzad pa yin no. / yum gsum ga'i gnod 'joms su grags pa bam po nyi shu rtsa bdun pa 'di la dpa' bos byas par bris mod / 'di ni dbyig gnyed gyis mdzad pa'i gzhung 'grel yin te / thub dgons su / gzhung 'grel gyi lung drangs pa rnams ji lta ba bzhin 'dir snang ba'i phyir dang / 'di'i gzhung 'grel gnod 'joms bya bar 'dod / ces brtoms par dam bca' mdzad pa'i phyir / 'di la yum gsum gnod 'joms su grags kyang / rgyas 'bring gnyis dang / khri brgyad stong pa'i bshad pa yin no zhes gsung.*

10. Brunnhölzl 2011b, 10.

Lama Chimpa and Alaka Chattopadhyaya, in the introduction to their translation of Tāranātha's (1575–1634) *History of Indian Buddhism*, say, "Daṃṣṭrāsena lived during the time of Devapāla [= late eighth, early ninth centuries],"[11] and in an additional note say he is the author of both Bṭ3 and Bṭ1 and that his "name occurs in various forms: Ācārya Diṣṭasena, Daṃṣṭasena, Daṃṣṭasyana, etc."[12] Hopkins presents Tsongkhapa's mature explanation of Daṃṣṭrāsena's views.[13] Brunnhölzl says, "The majority of Tibetan commentators in all schools except for the Gelugpa tradition accept Vasubandhu's authorship."[14] Leonard van der Kuijp nicely avoids the difficulties surrounding the issue by referring to "a rather controversial issue concerning the authorship of two important works."[15]

From a historical point of view, there is no room for disagreement. The version of Bṭ3 in the present Narthang, Kanxi (Tsalpa), and Golden (Thempangma) Tengyurs cannot, in its present form, have been written in its entirety by the Vasubandhu who wrote the *Treasury of Abhidharma* (*Abhidharmakośa*) because it references the opinion of Śāntarakṣita, who lived at least three hundred years later. The exact status of this passage in which Śāntarakṣita is named is yet to be fully investigated, but it was extant in the version available to Tsongkhapa circulating in 1392 because he points out this chronological anomaly at the beginning of the *Golden Rosary*, but just as an afterthought, not as a conclusive piece of evidence. What is particularly striking is that this passage is omitted from the later Dergé edition of the Tengyur (completed in 1744).[16]

The passage in question comes at the end of the Bṭ3's long commentary on the words "during the last of the five hundreds."[17] After explaining that a "five hundred" is one tenth of the five thousand years the doctrine of a tathāgata lasts, and counting each of the ten five-hundred-year periods as

11. Chimpa and Chattopadhyaya 1997, 268.

12. Chimpa and Chattopadhyaya 1997, 417n54.

13. Hopkins 1999, 225–33.

14. Brunnhölzl 2011a, 692–94n99.

15. Van der Kuijp 2013, 133n41.

16. *Gnod 'joms.* Dergé Tengyur 3808, Perfection of Wisdom vol. *pha*: 208b.

17. Cf. Nattier 1999; also Yuyama 1992 and Harrison 2006, 144n40. The passage is found in the Dergé edition of the various Perfection of Wisdom sūtras at *Eighteen Thousand* (Tōh 10), *kha*: 256; *Hundred Thousand* (Tōh 8), *ta*: 58a6; and *Twenty-Five Thousand* (Tōh 9), *kha*: 245b1.

a "chapter" and associating lower and lower attainments with each subsequent chapter, the author of the Bṭ3 then gives another opinion:

> Some say the measure of a human lifespan can be one hundred years. There, in the first fifty years, the color, shape, strength, intellect, and so on increase, and in the later fifty years they wane. Similarly, the end of the epoch, the time of the waning of the teaching, is like the later fifty years and hence is labeled "the last of the five hundreds."[18]

Although Bṭ3 does not say so explicitly, this is a citation from Vasubandhu's *Long Commentary on the Teachings of Akṣayamati* (*Akṣayamati-nirdeśaṭīkā*).[19] In the Golden Tengyur edition of Bṭ3, which also reflects the Narthang and Kanxi editions, it then says:

> When formulated like that [in Vasubandhu's *Long Commentary on the Teachings of Akṣayamati*], the duration of a tathāgata's teaching is two thousand five hundred years. The two commentaries (*ṭīkā*) appear to be contradictory. Śāntarakṣita's intention is that the good Dharma lasts from the first, or "Arhat," chapter up to the [fifth] "Samādhi" chapter. There is the explanation in the commentarial tradition and there is this other explanation. The general consensus is five thousand years.[20]

One way of explaining away this passage, if it is indeed by the author of Bṭ3 and not a later interpolation, may be to say the *Paddhati* (Bṭ1/Bṭ3) known to Haribhadra and Abhayākaragupta is by a later Buddhist writer having the name Vasubandhu (like the tantric Nāgārjuna). This would mean we would have to add yet another Vasubandhu to the ever-lengthening list!

18. *Gnod 'joms.* Dergé Tengyur 3808, Perfection of Wisdom vol. *pha*: 208; Pedurma 55:1131.

19. Jens Braarvig (1993, 2:587–89) transcribes the passage from Vasubandhu's *Akṣayamati-nirdeśaṭīkā* in a note and provides an excellent translation.

20. *Gnod 'joms.* Bstan 'gyur gser bri ma, vol. *pha*; 293b4–6, BDRC MW23702, *de de ltar byas na de bzhin gshegs pa'i bstan pa gnas pa'i dus lo nyis stong lnga brgyar 'gyur te / ṭīka 'di dang gnyis 'gal bar snang ba / shanta rakṣi ta'i bsam pa ni / dgra bcom pa'i le'u dang / ting nge 'dzin gyi le'u'i bar la dam pa'i chos gnas so zhes bya bar bsam pa yin te / 'chad pa'i lugs la ji skad 'chad / la la ji skad du 'chad de / spyir lo lnga stong mthun no.*

Alternatively, it may be that the kernel of Bṭ3, or the tradition of interpretation at the heart of Bṭ3, goes back to Vasubandhu, who is then said to be its author. This would be like saying Nāgārjuna is the author of the *Long Treatise on the Perfection of Wisdom* (*Dazhidu lun*).

One way or the other, on historical grounds, the Vasubandhu who lived circa 400 CE did not write the passage found in the Narthang and Kanxi editions. This also appears to be the opinion of Kano and Li, who say of Bṭ3 that it "has been influenced by Kamalaśīla's *Light of the Middle Way* (*Madhyamakāloka*)."[21] They consistently give Daṃṣṭrāsena as the author.

The Perfection of Wisdom

To give an account of Tsongkhapa's contribution to hermeneutics, defined in this context as a vehicle of explanation that conveys the meaning of the Perfection of Wisdom to ordinary beings, it is first necessary to identify the subject matter of the Perfection of Wisdom scriptures. As stated above, the Perfection of Wisdom scriptures say all phenomena are empty of an intrinsic nature. Included among phenomena is sacred scripture; in particular, the older, sacred, foundational Buddhist scripture. The Perfection of Wisdom does not mean when it says this foundational scripture is "empty" that it is nonexistent or useless. It accepts both foundational scriptures and the Perfection of Wisdom scripture itself conventionally. It does not say that either is to be rejected outright but that they are to be rejected as objects of negative attachment (*abhiniveśa, zhen pa*), where "negative attachment" means grasping at an absolute, assenting to an intrinsic nature where there is in fact only its absence. It implies that the conventional truth of a true statement is not undermined by the absence of any validity of the claim it makes to absolute authority. We will return to this later.

The long version of the Perfection of Wisdom does not reject foundational scripture; it incorporates it.[22] This is clear right from the beginning,

---

21. Kano and Li 2014, 140.

22. The compilers of the Perfection of Wisdom say the merit from writing out even a few of the words of the scripture in the form of a book surpasses the merit from infinite beings worshiping infinite reliquaries containing the remains of infinite buddhas for infinite years. Such passages do not mean that the compilers of the Perfection of Wisdom took a side in a putative fight between Hīnayānists defending authentic foundational scripture and Mahāyānists set on discrediting older established foundational texts in order to buttress a claim to authority. They

where it states that both arhats and bodhisattvas are in the immediate audience. Since arhats are those who have already attained the final goal explained in the foundational sacred texts that are the record of Śākyamuni Buddha's words, they would not be sitting there listening to a Perfection of Wisdom discourse because they would already know what it has to say. The Perfection of Wisdom scriptures repeat the foundational scriptures within, saying they have no claim to absolute authority.

This is what Ārya Vimuktisena is getting at when he says at the start of his *Commentary* (*Vṛtti*) explaining the *Twenty-Five Thousand Perfection of Wisdom* (*Pañcaviṃśatisāhasrikāprajñāpāramitā*) with the categories listed in the *Ornament for Realization* (*Abhisamayālaṃkāra*) that there are no topics in the Perfection of Wisdom that have not already been set forth in the fundamental texts.[23]

The Perfection of Wisdom scripture, then, does not reject the older, foundational sacred scriptures. It introduces no topic (*vastu*) that is not already found in the foundational scriptures. Its originality is in its explanation of the antidote to negative attachment (*abhiniveśa*) and what results from it.

The bodhisattvas together with the arhats in the immediate audience listening to the long Perfection of Wisdom discourse understand that the "not seeing" ("A son of a good family or daughter of a good family practicing the perfection of wisdom does not see form" and so on) extends not just to the topics of the fundamental scriptures ("form" and so on) but to the Perfection of Wisdom scripture, to the bodhisattva practices, and even to the result, perfect enlightenment. Not to see them and not to settle down in them means not to be negatively attached to them.

While clearly rejecting such attachments, the Perfection of Wisdom scriptures say they contain the most beneficial of all sacred texts and traditions, the origin of all that is good—statements that have led some to mistakenly positing a cult of the book—and that fake scriptures, fake practices, and fake enlightenment are all the work of Māra, the deceiver. As Nāgārjuna puts it in *Fundamental Verses on the Middle Way*:

---

are also not evidence that the compilers were members of a putative cult of the book (Schopen 2005) or took sides in a putative dispute between lay preachers located at reliquaries and traditional monks teaching in monasteries (Hirakawa 1990).

23. *Na hi tad astīha sūtre vastu yan na lakṣaṇaśāstreṣu parisaṃkhyātam.* See Pensa 1967, 12.

> The victorious ones say emptiness
> is expounded as the escape from [wrong] views.
> They say those who have emptiness
> as a [wrong] view are incorrigible.[24]

The Perfection of Wisdom also suggests that orthodox Vedic scripture is not to be rejected outright but only as an object of negative attachment as well. This is suggested, first, by the presence of Vedic gods listening to the discourse. Secondly, probably the compilers themselves, and certainly many authors in the commentarial tradition associated with the Perfection of Wisdom, were educated brahmans. Vedic orthodoxy would form part of their family identity, and nothing intrinsic to Vedic orthodoxy precludes a highly educated brahman with an ecumenical attitude and a complex religious and social identity from reposing faith in the Perfection of Wisdom as well. As I will attempt to show below, the basic hermeneutical principle to be gleaned from the Perfection of Wisdom scriptures is *cittotpāda*, the production of the thought of enlightenment rooted in compassion (= *bodhicitta*), so there is nothing theoretically that precludes orthodox Vedic scripture being treated in the same way as foundational Buddhist scripture. Its value derives from its value to those who read it, not from something intrinsic to its nature as spoken or written words.

In this context, it is noteworthy that the incorporation of elements of orthodox non-Buddhist scripture into Buddhist scripture coincides with the rise of Buddhist tantra. Similarly, the development of a distinctly Buddhist epistemological tradition coincides with a protracted debate with orthodox thinkers over the true sources of authority as it pertains to sacred scripture. Both occur in tandem with the spread of the Perfection of Wisdom.[25]

It is therefore possible, and even likely, that the compilers of the Perfection of Wisdom scripture did not reject the sacredness of orthodox Vedic scripture outright but only when it is an object of negative attachment,

---

24. *Mūlamadhyamakakārikā* 13.8, in Siderits and Katsura 2013, 145: *śūnyatā sarvadṛṣṭīnāṃ proktā niḥsaraṇaṃ jinaiḥ / yeṣāṃ tu śūnyatādṛṣṭis tān asādhyān babhāṣire.*

25. Vincent Eltschinger (2013), continuing a line of inquiry initiated by Eli Franco (1997), building on the work of Alexis Sanderson (1988 and 1994) and Ronald Davidson (2002a), explains both as the outcome of a zero-sum competition for patronage between different Buddhist groups and, after the collapse of the Gupta dynasty, between Buddhist and non-Buddhist groups.

leading to self-serving, socially destructive action. This interpretation conforms with the general tenor of the Perfection of Wisdom.

The Ornament for Realization's *Interpretation of the Perfection of Wisdom*

Historically, the orthodox sacred scriptures on the Indian subcontinent are the Vedas, which were held to be qualified by two profound attributes: first, they are eternal and not produced by any human or other agency, and second, the relation between the words of the Vedas and their meaning is eternal and fixed, so they are inherently true without deriving their authority from any other source.

The great contribution of the *Ornament of Realization* attributed to Maitreya is its presentation of bodhicitta as the principle the Perfection of Wisdom scriptures offer as a *clavis hermeneutica*, a key to interpretation, to compete with the orthodox claim that the authority of a sacred scripture is intrinsic to it, that the meaning of sacred scripture is intrinsically fixed in the words—the "authorlessness of the semantic relation" of "non-Buddhist doctrines such as the Mīmāṃsakas."[26]

The *Ornament of Realization* is not a text cited frequently in Sanskrit outside the narrow range of the Indian Perfection of Wisdom commentarial tradition. Viewed from the perspective of the long literary and intellectual developments that come after it both in India and Tibet, however, it is possible that its importance has not been adequately acknowledged, both because of its influence on the Buddhist epistemological tradition and on the development of distinctive literary genres.

In the Buddhist epistemological school of Dignāga and Dharmakīrti, which rejects Vedic authority, the validity of an ordinary person's statement, which originates in the speaker's intention, derives from a direct perception or a valid inference that authorizes the statement as true. The situation is more complex, however, when it comes to statements of extraordinary persons with an insight into things beyond ordinary understanding—for example, the source of authority for the words of a sacred text like one of the Perfection of Wisdom scriptures.

Western scholarship has expended considerable effort discussing the

---

26. Eltschinger 2013, 258.

problem faced by the Buddhist epistemological school in this regard[27] because, even though it is axiomatic that Buddhist faith should not be in the person of the Buddha but in the Buddha's teachings, and those teachings should be validated through the reliable perceptions gained in an individual's yogic practice, still the authority vested in the Buddha's statements are because of the Buddha's knowledge—omniscience—and how can anyone be certain about the mental state of anybody else, especially a state like omniscience that no one except a buddha can ever have?

The solution is found in the guiding principle for the interpretation of the Perfection of Wisdom scriptures as explained in the *Ornament of Realization*—namely, bodhicitta, the production of the thought of enlightenment. Both Dharmakīrti in his explanation of Dignāga's survey of the Perfection of Wisdom scriptures[28] and Candrakīrti in his explanation of Nāgārjuna's[29] identify *karuṇā* (compassion)—the *kāma* (wanting) of the Perfection of Wisdom scriptures[30]—as the origin of a buddha's omniscience. This origin is the mother perfection of wisdom explained explicitly and insistently in the *Ornament of Realization*. As the origin of omniscience, it is the source of authority for statements made by one with that level of knowledge.

The origin in the Perfection of Wisdom is a unification of compassion (*karuṇā*) or method (*upāya*) and wisdom (*prajñā*) (of the conventional and the ultimate). This unification undercuts the absolute truth of every profound doctrine—as the doctrine itself, as an understanding of doctrine, and as a practice of the doctrine. The underlying unifying *dharmatā* is the absence of any intrinsic nature (*svabhāva*) of the sort that would provide

---

27. See the summary in McClintock 2010, chapters 4–6.

28. Dharmakīrti, *Commentary on Reliable Cognition* (*Pramāṇavārttika*), 2.34, *sādhanaṃ karuṇā*, translated in Franco 1997, 159, as "Compassion is the proof [of the Buddha being a means of knowledge]."

29. Candrakīrti, *Entering the Middle Way* (*Madhyamakāvatāra*), 1.1–2, translated by Thupten Jinpa in Tsongkhapa 2021a, 36–45: "Śrāvakas and middle-level buddhas arise from sovereign sages. Buddhas are born from bodhisattvas. The compassionate mind and nondual cognition as well the awakening mind: these are causes of bodhisattvas. As compassion alone is accepted to be the seed of the perfect harvest of buddhahood, the water that nourishes it, and the fruit that is long a source of enjoyment, I will praise compassion at the start of all."

30. *Pañcaviṃśatisāhasrikāprajñāpāramitā* (Kimura 2007–9, 28): *sarvākāraṃ śāriputra sarvadharmān abhisaṃboddhukāmena bodhisattvena mahāsattvena prajñāpāramitāyāṃ yogaḥ karaṇīyaḥ.*

any *dharma* (phenomenon) with its own unique identity, independent of anything else. It explains, or is indivisible from, the *upāya*, the different doctrines that form the body of sacred scriptures and effective practices known as Buddhism. The origin (*mātṛ*), the object of Maitreya's opening verse of homage in his *Ornament of Realization*, is thus *prajñāpāramitā*, which provides authority to a scripture. It is an authority that replaces the orthodox Vedic assertion that a true sacred scripture has no beginning and that the words of sacred scriptures relate to their contents in an absolute and immutable way.

This explains in large part why Tsongkhapa at the start of his *Golden Rosary* says that Dignāga's *Summary of the Perfection of Wisdom* (*Prajñā-pāramitāpiṇḍārtha*) is indebted to Maitreya and thus not a trailblazing commentary, and also his statement in his short account of his intellectual and spiritual development *Realization Narrative* (*Rtogs brjod 'dun legs ma*):

> Having seen [that what others said was wrong], I investigated this
>   matter further.
> I found a joy and a certainty that the "Establishing Valid Cogni-
>   tion" (*pramāṇasiddhi*) [chapter of Dharmakīrti's *Commentary on
>   Reliable Cognition* (*Pramāṇavārttika*)],
> through explaining the order in which [saṃsāra] comes into being
>   and the order in which it is reversed,
> established for those seeking liberation the intended mean-
>   ing of [Dignāga's] *Compendium of Reliable Cognition*'s
>   (*Pramāṇasamuccaya*) opening homage:
> that the Lord Buddha is an authority and, on account of that,
> that his teaching alone is the point of entry for those seeking
>   liberation.[31]

The *Ornament of Realization*'s contribution, then, is its clear articulation of *cittotpāda* as an alternative grounding for the authority of sacred scripture. It interprets the Perfection of Wisdom as saying sacred scripture has no validity in itself but only insofar as it is of benefit to those for whom it is intended.

---

31. Tsong kha pa, *Rtogs brjod 'dun legs ma*, 78.

Tsongkhapa's Historical Context

Tsongkhapa was influenced by a confluence of historical factors, among which is the final redaction of the Buddhist canon and debates around the issue of canonical authenticity. The authority of Buddhist foundational scriptures and later Mahāyāna scriptures, including the tantric scriptures, a deeply contested issue in India, had been largely resolved in Tibet by the time Tsongkhapa wrote his *Golden Rosary*.[32] Still, the continual formation of new sacred scriptures through tales of discovery or claims of supernormal modes of cognition that is a distinctive feature of the larger Tibetan cultural region ensured that the question of canonical legitimacy remained.[33]

The second historical circumstance that provides a context for Tsongkhapa's contribution to hermeneutics is the dominance of the Perfection of Wisdom interpretative tradition started by Ngok Lotsāwa Loden Sherab (1059–1109) at Sangphu Monastery. This tradition, with its many branches, privileges Maitreya's *Ornament of Realization* and Haribhadra's *Clear Meaning Commentary (Vivṛti)*. In Tibet during the twelfth to fourteenth centuries, an aspiring scholar and teacher had to demonstrate expertise in a number of subjects during visits to famous seats of learning. One of these subjects was the Perfection of Wisdom, in essence the Sangphu tradition. Tsongkhapa's *Golden Rosary* is a demonstration of that expertise. According to the received Sangphu tradition, Haribhadra, the author of the *Clear Meaning Commentary* on the *Ornament*, criticized Vasubandhu for writing from an incomplete Mind Only perspective.

The third circumstance is the rediscovery by Tsongkhapa's main teacher and friend Rendawa Shönu Lodrö of the tradition of exegesis going back to the translator Patsab Nyima Drak (b. 1055) that privileges Candrakīrti's exegesis of the works of Nāgārjuna. This had a great influence on Tsongkhapa, and already at the start of his *Golden Rosary*, it informs his identi-

32. Under the guiding hand of Butön the mass of scriptures in translation had been divided into the collection of translations of scripture said by a buddha (Kangyur) and translations of commentaries on words said by a buddha (Tengyur) and had become in most respects a closed canon.

33. The importance of this constant, known best through the distinct "treasure" (*gter ma*) genre, in the life of Tsongkhapa has been made clear by the recent biography by Thupten Jinpa (2019).

fication of Nāgārjuna, as distinct from Maitreya, as providing a different trailblazing explanation.

The fourth circumstance is Dölpopa Sherab Gyaltsen's rediscovery and popularization of the B_ṭ1 and B_ṭ3 Perfection of Wisdom exegesis. Even though B_ṭ3 itself supplies an outline for, and glosses important words and passages in, the Perfection of Wisdom scriptures, the *Ornament of Realization*, accepted universally in Tibet by the eleventh century to have been written by Maitreya and popularized by Ngok's Sangphu tradition, had become so central that B_ṭ3 and B_ṭ1 were already receding into relative obscurity. A brilliant polemicist, Dölpopa used B_ṭ3's exegesis as a nontantric scriptural basis to explain his distinctive and influential doctrine of extrinsic emptiness (*gzhan stong*) propounded in the works of Maitreya, Vasubandhu, and Nāgārjuna.

Dölpopa greatly admired the *Kālacakra Tantra* and Puṇḍarīka's *Stainless Light* (*Vimalaprabhā*) commentary on it as the pinnacle of Buddhist scripture. Rendawa, on the other hand, at least in the earlier part of his life, characterized the *Kālacakra Tantra* as a non-Buddhist scripture. This was an extreme position that Tsongkhapa never accepted, but Rendawa's attitude to sacred scripture undoubtedly influenced Tsongkhapa's thinking about this subject.

Tsongkhapa's Contribution to Hermeneutics

Tsongkhapa's explicit contribution to hermeneutics is set forth in his *Essence of Eloquence* (*Legs bshad snying po*). There, his presentation, drawing on the *Unraveling the Thought* (*Saṃdhinirmocana*) and *Teachings of Akṣayamati* (*Akṣayamatinirdeśa*) sūtras, the former presenting the three wheels of the Dharma and the latter distinguishing the ultimate and the conventional, is of a hermeneutics based on the identification of definitive statements and provisional statements, those requiring interpretation. It is a magisterial presentation using traditional categories. The work has been translated into English by Thurman (1984) and again partly by Hopkins (1999). In this work Tsongkhapa is not concerned with the interpretation of contested sacred scripture, or sacred scripture in general, as were the compilers of the Perfection of Wisdom or the author of the *Ornament of Realization*. He is concerned with the interpretation of a received canon.

Tsongkhapa sets aside tantra entirely and passes quickly over the

Kangyur, concerning himself primarily with the treatises (*śāstra*). He accepts all to be authentically Buddhist, and to that extent of equal value, but he grades them on a scale from lower to higher based on the extent to which a treatise properly articulates the Buddha's actual intention as it pertains to ultimate and conventional truth. His main concern is with the most important Mahāyāna commentaries. Crucially, he puts works by Maitreya, Asaṅga, and Vasubandhu into a lower Mind Only category and works by Nāgārjuna as interpreted by Bhāviveka into a category just below the highest category. The highest grade he reserves for works in accord with the exegesis of Nāgārjuna by Candrakīrti, works that propose an especially strong version of emptiness.

Buddhist scripture sets forth a practice and a result. The *practice* takes place in an imperfect and impure state. The *result* describes a perfect pure state. The explanation of how the change from the impure to the pure takes place gives rise to different traditions of interpretation. In Tibet, the explanations employ the conventional and ultimate terminology of the Middle Way; the imaginary, dependent, and thoroughly established terminology of the Mind Only; and the terminology of buddha nature or tathāgatagarbha.

According to Dölpopa in his Perfection of Wisdom commentaries, all these three traditions of interpretation have always been one unified Great Middle Way. Dölpopa says not just tantra and the scriptures privileged by the tathāgatagarbha tradition but also the Perfection of Wisdom and its commentarial tradition clearly teaches this Great Middle Way where change is impossible if the imaginary conceptual world is endowed with any reality whatsoever. Dölpopa says Bṭ3's three-nature terminology conveys this decisively. He characterizes the *Questions of Maitreya* (*Maitreyaparipṛcchā*), chapter 83 of the *Eighteen Thousand Perfection of Wisdom* (*Aṣṭādaśaprajñāpāramitā*), in which the three-nature terminology is explicitly used, as the Buddha's own commentary on his own works (*rang 'grel*) and hence not open to challenge. Dölpopa, as a polemical strategy, says that since the skill of a buddha is so great, definitive statements and statements that require interpretation are not necessary. A buddha is capable of making a topic clear because a buddha is a supremely skillful and supreme orator.

In his *Essence of Eloquence*, working out ideas already germinating in his *Golden Rosary*, Tsongkhapa uses the rediscovered exegesis of Nāgārjuna by Candrakīrti as a vehicle to reject Dölpopa's unified Great Middle Way explanation and propose in its place a thoroughgoing Consequentialist (*thal 'gyur pa*) version of emptiness.

Hopkins sums up Tsongkhapa's explanation of the real meaning of the passages Dölpopa cites from Bṭ3 to buttress his extrinsic-emptiness position:

> In sum, the meaning is that although the *Conquest Over Objections* [=Bṭ3] describes how emptiness appears to a consciousness of direct realization, it does not present how to get at that state through reflecting on phenomena and how they are empty of an imputational nature.[34]

When presenting his own understanding of the ultimate truth (*yongs grub*) and how it is balanced with conventional reality (*gzhang dbang*), it is noteworthy that Tsongkhapa does not simply reject Bṭ3 as wrong, as he does Dölpopa's interpretation of it. Rather, he interprets it as fitting within his new graded framework that will culminate in the Prāsaṅgika presentation of emptiness, a quasi-nihilistic ultimate capable of undercutting all negative attachment to scriptures, together with a presentation of authority that will retain the value of the scriptural analysis he is engaged in. Finally, Tsongkhapa locates authority only in a compassionate principle qualified by its own lack of any intrinsic authority.

In his *Essence of Eloquence*, Tsongkhapa is not concerned with the validity or invalidity of treatises but with their relative benefit to a listener or reader. This hermeneutic principle, in the sense of a principle that indicates why a statement is authoritative or true, is set forth more explicitly by Tsongkhapa at the beginning of his most famous work, the *Great Treatise on the Stages of the Path* (*Lam rim chen mo*), where he says, "This advice, in general, is the advice in the *Ornament of Realization* composed by the venerable lord Maitreya,"[35] filtered through Atiśa's *Lamp for the Path to Enlightenment* (*Bodhipathapradīpa*). The *Great Treatise*'s tripartite path structure developed specifically for a Tibetan audience is modeled on the

---

34. Hopkins 1999, 230, note c.

35. Tsong kha pa, *Lam rim chen mo*, 2: *gdams ngag 'di spyir rje btsun byams pas mdzad pa'i mngon par rtogs pa'i rgyan gyi gdams ngag yin la.*

three types of persons associated with the three types of knowledge first set forth clearly in the *Ornament of Realization.*

In the *Great Treatise,* written at about the same time as the *Essence of Eloquence,* bodhicitta operates as an interpretative principle to give legitimacy to an entire range of statements and practices: even ordinary (*'jig rten pa*) statements directed toward ordinary beings of "small capacity." These include statements describing a common moral code rejecting ten non-virtues and statements explaining the drivers of foolish conduct by ordinary people, the so-called eight worldly dharmas (*'jig rten gyi chos brgyad*). Tsongkhapa goes so far as to use bodhicitta as an interpretative principle to give legitimacy to a system of meditation, tranquil abiding (*śamatha*), that he describes as a practice shared with non-Buddhists. The same principle in his accompanying *Great Exposition of Secret Mantra* (*Sngags rim chen mo*) leads him to say that imagining oneself as a deity, the defining characteristic of a Buddhist tantric scripture, is a practice shared by Buddhists and non-Buddhists. Statements and practices are differentiated by whether bodhicitta is the motiving factor. It is also noteworthy that the last major work of Tsongkhapa setting forth this view is his *Illuminating the Intent* (*Dgongs pa rab gsal*), a commentary on Candrakīrti's *Entering the Middle Way,* the opening lines of which, cited above, praise compassion as the origin of buddhas and all else that is good.

Tsongkhapa did not oppose Dölpopa and his followers the way that Buddhists in classical India opposed followers of non-Buddhist orthodoxy. Tsongkhapa would certainly have been familiar with the great benefit of Dölpopa's view of extrinsic emptiness as a basis for generating great compassion and bodhicitta. After all, what could be sadder than the idea that all beings suffer in a stream of different forms of life from the very beginning just because of their ignorance of their true nature—Dölpopa's consummate nature?[36] So, his rejection of Dölpopa's assertion that Bṭ3 is a commentary by the Great Middle Way master Vasubandhu and his oblique rejection of Dölpopa's emptiness view even at the beginning of his earliest major commentary is not a blanket rejection of the sacredness of Dölpopa's tradition. It is an oblique way of saying that Dölpopa's "profound extrinsic emptiness endowed with the supreme of all aspects" may be a way to con-

---

36. This is also called the primordial enlightened being (*ādibuddha*) and Samantabhadra.

vey the meaning of the Perfection of Wisdom but is to be rejected when it is the basis of a negative attachment.

Tsongkhapa's complicated way of presenting the two complementary hermeneutics he accepts as suitable for interpreting the Perfection of Wisdom—Nāgārjuna's explanation of the ultimate emptiness and Maitreya's explanation of compassionate skillful means as the three knowledges (the *all-knowledge* of śrāvakas, the *knowledge of paths* of bodhisattvas, and the *knowledge of all aspects* of buddhas) underpinned by emptiness—in his early Perfection of Wisdom commentary, the *Golden Rosary*, opened him up to a series of criticisms, starting with Rongtön Sheja Kunrik's (1367–1449) observation that Maitreya cannot both propound a mistaken (lesser) point of view and at the same time correctly convey what the Perfection of Wisdom says. This leads Tsongkhapa in his later work, through his student Gyaltsab Jé (1364–1432), to propound the view that Maitreya and his student Asaṅga, which the *Essence of Eloquence* says are the main proponents of the Mind Only, are in fact, in the *Sublime Continuum* (*Uttaratantra*), writing from an ultimately defensible Prāsaṅgika perspective. In this way Tsongkhapa accounts more fully for the buddha-nature tradition. He presents a more refined view of the *tathāgatagarbha* by interpreting some scriptural statements as referring to emptiness and others to a functioning potential (*nus pa*).

His hermeneutics that balances emptiness and bodhicitta also leads Tsongkhapa, again through his student Gyaltsab, to develop a distinctive epistemology that is not undercut by a strong view of emptiness but is, in his explanation, buttressed by it. This epistemology accords to every cognitive state a validity relative to what appears to it (*rang gi snang yul la tshad ma*) while refuting the establishment of any object as authoritative beyond a worldly, conventionally accepted authority. In the context of sacred scripture, it asserts a statement must meet a number of criteria to be deemed definitive, among them that it is not undercut by statements articulating the view of emptiness Tsongkhapa finds in Candrakīrti's interpretation of Nāgārjuna.

As for Maitreya's *Ornament of Realization*, it is left in the position it occupied before Dölpopa, propounding a point of view set forth by Haribhadra and Ārya Vimuktisena that is not quite wrong and not quite right either, a rather nice way of leaving a student with the insight that sacred traditions are never to be objects of a deluded attachment.

10. Jé Tsongkhapa's Teachings and Translations in Mongolian

BATAA Mishig-Ish

ACCORDING TO ANCIENT sources, Buddhism was introduced to Mongolia during the first and second centuries of the Common Era.[1] However, the principal teachings of the Lord Buddha were more profoundly absorbed by Mongolians through Jé Tsongkhapa's teachings. Following in the footsteps of the Tibetans, Mongolians adopted Jé Tsongkhapa's path to enlightenment via the Geluk tradition in the second half of the sixteenth century. As one of the major beneficiaries of Jé Rinpoché's teachings, Mongolians have historically studied and practiced them, in both the Tibetan and Mongolian languages, throughout the Mongolian-speaking territories, including today's Mongolia, Inner Mongolia, Buryatia, and Western (Oirat) Mongolia. In this paper, I explore how Jé Tsongkhapa's different versions of *lam rim* and related texts have been used by Mongolians for centuries.

Following its translation from Tibetan into Mongolian in the early seventeenth century, the Kangyur began to circulate in woodblock prints due to a decree of Ligden Khan (1588–1634), the khan of the Northern Yuan dynasty, in 1629. The completion of the Kangyur translation led to the translation of the Tengyur beginning in 1720, involving several dozen

---

1. Zava Damdin's *Golden Chronicle: A History of Holy Dharma in the Land of Mongolia* mentions that Buddhism was introduced to the ancient Mongols during the Hun or Xiongnu dynasty in the second century CE. Anandyn Amar's *Brief History of Mongolia* states that "the Hun soldiers carried with them an icon of the Buddha. It was likely that they had faith in Buddhism" (Amar 2015, 11). The scholar Shagdaryn Bira also mentions that "based on Zava Damdin's account, it was correct to assume that early Buddhism was introduced to the Mongols through the Khotans of Central Asia in the second and third century AD" (Zava Damdin 2014, 13 and 46). Since Khotan bordered the Kushan Empire during that period, it is very likely that it was influenced by the Buddhist religion and culture of this neighbor.

renowned translators and scholars. The Mongolian Tengyur was printed in Beijing in 1749. The translation of Kangyur and Tengyur into Mongolian served as the foundation for the dissemination of Jé Tsongkhapa's writings in Mongolia following the introduction of the Geluk tradition of Buddhism starting in the seventeenth century.

Following the enormous task of translating the Kangyur and Tengyur over several decades, the Mongolian translation of Jé Tsongkhapa's collected works, compiled in twenty volumes, was also completed in the eighteenth century. This was then published as woodblock prints prepared in Beijing in the second half of the eighteenth century. This important project was undertaken by a collective of Mongolian scholars and translators including Thupten Guush, Minjuur Choirje, Kharachin Guush Sandui Baldan, and Ordos Erdene Mergen Guush Gungaadonrov. This classical Mongolian translation of the collected works of Jé Tsongkhapa has survived until today and contains 211 individual writings and texts.

Different Translations of the Lam rim chen mo

The first volume of the Mongolian collected works begins with the *Great Treatise on the Stages of the Path*, or *Lam rim chen mo*, the most studied and widely revered work of Jé Tsongkhapa. Numerous *lam rim* texts, including the *Lam rim chen mo*, the *Middle-Length Treatise on the Stages of the Path* (*Lam rim 'bring*), and the *Abbreviated Stages of the Path* (*Lam rim bsdus don*, also known as the *Songs of Spiritual Experience*) and their commentaries, can still be found throughout Mongolia, in both the Tibetan and Mongolian languages. Most of these widespread *lam rim* volumes are woodblock prints; however, a few are handwritten. It is of great historical import to study how the different Mongolian translations of the *Lam rim chen mo* were disseminated and used by Mongolians over the past four centuries.

Distinguished scholars and monks such as Altangerel Ubashi, Minjuur Agramba, Zaya Paṇḍita Namkhaijamts of Oirat, Agvangalsanjamba of Buryatia, Mergen Guush Gungaadonrov, and Mergen Lama Agvaanlodoijamts[2] translated the *Lam rim chen mo* into Mongolian between the sev-

---

2. Some of the above names are Tibetan in origin—e.g., Namkhaijamts is Namkhai Gyatso, Agvangalsanjamba is Ngawang Kalsang Jampa, and Agvaanlodoijamts is Ngawang Lodrö

enteenth and the nineteenth centuries. There may have been as many as a dozen different Mongolian translations of the *Lam rim chen mo*, but unfortunately many of the earliest translations of this and other *lam rim* texts, along with other Buddhist scriptures, did not survive the destructive persecution of Buddhism in Mongolia in the 1920s and 1930s. The systematic destruction of Buddhist texts and scriptures was one of the most devastating policies of the Soviet-guided government to completely eliminate Buddhism in Mongolia during that period.

In an attempt to locate the existing Mongolian versions of the *Lam rim chen mo*, I have been able to track down four versions of the existing translations in classical Mongolian script. (1) The first of the four versions is a Mongolian translation printed in Beijing in the eighteenth century as part of the collected works (see figure 7). (2) Around the same time, another finely printed version of the *Lam rim chen mo* could be found in both Inner and Outer Mongolia. This version was printed in the Western Tümed banner, or administrative region, of Inner Mongolia in the seventeenth century. *Lam rim* translations like the Tümed version continued to be printed at different monastic institutions throughout Mongolia (see figure 1). (3) Another *Lam rim chen mo* version was published in Aga province, Buryatia, in the early nineteenth century. This particular version was extensively distributed throughout central Mongolia and Buryatia (see figure 5). (4) One of the rarest of the Mongolian *Lam rim chen mo* is the *tod* (clear) script woodblock version from the seventeenth century (see figure 3). *Tod* script was widely used by the Oirat and Kalmyk people in Western Mongolia. The script was created by Zaya Paṇḍita Namkhaijamts (Namkhai Gyatso, 1599–1662), a prominent Oirat scholar, based on the distinctive dialect of the Oirat Mongols.[3] *Tod* script closely resembles the old or traditional Mongolian script.

Several of these *Lam rim chen mo* translations from disparate locations are presented in the following images. Figure 1 shows the Tümed version from a printing in 1821 at a monastery in the western part of what is now Hohhot, the current capital city of Inner Mongolia.[4]

Gyatso. They spellings here are phonetic transcriptions of the Cyrillic writing system of modern Mongolian. Many Mongolians are still given Tibetan names at birth.

3. Not to be confused with Khalkha Zaya Paṇḍita Luvsanprinlei (Losang Trinlé, 1642–1715).

4. This scripture is currently owned by R. Otgonbaatar, researcher at the Institute of Language and Literature of the Mongolian Academy of Sciences.

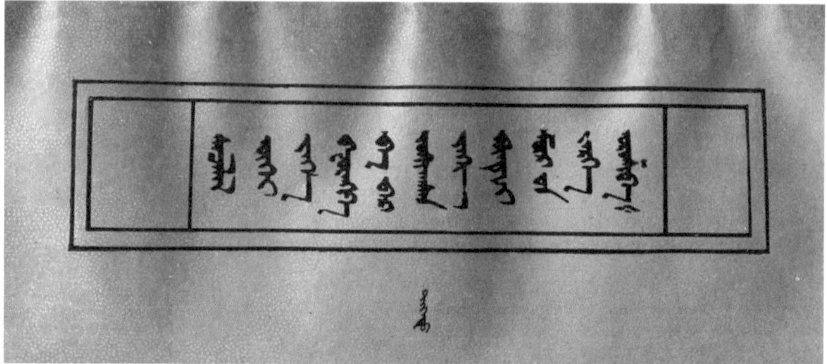

Figure 1. Mongolian translation of *Lam rim chen mo*.

Figure 2. Woodblock-printed *lam rim* in traditional Mongolian script.

Zaya Paṇḍita Namkhaijamts's translations of the *Lam rim chen mo* (*tod: Bodi muriin ue*) and other *lam rim* commentaries into *tod* script in the seventeenth century are depicted in figure 3.

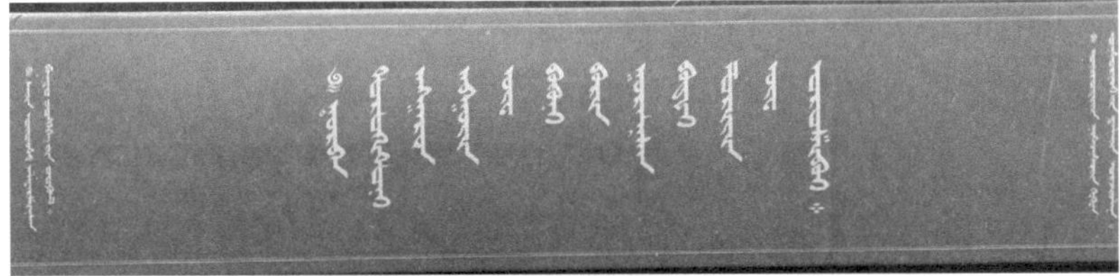

Figure 3. Mongolian translation of a *lam rim* work in *tod* (clear) script.

Although *tod* script has a strong resemblance to classical Mongolian script, it has certain distinguishing characteristics associated with Oirat Mongolian dialect and vernacular.

Figure 4. Handwritten pages of a *lam rim* in *tod* script.

As noted above, the *Lam rim chen mo* was translated into Mongolian by the well-known Buryat monk Agvangalsanjamba (Ngawang Kalsang Jampa) and woodblock printed in Aga province in Buryatia in the nineteenth century (see figure 5).

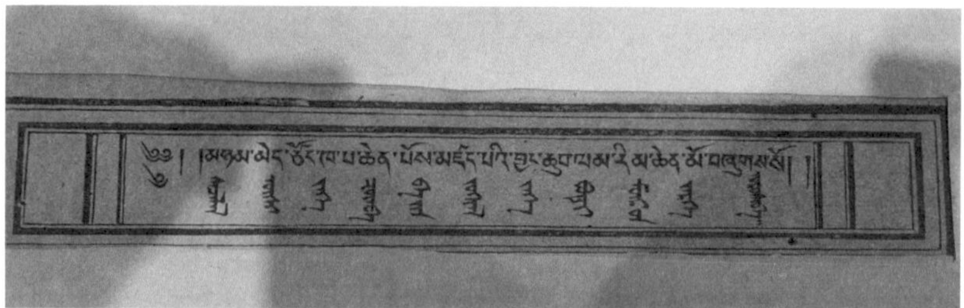

Figure 5. A *Lam rim chen mo* printed in Buryatia.

Gombojav Tsybikov's Russian translation of the *Lam rim chen mo* in the early twentieth century is the first time the work was translated into Russian. Gombojav's translation was likely based on Agvangalsanjamba's Mongolian translation and on the Tibetan version.

Figure 5 is an example of the word-by-word translation method, which was one of the key methods used by Mongolian translators; it is simple substitution, replacing Tibetan words with Mongolian ones based on an established lexical key but keeping the Tibetan sentence structure.

Figure 6. Woodblock-printed *lam rim* in Mongolian.

Most scholars agree that there are at least two different Mongolian translations of the *Lam rim chen mo* preserved in Beijing print formats. I was able to locate only one, which is in the classical Mongolian script (see figure 7).

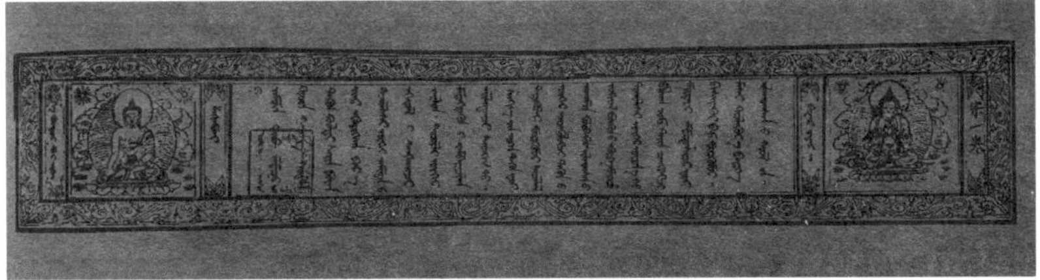

Figure 7. *Lam rim* printed in Beijing.

The *Lam rim chen mo* was also translated by the famous Mongolian translator Mergen Lama Agvanlodoijamts (Ngawang Lodrö Gyatso), but no copy of his translation was found.

Other Lam rim Texts and Commentaries

One of the earliest introductions to teachings on the stages of the path in Mongolian was a translation of the seventh-century *Bodhicaryāvatāra* of Śāntideva. This classical Indian treatise in verse was translated into Mongolian in the early fourteenth century by the Uighur Paṇḍita Chökyi Öser. In the 1960s, the scholar Tsendiin Damdinsuren stated that twelve pages of the *Bodhicaryāvatāra* in classical Mongolian script were discovered in the Turfan cave repository in the early twentieth century by German scholars.[5]

In 1578, Altan Khan (1507–82) of the Tümed tribe officially invited and warmly welcomed the Third Dalai Lama Sönam Gyatso (1543–88) to Chabcha Monastery, located south of Lake Kokonor. According to Zava Damdin's *Golden Chronicle*, during the Dalai Lama's first visit to Mongolian territory, around forty Mongolian monks made a special request to him to give an initiation of his *Essence of Refined Gold*, or *Lam rim gser zhun ma*.[6] Historically, this was the earliest *lam rim* teaching directly transmitted by the Third Dalai Lama to the Mongolian monks.

As noted above, Mongolian translations of *lam rim* texts were made between the seventeenth century and nineteenth centuries. Ubashi

5. Damdinsuren 2008, 8–11. Damdinsuren discovered the pages among the works in the Turfan Collection at the Berlin Library in 1952. The Turfan Collection was housed in Germany from early in the twentieth century but remained unstudied until after World War II.

6. Full title: *Byang chub lam gyi rim pa'i khrid yig gser gyi yang zhun*. Zava Damdin 2014, 141.

Altangerel's translation of the *Lam rim chen mo*[7] is probably one of the first Mongolian translations of the text, made in the late sixteenth century. One of the earliest *lam rim* commentaries by a Mongolian was the *Stages of the Path Instructions that Dispel Mental Darkness* (*Lam rim gyi 'khrid blo yi mun sel*), written by Lamyn Gegeen Luvsandanzanjantsan (Losang Tenzin Gyaltsen, 1639–1703) in the late seventeenth century.

In addition to translations of the core *lam rim* texts, an even greater number of commentarial treatises were written by Mongolian scholar monks for centuries. In his doctoral thesis, Lama Dr. G. Myagmarsuren mentions the names of over twenty Mongolian scholar monks who had written several dozen commentaries on Tibetan *lam rim* texts.[8] Unfortunately, many of these texts are not thoroughly studied and researched. Here I mention only one of the well-studied treatises, Qahar Geshe Luvsanchultem's (Chahar Geshé Losang Tsultrim, 1740–1810) *Exposition on the Four Qualities of the Path to Enlightenment.*[9]

The Practice of Lam rim Teachings

Historically, Mongolian monks have thoroughly studied Jé Tsongkhapa's teachings, especially the *lam rim* texts. The language sources for this long tradition can be divided into the three categories. First, intellectual monks and scholars, who were highly proficient in the Tibetan language, not only read and studied them in Tibetan but also wrote various commentaries in that language. According to the late Khambo Lama Gombojav's provisional account, 208 Mongolian monks composed works in Tibetan.[10] Contemporary research suggests that well over three hundred individual scholar monks wrote their works in the Tibetan language. Many of these works were commentaries on and interpretations of *lam rim* teachings.

---

7. Luvsantseren 1976, 501–4.

8. Myagmarsuren is a Mongolian scholar lama who specializes in the study of *lam rim* texts in different languages. He completed his doctoral program at Inner Mongolia University in 2017 and recently converted his doctoral dissertation into a book titled *The Uppermost Manuscript of the Collected Lamrim Scriptures*. See Myagmarsuren 2021, 17–18 and 25–29.

9. *Бодь мөрийн зэргийн дөрвөн эрдмийн тайлбарыг номлосон бэрх утгийг тодотгогч* (*Byang chub lam gyi che ba bzhi'i rnam gzhag bshad pa gnad don gsal byed*).

10. Gombojav 1959.

Compilation of the list of Mongolian scholars who produced works related to *lam rim* in Tibetan in ongoing and not yet complete.

The second language source is people without proficiency in Tibetan who relied on Mongolian translations. Such people were the major beneficiaries of Mongolian translations of the *lam rim* teachings. Both the woodblock editions of Mongolian translations and the handwritten versions were commonly distributed among laypeople.

Third, oral transmission or oral translation was employed by Mongolian translator monks to disseminate *lam rim* teachings throughout Mongolian-speaking regions, often in the form of stories and illustrations. The scholar B. Rinchen notes that "in 1934, a person named Sanjsuren orally translated Tsongkhapa's *lam rim*. The content was the same as the woodblock-printed *lam rim* in Mongolian, but its composition was more pleasant."[11] So apparently there was a practice by skillful translators to orally interpret the texts directly and recite them to listeners in the Mongolian language.

In addition to written *lam rim* teachings, a dozen biographies of Jé Rinpoché were written by Mongolian monks. One of the most famous is the *Great Biography of Jé Tsongkhapa* (*Rje tsong kha pa'i rnam thar chen mo*) by Qahar Geshe Luvsanchultem. This was written in the Cagar banner, Inner Mongolia, in 1791 and was woodblock printed in Mongolian script in 1870.[12]

In terms of traditional translation methodology, two types of translation for *lam rim* texts are commonly found. First is the word-by-word translation style mentioned above, a mechanical substitution preserving the syntax of the source language. However, most translations strove to convey the meaning and the content of the teachings in the target language.

In addition, there are contemporary translations published in Cyrillic Mongolian script. These modern translations avoid obscure classical terminologies and phrasings, replacing them with modern words and expressions that are easily understandable by today's Mongolians. There are about ten different contemporary translations of *Lam rim chen mo* currently available in Mongolian.

11. Myagmarsuren 2021, 202.

12. Cha har dge shes Blo bzang tshul khrims, *Rje thams cad mkhyen pa tsong kha pa chen po'i rnam thar go sla bar brjod pa bde legs kun gyi 'byung gnas.*

Conclusion

Historically, Jé Rinpoché's *Lam rim chen mo* has been the fundamental source of Buddhist teachings not only in today's Mongolia but also in Inner Mongolia, Buryatia, and Kalmykia. Because its teachings on transformative practices were long implanted in the minds and hearts of Mongolians, Buddhism in Mongolia was not utterly destroyed by the oppressive Communist regime that lasted seven decades.

According to the ancient history of Mongolia, Buddhism was first introduced to Mongolian nomads during the Xiongnu Empire in the second century via Central Asia, presumably through contacts with the Buddhist culture of the Kushan Empire in Greater Gandhāra. Sources such as Zava Damdin's *Golden Chronicle*, Amar's *Brief History of Mongolia*, and Bat's *Oral History of Buddhism in Mongolia and Tibet* provide confirming details of this early introduction in the period between the second and ninth centuries.[13] And Tibetan Buddhism, especially the Sakya school, had a great deal of influence during the Yuan dynasty, which lasted from 1271 to 1368. However, the essence and fullest extent of the Buddhadharma and teachings were transmitted from Tibet to Mongolia with the spread of Jé Tsongkhapa's path of enlightenment.

13. Amar 2015 (first published in 1934), Zava Damdin 2014 (from the early twentieth century), and Bat 2012 (consisting of the oral stories of Agvaanchoidor [Ngawang Chödor], a scholar and monk from Inner Mongolia).

11. Learning, Living, and Teaching Bodhicitta: Jé Tsongkhapa's Contribution to Spreading Compassion in the World

Bhikṣuṇī Thubten Chodron

THIS PAPER WILL begin with full disclosure by the author: I'm an unabashed Lama Tsongkhapa fan. While this conference features many academic scholars I greatly respect, I would like to speak as a practitioner and as someone who spends a good amount of time sharing the Buddhadharma with people from diverse walks of life in the West. I will share with you in a more personal way how Jé Rinpoché's teachings—especially those on great compassion and bodhicitta—and the example of his life have inspired and continue to inspire me and many others. I will also discuss how Jé Tsongkhapa's explanation clarifies aspects of compassion that have often been confusing for some Westerners.[1] And in conclusion, I will share some thoughts about how all of us can uphold Jé Tsongkhapa's teachings in a global culture where everything is in constant flux.

Jé Tsongkhapa emphasized building a strong foundation before entering the Vajrayāna. When he did retreat in Ölkha from 1392 to 1395, his focus was on not only the preliminary practice of prostrations, maṇḍala offerings, and so on but also the practices of renunciation of saṃsāric duḥkha, bodhicitta, and the wisdom realizing emptiness, which are the principal aspects of the path. During this retreat he read many sūtras on compassion, bodhicitta, and bodhisattva conduct, and in his meditation he cultivated the aspirations, attitudes, attributes, and deeds of bodhisattvas.

---

1. While finding an accurate term for a group of diverse individuals is difficult, here "Westerner" indicates anyone, no matter their race, ethnicity, socioeconomic status, and so forth, who has grown up in a Judeo-Christian culture.

Transforming our mind is no easy endeavor and requires great inner strength, perseverance, and courage. Jé Tsongkhapa's life illustrates that: he spent years doing these practices, continuing to do them after he began tantric practice. He diligently cultivated compassion, overcoming all obstacles that could interfere with it, such as possessive attachment, resentment, self-pity, and self-centeredness. Without discouragement he contemplated the two major factors in generating bodhicitta—awareness of the duḥkha of sentient beings and a strong feeling of affection and heartwarming love toward them—so that effortlessly all sentient beings had a place in his heart. This is an excellent role model for us, especially for those people in the West who want the quick, cheap, and easy way to accomplish our goals.

Jé Tsongkhapa was the true nonsectarian who learned from whomever he could. This is reminiscent of Sudhana, the principal character in the *Array of Flowers Sūtra* (*Gaṇḍavyūha Sūtra*), the thirty-ninth chapter of the *Flower Ornament Sūtra* (*Avataṃsaka Sūtra*). The youth Sudhana sought the truth, and on a lengthy pilgrimage, spoke to fifty-three spiritual friends, each of whom enhanced Sudhana's knowledge and understanding before sending him on to the next spiritual mentor. Similarly, Jé Tsongkhapa traveled widely, studying with a wide range of spiritual mentors, each of whom contributed to his knowledge and understanding.

Like Sudhana, Jé Tsongkhapa didn't simply accept what all these spiritual mentors said—he thought about their teachings deeply, debated them, and importantly, meditated on them and put them into practice. In that way, he gradually discerned the Buddha's intent. Also, like Sudhana, Jé Tsongkhapa cultivated the bodhisattva aspirations, unshakable resolves, deeds, and ethical restraints, and on this basis he taught the Dharma widely. And just as Sudhana had mystical visions, so did Jé Rinpoché.

Not only were his actions motivated by great compassion and bodhicitta, he also taught the method to generate bodhicitta and encouraged his students to practice it. Highlighting bodhicitta as one of the three principal aspects of the path emphasized its great importance as the key to the Mahāyāna. In addition, he harmonized the two ways of cultivating bodhicitta—the seven cause-and-effect instructions and equalizing and exchanging self and others—so that they could be practiced together. He put them in a combined order for contemplation: (1) develop equanimity toward friends, enemies, and strangers, (2) recognize all sentient beings as having been your mother, (3) remember the love and kindness of others both when they were your mother and when they were not, (4) wish to repay that kindness, (5) equalize self and others, (6) examine the disadvantages of self-centeredness and (7) the benefits of cherishing others, (8) exchange self and others, (9) take others' suffering, with special emphasis on compassion, (10) give away your own happiness, with special emphasis on love, (11) develop the great resolve, and (12) generate bodhicitta.

Jé Tsongkhapa said that initially the practices to cultivate bodhicitta were challenging, but through perseverance, his bodhicitta became effortless. Enthusiastic to share the precious jewel of bodhicitta, he asked Mañjuśrī's permission to teach it to others, but Mañjuśrī recommended that he focus on his own practice instead, because subduing the unruly minds of sentient beings was difficult. He followed Mañjuśrī's advice and began to teach bodhicitta later when conditions were conducive.

Great compassion and bodhicitta figure strongly in the aspirational prayers he made to be reborn in Amitābha Buddha's pure land Sukhāvatī, which he asked the monks of Ganden Monastery to recite shortly before he passed away:

> Though born in pure Sukhāvatī, I pray to be able to journey to impure realms with unhindered miraculous power motivated by fierce compassion, there to teach every living being the Dharma according to their disposition and so bring them to that immaculate path hailed by the Buddha. By quickly perfecting these exalted practices, for the benefit of countless living beings, may I easily attain the awakened state of a buddha. . . .
>
> Furthermore, in every life, having put an end to all self-preoccupied ways of thinking and to all laziness and weakness regarding the powerful practices of the bodhisattva, may I possess bodhicitta wise in the accomplishment of supreme courage and the willingness to dedicate myself to others. As the noble Avalokiteśvara has done, may I perfect every bodhisattva practice. . . .
>
> To perfect the bodhisattva practice that dispels all laziness, may I in every life first generate bodhicitta, and by powerful

endeavor undistracted for even an instant, may I reach great awakening as the unparalleled Śākyamuni has done.[2]

Not only does this sampling of verses teach us about compassion, but being heartfelt aspirations, they illustrate how Jé Tsongkhapa himself regarded life, death, and his mother sentient beings.

What touches me the most, as a practitioner, regarding Jé Rinpoché's explanation of bodhicitta is his emphasis on Śāntideva's equalizing and exchanging self and others, which I find more suitable for a modern, secular audience. It is clear that Jé Tsongkhapa's approach has influenced His Holiness the Dalai Lama in that His Holiness emphasizes the role of reasoning in all aspects of the Dharma, including topics that may be considered more "emotional," such as great compassion.

"If you want to be selfish," suggests His Holiness, "take care of others."[3] The reasoning behind this advice opens a welcome door for a Western audience that often thinks that to be genuinely compassionate, one has to suffer and that one's own well-being in every aspect of life has to be renounced in order to be altruistic.

Here "being selfish" does not refer to the self-centeredness that most of us suffer from; it means fulfilling one's own spiritual aims as well as experiencing happiness in this life as a byproduct. The reasoning that our own and others' happiness are linked—that happiness is not a limited resource that I must give up for you to have it—is refreshingly appealing. The idea that the self-centered attitude is my true enemy and that other living beings are the cause of my well-being can be verified through deeply examining our own life experience. The notion that true compassion doesn't involve the personal distress that arises when we can't bear to see others suffer opens us to see that living with compassion brings tremendous joy and optimism.[4]

---

2. Tsongkhapa 2001, 87, 93.

3. This is a sentiment that I have heard His Holiness express in oral teachings many times.

4. *Karuṇā* is the Sanskrit term for compassion. *Kaṃ* means "happiness" and *ruṇa* means "block." That is, one finds the suffering of others unbearable such that one's own happiness is blocked. This is an etymological description of compassion; however, the definition of *karuṇā*—the wish for sentient beings to be free of duḥkha and its causes—doesn't indicate that one must be miserable when feeling compassion. Although bodhisattvas cannot bear to see others suffer, they know that the suffering has causes and that these causes can be eliminated. Therefore they do not

Bodhicitta is about fulfilling both our own and others' purpose. There is no virtue in our suffering for suffering's sake. Rather, seeing the drawbacks of self-centeredness and the benefits of cherishing others, we can work for the welfare of everyone. To do so, we must learn to live in a balanced way. We can set priorities without feeling guilty or believing we are selfish. We can rest when tired so that we can return later to our Dharma practice or altruistic actions. Even doing everyday activities such as bathing, walking the dog, and sitting in a traffic jam can be imbued with bodhicitta. Presenting compassion in this way is psychologically healing for many people in highly demanding cultures.

Unpacking Candrakīrti's Homage to Great Compassion

Jé Tsongkhapa's brilliance in teaching great compassion and bodhicitta shines in his *Illuminating the Intent* (*Dgongs pa rab gsal*), his extensive commentary on Candrakīrti's *Entering the Middle Way* (*Madhyamakāvatāra*). Here, depending on Candrakīrti's autocommentary, Jé Tsongkhapa unpacks and clarifies the meaning of Candrakīrti's homage to great compassion. There is much to say, but I will cite only a few verses and give a brief explanation here.

Candrakīrti points to great compassion as the root of the other two causes of bodhisattvas—bodhicitta[5] and nondual understanding[6]—and as the essential factor at the beginning, middle, and end of the bodhisattva path.

> Compassion alone is seen as the seed
> of a conqueror's rich harvest, as water that nourishes it,

feel despair. However, when ordinary beings fall into personal distress or despair, it is because others' suffering frightens them and they feel uncomfortable witnessing it. With personal distress the focus is on one's own discomfort, whereas with compassion the focus in on others' pain, which triggers compassion for the person.

5. Here "bodhicitta" refers to bodhicitta like sugarcane bark. Sugarcane bark is sweet, but its sweetness doesn't measure up to that of actual sugarcane. Similarly, contrived bodhicitta wishes to attain full awakening for the benefit of all sentient beings, but it doesn't have the strength and power of actual bodhicitta.

6. Nondual understanding is a conceptual realization of emptiness that is free from the two extremes of absolutism and nihilism. It still has the appearance of subject and object and is not nondual in that sense.

and as the ripened fruit that is the source of long enjoyment.
Therefore, at the start I praise compassion.[7]

Jé Tsongkhapa explains that at the beginning of our practice, great compassion is likened to a seed in that it gives rise to the great resolve to protect all sentient beings from the duḥkha of saṃsāra and lead them to full awakening. Based on this, we generate bodhicitta, the strong determination to attain buddhahood in order to lead others to that state. To actualize this aspiration, we must amass the two collections of merit and wisdom and engage in the six perfections—especially the perfection of wisdom. This leads us to learn, contemplate, and meditate on nondual wisdom. This is the sequence followed by those of modest faculties. Those with sharp faculties first generate nondual understanding followed by bodhicitta. In both cases, compassion is the root of the other two causes of a bodhisattva and is the seed that bears the fruit of buddhahood.

In the middle of our practice, great compassion is like nourishing water that sustains the sprout of bodhicitta. It prevents the discouragement that could arise from thinking of the great amount of time and energy required to amass the two collections and accomplish the six perfections. Compassion keeps our heart connected to the practice so we do not waver in developing all the vast causes needed to attain full awakening.

At the conclusion of the path, great compassion resembles ripe fruit. It enables the buddhas to enact their awakening activities to benefit sentient beings for as long as saṃsāra remains by manifesting as the two form bodies of buddhas—the enjoyment and emanation bodies.

By stressing that we must immerse ourselves in great love and compassion over a long period of time and create a variety of causes and conditions in order to attain them, Jé Tsongkhapa's explanation is a counterbalance to the impatience to do things quickly and easily that some Westerners experience. It will help them to understand that having a few strong experiences of compassion in meditation is not the realization of great compassion or bodhicitta. This prevents practitioners from becoming complacent or proud and stopping their meditation on compassion.

Candrakīrti pays homage to three types of compassion: the compassion observing sentient beings, the compassion observing phenomena, and the

7. *Madhyamakāvatāra* 1.2, in Tsongkhapa 1980, 102.

compassion observing the unapprehendable. This section is especially powerful for generating great compassion:

> Like a bucket in a well, migrators have no autonomy;
> first, with the thought "I," they cling to a self;
> then, with the thought "mine," they become attached to things;
> I bow to this compassion that cares for migrators.

> [Homage to that compassion for] migrators
> seen as evanescent and empty of inherent existence
> like a moon in rippling water.[8]

All three types of compassion have both an observed object (*ālambana*) and a subjective aspect (*ākāra*). The observed object is the basic object that the mind focuses on, whereas the subjective aspect is the way the mind relates to that object. All three types of compassion observe sentient beings, and all three have the subjective aspect of wanting to protect them from saṃsāric duḥkha.

The first compassion observes just sentient beings who are afflicted by one form of duḥkha after another. The last two types of compassion focus on sentient beings qualified by specific attributes. "Qualified by" means that a quality appears to that mind through the force of previously having brought that attribute to mind. Before the second compassion can arise in the mind, we must first ascertain that sentient beings are impermanent—not static for even a moment; for the third compassion to arise, we must first ascertain that sentient beings lack inherent existence. These two compassions do not apprehend sentient beings as impermanent or as lacking inherent existence; rather these attributes appear to the compassionate mind because the person has previously ascertained impermanence and emptiness.

Here the wisdom side of the path, which involves the realizations of impermanence and selflessness (in the case of the second compassion) and of emptiness (for the third compassion), accompanies the method side of the path, adding depth to our compassion.

---

8. *Madhyamakāvatāra* 1.3–4, in Tsongkhapa 1980, 116 and 120.

Compassion observing sentient beings[9] focuses on sentient beings who migrate from one saṃsāric realm to another under the control of ignorance, afflictions, and karma. Saṃsāra comes about when, with the thought "I," we cling to the self as an inherently existent person. Whereas the mere *I* or person exists by being merely designated in dependence on the aggregates, the identity view (*satkāyadṛṣṭi*) grasps it to exist inherently, with its own essence that is independent of all other factors.

Viewing the aggregates as under the control of an inherently existent person who regards things as "mine," the identity view then grasps *mine* as inherently existent. From this, attachment to what makes *me* happy and anger at what disrupts *my* happiness or causes *me* pain, as well as all other afflictions, arise. When conjoined with the mental factor of intention (*cetana*)—which is karma—afflictions such as craving, hatred, jealousy, pride, deluded doubt, and heedlessness create the paths of action that leave karmic seeds on our mindstream. The ripening of these seeds leads to our future rebirths, what we experience in those lives, our habitual actions, and the type of places we inhabit. Seeing that sentient beings are trapped in this cycle of constantly recurring problems inspires us to generate the compassion that cares for migrators.

For Westerners raised in theistic religions—as indeed for everyone— this explanation of the origin and development of saṃsāra is necessary in order to properly understand great compassion and bodhicitta. If we don't have the correct understanding of rebirth in saṃsāra, how can we have great compassion that wants to protect sentient beings from saṃsāric duḥkha? How can we generate the aspiration to become a fully awakened buddha with the four buddha bodies if we believe in a creator god whose will is the cause of happiness and sorrow or if we believe that the mind ceases completely after death?

Six analogies that compare the experience of migrating sentient beings to a bucket in a well give a different perspective on how sentient beings suffer in saṃsāra; meditating on these stimulates great compassion within us.

(1) Just as a bucket in a well is tied by a strong rope, sentient beings are tightly bound to saṃsāra by afflictions and karma. Although we wish for

---

9. *Compassion observing sentient beings* is a contraction of "compassion observing just sentient beings." "Just" indicates that this compassion observes only sentient beings, not sentient beings qualified by being either impermanence or emptiness, like the other two types of compassion.

happiness and freedom from suffering, afflictions such as greed, anger, and confusion overwhelm our minds and influence us to act against our own best interests and, as a result, to experience duḥkha.

(2) Just as the operator of a pulley moves the bucket in the well, the afflictive mind propels sentient beings into various rebirths, where we find ourselves in situations of conflict and pain. Although we see ourselves and others as independent beings in control of our lives, in fact afflictions and karma are our overlords and control us.

(3) Just as the bucket continuously goes up and down in the deep well, sentient beings wander unremittingly in saṃsāra, from the highest formless realm to the lowest hell realm.

(4) The bucket descends easily, but great exertion is needed to pull it up. Similarly, sentient beings easily fall to lower rebirths, but must exert great energy to create the causes for a fortunate rebirth. Attachment and anger arise easily, whereas great effort is needed to train in their antidotes.

(5) Just as the bucket cycles without a discernible beginning or end, sentient beings cycle through the three sets of "thoroughly afflictive links" where the end of one and the beginning of another are difficult to distinguish. These three sets refer to the twelve links of dependent origination. They are the paths of afflictions (ignorance, craving, and grasping), the paths of karma (formative actions and renewed existence), and the paths of duḥkha (consciousness, name and form, six sources, contact, feeling, birth, and aging and death). One set of twelve links is so intertwined with many other sets that it is difficult to distinguish them.

(6) The bucket is constantly battered and punctured as it knocks against the sides of the well. Likewise, sentient beings are battered by the three kinds of duḥkha: The duḥkha of pain is painful physical and mental feelings; the duḥkha of change is the fleeting nature of our pleasure and the ease with which a happy situation transforms into an uncomfortable one; and the pervasive duḥkha of conditioning is having a body and mind under the control of afflictions and karma.

To get a deep experience of this meditation, it is necessary to think first that we ourselves are like a bucket in a well. For those Westerners who tend to be intellectual, this makes saṃsāric duḥkha real and personal. It also clarifies that duḥkha is much more than gross physical and mental suffering and forces them to look more closely at what Western society considers happiness and success.

We then expand our mind to understand that all sentient beings are tormented by duḥkha. Combining this with heartwarming love that views sentient beings as endearing, we generate the three thoughts that are found in the meditation on immeasurable compassion: How wonderful it would be if all sentient beings were free from duḥkha and its causes. May they be free from duḥkha and its causes. I shall cause them to be free from duḥkha and its causes. Our compassion is now fearless and unmarred by self-preoccupation. We are determined to act, and our actions will now correspond to our aspirations.

With each of the three types of compassion, we progressively generate the above three thoughts. The third thought that "I shall cause them to be free" is the great compassion that Candrakīrti refers to in his homage. From it, bodhicitta flows easily.

In the West, many people tend to confuse compassion with pity, feeling sorry for someone they consider inferior. Some people think compassion makes us weak: our constant wish to please others will open the door for them to take advantage of us. Others confuse compassion with personal distress, where people become so emotional when seeing others' pain that they cannot reach out to help. Jé Tsongkhapa's explanation clarifies these misconceptions by showing that great compassion makes us clear-minded, confident, and able to act.

The lines "[Homage to that compassion for] migrators / seen as evanescent and empty of inherent existence / like a moon in rippling water" speak of the second and third forms of compassion. Reading those lines as "I pay homage to the compassion that views beings as subject to moment-by-moment disintegration, as fluctuating as the reflection of the moon in water that is being stirred by wind" is paying homage to the compassion observing phenomena. Reading the lines as "Homage to the compassion that views beings who, although appearing to exist inherently, are like the reflection of the moon in water, devoid of inherent existence" is paying homage to compassion of the unapprehendable.[10]

In the phrase *compassion observing phenomena*,[11] the collection of aggregates is the referent of the term "phenomena." The observed object

---

10. *Madhyamakāvatāra* 1.3–4, in Tsongkhapa 1980, 116 and 120.

11. *Compassion observing phenomena* is a contraction of "compassion observing sentient beings who are designated on just phenomena, such as the aggregates."

of this compassion is sentient beings qualified by impermanence; sentient beings qualified by lacking a permanent, unitary, and independent self; or sentient beings who lack a self-sufficient, substantially existent self, depending on whether compassion is affected by an understanding of impermanence; of the lack of a permanent, unitary, and independent self; or of the absence of a self-sufficient, substantially existent self.

The rippling of the water indicates both the gross impermanence of death that all of us are subject to and the subtle impermanence of not remaining the same from moment to moment. When we realize that sentient beings change moment by moment, we implicitly know that they do not have a permanent, unitary, and independent self or soul, as asserted by non-Buddhists. If sentient beings are not independent, they must be dependent—in this case on their aggregates, the body and mind. This dependent self is not a different entity from the aggregates that compose it. Sentient beings are designated just on the collection of their impermanent aggregates. In this context, being designated just on the collection of aggregates eliminates their being self-sufficient, substantially existent selves that are separate entities from their aggregates.

Blind to this transitory nature, we cling to the notion that we and everything around us is reliable and unchanging. Holding what is impermanent to be permanent makes the mind inflexible; we refuse to accept the reality of a situation that doesn't agree with our expectations. In addition, everything we seek security in is changing with every passing moment. Observing that sentient beings suffer intensely by holding what is impermanent as permanent, bodhisattvas experience compassion for sentient beings.

When sentient beings appear to our mind as changing moment to moment or as lacking self-sufficient substantial existence, the quality of our compassion for them changes. On the one hand, we understand more clearly how and why they suffer by grasping themselves as permanent or as self-sufficient, substantially existent persons. On the other hand, we know that they can change and develop their good qualities because they are not fixed, static beings with a substantial self.

Compassion observing the unapprehendable[12] arises after a practitioner

12. *Compassion observing the unapprehendable* is a contraction of "compassion observing sentient beings qualified by lacking true existence, which is unapprehendable although it is the object conceived by the grasping of true existence."

meditates on emptiness, when the mind understanding the emptiness of sentient beings informs the compassion wishing to protect all sentient beings from saṃsāric duḥkha. At that time, the observed object of the mind of compassion is sentient beings qualified by the lack of inherent existence. Compassion does not apprehend emptiness, although emptiness appears to it when the person has previously ascertained sentient beings to be empty of inherent existence. This compassion is so called because sentient beings appear qualified by lacking inherent existence. Inherent existence is unapprehendable because it doesn't exist; nevertheless it is the conceived object of the erroneous mind grasping inherent existence.

In the context of this compassion, the analogy of the moon's reflection in water emphasizes the illusory nature of sentient beings: just as the moon reflected in water falsely appears to be a real moon although it isn't, sentient beings falsely appear to be inherently existent, although they are not. Although persons appear to be "real," having their own essential nature, they are actually reflections of their previously created karma. The water represents the ocean of the identity view that grasps *I* and *mine* as inherently existent. This ocean is fed by the powerful river of ignorance grasping the five aggregates as inherently existent. While sentient beings struggle to stay afloat, the powerful winds of distorted conceptions agitate the water where sentient beings appear as reflections of their virtuous and nonvirtuous karma. Unaware that they lack inherent existence, sentient beings grasp themselves and all other phenomena as inherently existent and generate afflictions that bind them in saṃsāra. Seeing sentient beings as qualified by being empty of inherent existence, and knowing that they suffer due to grasping themselves and everyone and everything around them as inherently existent entities, bodhisattvas generate strong compassion, wanting sentient beings to be free from ignorance, afflictions, polluted karma, and all the duḥkha that these cause.

Although there is no moon in the water of a still pond, the reflection exists as a dependent arising, the product of the water, moon, and light coming together in a certain arrangement. Just as there is no inherently existent person in either the body or mind, or in the collection of the two, a person still exists. The *I* is a dependently arising product of conceiving and designating the person in dependence on the collection of physical and mental aggregates.

Jé Tsongkhapa's explanation of the three types of compassion is designed to stimulate us to actively reduce and eventually eradicate sentient beings' duḥkha and its causes. For most people in the West, the ideas of compassion observing phenomena and compassion observing the unapprehendable are completely new. The Buddhist analysis of suffering and its origins, and of awakening and the paths to attain it, requires in-depth questioning of assumptions and beliefs. It also requires opening to a very different worldview—one in which the causes of our misery lie in our own mind and the path to bliss involves purifying the mind. Jé Tsongkhapa's clear explanation of this is a true light illuminating the darkness of our minds.

Taking the meaning of compassion to heart increases our respect and admiration for great compassion and for the bodhisattvas who possess it. It also enables us to see sentient beings the way bodhisattvas see them and to respond with similar love and compassion. Because the buddhas cultivated such great compassion as well as the wisdom realizing emptiness, they attained buddhahood and continue to turn the wheel of Dharma to benefit us sentient beings. We can do the same.

The fact that sentient beings do not exist inherently does not mean that sentient beings do not exist, which would make generating compassion useless. Rather, sentient beings exist falsely like illusions, appearing to truly exist but existing dependently.

Clarifying Misconceptions Concerning Compassion

People who did not grow up as Tibetan Buddhists often hold misconceptions about compassion that frequently stem from the cultural and/or religious environment in which they were raised. Jé Rinpoché's teachings clarify these in a way that illustrates how wisdom and courage counteract these misconceptions and shows the way for ordinary beings and āryas to live with compassion.

> **Misconception 1:** Compassion is sentimental and emotional. If you're compassionate, you're a pushover or a doormat.
>
> **Buddhist response:** Our worldly attitude believes that if we're compassionate, everyone will take advantage of us. They will walk all over us, and we won't be able to stick up for ourselves because we're so kind. That's not what Jé Rinpoché teaches or what he shows through the example of his life. Being a bodhisattva

requires incredible self-confidence and inner strength. If we're compassionate, we may have to risk other people's anger when we try to do what is beneficial for them but they don't like it. We have to be willing to risk our reputation to do what we know in our heart is good for others in the long term.

Misconception 2: To be truly compassionate, you have to suffer.
Buddhist response: This is the model in Christian society, where we see Jesus suffering on the cross. If we feel any happiness at all, we're being selfish. This is not the Buddhist approach; in fact, bodhisattvas on the first ground are called the Joyous Ones because genuine bodhicitta brings joy and happiness in their minds.[13] We can be happy and compassionate at the same time. When Buddhist scriptures say that bodhisattvas can't endure the suffering of others, it means that their wish to alleviate others' suffering is so strong that they won't procrastinate in helping them. But bodhisattvas do not fall into personal distress when witnessing others' misery, for doing so would impede their ability to reach out and be of benefit. Personal distress confines us in our own feelings, whereas compassion focuses on others and cares about their experience.

Misconception 3: You must have compassion for everybody else but never for yourself. Taking care of yourself is selfish.
Buddhist response: In Buddhism, practicing the bodhisattva path involves accomplishing the purposes of ourselves and of others. It's not an either-or situation. Attaining a buddha's truth body (*dharmakāya*) fulfills our own purpose by purifying our mind and developing all excellent qualities. Attaining a buddha's form body (*rūpakāya*) fulfills others' purpose by manifesting in a multitude of different forms to benefit others. Bodhicitta requires first having compassion for our own suffering in saṃsāra, which motivates us to free ourselves from defilements. When we extend that understanding of suffering to others, we want to free them

---

13. *Mahāyānasūtrālaṃkāra* 21.32: "[The first bhūmi] is called Joyous because supreme joy arises on seeing that enlightenment is imminent and one can now truly benefit beings."

from saṃsāra as well, as that is the best way to benefit them. We need to take care of ourselves in a healthy way to practice the Dharma and be of service to sentient beings. That isn't selfishness.

Misconception 4: Compassion is an easy practice.

Buddhist response: Some people think that renunciation and compassion are practices for beginners. They want to learn tantra, mahāmudrā, and dzokchen. Jé Rinpoché showed us that we need consistent and repeated meditation to genuinely transform our minds. The three principal aspects of the path—renunciation, bodhicitta, and wisdom—are not easy practices. They're not practices to rush through so we can go on to tantra because we're sophisticated practitioners. The three principal aspects of the path are not so easy when we really try to practice them and transform our mind. His Holiness says it's easy to understand teachings on compassion and bodhicitta but generating these states of mind is very difficult.

Misconception 5: People should appreciate our compassion.

Buddhist response: Seeking praise or gratitude for compassionate help we've given takes the joy out of giving. We may try to mask this self-centered wish but still feel forlorn and unappreciated if others don't thank us or tell others how kind we were. His Holiness the Dalai Lama says that he is the primary beneficiary of his compassion for others because acting with compassion brings happiness to his own mind; he feels content and knows his life has meaning. Plus, showing kindness to others improves our relationships with them. Since we cannot make others benefit from our aid, counting on their appreciation is foolish.

Misconception 6: Compassion leads to burnout.

Buddhist response: Some people say that they become fatigued from being compassionate and need to stop their compassionate activities and rest. However, if we "burn out from compassion," our compassion wasn't real compassion. Genuine compassion gives us consistent mental and emotional energy. We may get physically tired and need to rest, but we don't want to take a break from cultivating and acting with compassion. Śāntideva counsels us to rest when we need to so that later, with joy, we can resume our compassionate work.

There are many other ways in which Jé Rinpoché's teachings help to clarify what compassion is, especially in his work *Illuminating the Intent*.[14]

Upholding Jé Tsongkhapa's Teachings in the Modern World

An important topic related to compassion is ethical conduct. One of Jé Rinpoché's foremost contributions to Buddhism in Tibet was reviving the Vinaya (monastic discipline). In our day too, the importance of ethical conduct needs to be emphasized; unfortunately, there have been many scandals in recent years due to some monks' improper behavior. I am often invited to teach in East Asia and Southeast Asia, and unfortunately Tibetan Buddhism does not have a good reputation among many people there. This has to do primarily with people hearing that tantric practitioners drink and have sex. Unfortunately, some monks and lay teachers confirm this through their behavior and have sexual relationships with students.

Many lamas travel to this region and give initiations. They ring bells, play drums, hand out protection cords and long-life pills, but they don't teach the Dharma. As a result, some Buddhists think that Tibetan Buddhism isn't really Buddhism but is closer to magic and fortunetelling. This makes me sad because our tradition is so rich.

The behavior of some monastics and lay teachers in these areas has also led to many people slandering Tibetan Buddhism in general, as well as His Holiness the Dalai Lama. This occurs because some monks do not keep their precept to abstain from sexual conduct. This may be difficult to acknowledge, but I bring it up because it's an important issue that needs to be addressed and corrected. All of us are responsible for upholding Jé Rinpoché's legacy, whether we are ordained or lay, scholars or practitioners. To pass this legacy to future generations, ethical conduct is crucial, especially on the part of monastics.

Another difficult topic is monastics visiting these regions to seek dona-

14. Please see Dalai Lama and Thubten Chodron 2020 and Kolts and Thubten Chodron 2015.

tions, supposedly for their monasteries but actually for their own pockets or for their families. Other monks and lay teachers ask followers to purchase expensive items for them. This too gives people a bad impression of Tibetan Buddhism.

Those among us who appreciate and revere Jé Rinpoché will do our best to put his teachings—especially those on ethical conduct and compassion—into practice. I was born and grew up in America at a time when the Dharma was hardly known there. As a young person, I was looking for meaning, and Jé Rinpoché's teachings gave purpose and meaning to my life. His teachings have the ability to help individuals, societies, and the world, but for that to happen we have to show through our example that these teachings function to subdue unruly minds and harmful actions. We must each do our part. May all our efforts enable Jé Rinpoché's teachings and the Buddha's precious Dharma to continue to flourish in the world.

To close, I would like to share with you a passage from Jé Tsongkhapa's *Great Treatise on the Stages of the Path*:

> Whether you plant the roots of the Mahāyāna or not, or whether you have genuinely entered the Mahāyāna or not, is all founded upon this [bodhicitta]. Therefore, always consider what you should do to develop this. It is excellent if you do develop this; if you have not, do not let it remain that way. Always rely on a teacher who gives this kind of teaching. Always associate with friends who are training their minds in this way. Constantly look at the scriptures and commentaries that describe this. Amass the [two] collections [of merit and wisdom] as causes for this. Clear away the obstructions that prevent this. Moreover, if you train your mind in this way, you will definitely acquire all the seeds for developing this, so this work is not insignificant; take joy in it.[15]

What better way is there to live than to generate bodhicitta? We live in challenging times, when ideologies of hate and prejudice are prevalent. We must not allow ourselves to fall under their sway but nourish the seeds of love, compassion, and altruism in ourselves and then share the fruit of doing so with all living beings. In encouraging and showing us the way to

15. Tsongkhapa 2004, 59.

do this, Jé Tsongkhapa's activities in the snowy lands of Tibet nearly seven hundred years ago profoundly affect the lives of countless beings in the world today. The best way to express our gratitude to him is to learn, contemplate, meditate on, and embody his teachings in our lives.

Table of Tibetan Transliteration

Akhuching Sherab Gyatso	A khu ching Shes rab rgya mtsho
Amé Shab Ngawang Kunga Sönam	A mes zhabs Ngag dbang kun dga' bsod nams
Ar Jangchup Yeshé	Ar Byang chub ye shes
Barawa Gyaltsen Palsang	'Ba' ra ba Rgyal mtshan dpal bzang
Bodong Tsöndrü Dorjé	Bo dong Brtson 'grus rdo rje
Bötrul Dongak Tenpai Nyima	Bod sprul Mdo sngags Bstan pa'i nyi ma
Butön Rinchen Drup	Bu ston Rin chen grub
Chabcha Monastery	Chab cha theg chen gling
Chahar Geshé Losang Tsultrim	Cha har dge shes Blo bzang tshul khrims
Changkya Rölpai Dorjé	Lcang skya Rol pa'i rdo rje
Chenga Chökyi Gyalpo	Spyan snga Chos kyi rgyal po
Chim Namkha Drak	Mchims Nam mkha' grags
Chingphu	'Ching phu
Chöjé Döndrup Rinchen	Chos rje Don grub rin chen
Chomden Rikpai Raldri	Bcom ldan Rig pa'i ral gri
Dergé Tengyur	sde dge bstan 'gyur
Desi Sangyé Gyatso	Sde srid Sangs rgyas rgya mtsho
Dölpopa Sherab Gyaltsen	Dol po pa shes rab rgyal mtshan
Drepung	'Bras spungs
Drigung Kagyü	'Bri gung bka' brgyud
Dro Lotsāwa Sherab Dra	'Bro lo tsā ba Shes rab grags
Drukpa	'Brug pa
Dudjom Rinpoché	Bdud 'joms rin po che
Dulnakpa Palden Sangpo	'Dul nag pa Dpal ldan bzang po

Dzeme Rinpoché	Dze smad rin po che
dzokchen	rdzogs chen
Gampopa Sönam Rinchen	Gam po pa Bsod nams rin chen
Ganden Phodrang	Dga' ldan pho brang
Ganden Shartsé	Dga' ldan shar rtse
Gelukpa	Dge lugs pa
Gen Losang Gyatso	Rgan Blo bzang rgya mtsho
Gen Nyima	Rgan Nyi ma
Geshé Lhundub Sopa	Dge bshes Lhun grub bzod pa
Getsé Mahāpaṇḍita Gyurmé Tsewang Chokdrup	Dge rtse mahāpaṇḍita 'Gyur me Tshe dbang mchog grub
Gö Khukpa Lhetsé	'Gos Khug pa lhas btsas
Gomang	Sgo mang
Gomchen Ngawang Drakpa	Sgom chen Ngag dbang grags pa
Götsangpa Gönpo Dorjé	Rgod tshang pa Mgon po rdo rje
Gungru Gyaltsen Sangpo	Gung ru Rgyal mtshan bzang po
Gyaltsab Jé	Rgyal tshab Rje
Jamsar Sherab Öser	'Jam gsar Shes rab 'od zer
Jamyang Tashi Palden	'Jam dbyangs Bkra shis dpal ldan
Jé Rinpoché	Rje rin po che
Jetsun Rendawa	Rje btsun Red bda' ba
Joden Sönam Lhundrup	Jo gdan Bsod nams lhun grub
Jonang	Jo nang
Ju Mipham	'Ju Mi pham
Kachen Yeshé Gyaltsen	Dka' chen Ye shes rgyal mtshan
Kadam	Bka' gdams
Kagyüpa	Bka' brgyud pa
Kangyur	Bka' 'gyur
Karma Kamtsang	Kar ma kam tshang
Karmapa Rölpai Dorjé	Karma pa Rang byung rdo rje
Khedrup Jé	Mkhas grub Rje
Khenchen Jikmé Phuntsok	Mkhan chen 'Jigs med phun tshogs
Khensur Pema Gyaltsen	Mkhan zur Padma rgyal mtshan
Khön Könchok Gyalpo	'Khon Dkon mchog rgyal po
Khyungpo Lhepa Shönu Sönam	Khyung po lhas pa Gzhon nu bsod nams
Kumbum	Sku 'bum

Kunga Döndrup	Kun dga' don grub
Kyabjé Trijang Rinpoché	Skyabs rje Khri byang rin po che
Labrang	Bla 'brang
Lati Rinpoché	Bla ti rin po che
Lekyi Dorjé	Las kyi rdo rje
Lhodrak Drupchen	Lho drag grub chen
Lochen Rinchen Sangpo	Lo chen Rin chen bzang po
Longchen Rabjampa	Klong chen Rab 'byams pa
Losang Tenzin Gyaltsen	Blo bzang bstan 'dzin rgyal mtshan
Losang Trinlé	Blo bzang 'phrin las
Maja Jangchup Tsöndrü	Rma bya Byang chub brtson 'grus
Malgyo Lotsāwa Lodrö Drakpa	Mal gyo lo tsā ba Blo gros grags pa
Marpa Chökyi Lodrö	Mar pa Chos kyi blo gros
Marpa Chökyi Wangchuk	Mar pa chos kyi dbang phyug
Marpa Dopa	Mar pa Do pa
Marpa Kagyü	Mar pa bka' brgyud
Milarepa	Mi la ras pa
Naktso Tsultrim Gyalwa	Nag tsho Tshul khrims rgyal ba
Namkha Gyaltsen	Nam mkha' rgyal mtshan
Namkhai Gyatso	Nam mkha'i rgya mtsho
Narthang	Snar thang
Neringpa	Ne rings pa
Ngawang Chödor	Ngag dbang chos rdor
Ngawang Kalsang Jampa	Ngag dbang skal bzang byams pa
Ngawang Lodrö Gyatso	Ngag dbang blo gros rgya mtsho
Ngawang Nyima	Ngag dbang nyi ma
Ngawang Tsultrim	Ngag dbang tshul khrims
Ngok Loden Sherab	Rngog Blo ldan shes rab
Nöjom Khenpo	Gnod 'joms mkhan po
Nup Sangyé Yeshé	Gnubs Sangs rgyas ye shes
Nyaön Kunga Pal	Nya dbon Kun dga' dpal
Nyethang	Snye thang
Nyingma	Rnying ma
Ölkha	'Ol kha
Padé	Dpa' sde

Panchen Lama Losang Chökyi Gyaltsen	Paṇ chen bla ma Blo bzang chos kyi rgyal mtshan
Paṇḍita Chökyi Öser	Paṇḍi ta Chos kyi 'od zer
Patsab Nyima Drak	Pa tshab Nyi ma grags
Pawo Tsuklak Trengwa	Dpa' bo Gtsug lag phreng ba
Phakmodrupa	'Phag mo gru pa
Phangthang Kamé	'Phang thang ka me
Phodrang Thongthangden	Pho brang thong thang ldan
Phukdrak	Phug brag
Ramoché	Ra mo che
Rechungpa Dorjé Drak	Ras chung pa Rdo rje grags
Rendawa	Red bda' ba
Rinchen Sangpo	Rin chen bzang po
Rongtön Sheja Kunrik	Rong ston Shes bya kun rig
Rongzom Chökyi Sangpo	Rong zom Chos kyi bzang po
Sachen Kunga Nyingpo	Sa chen kun dga' snying po
Sakya	Sa skya
Sakya Paṇḍita Kunga Gyaltsen	Sa skya paṇḍi ta Kun dga' ryal mtshan
Samyé	Bsam yas
Sangphu Monastery	Gsang phu
Segyü	Srad brgyud
Shabkar Tsokdruk Rangdröl	Zhabs dkar Tshogs drug rang grol
Shākya Chokden	Shākya Mchog ldan
Shangpa Kagyü	Shangs pa bka' brgyud
Sherab Sengé	Shes rab seng ge
Sönam Gyatso	Bsod nams rgya mtsho
Song Rinpoché	Zong rin po che
Tara Rinpoché	Rta ra rin po che
Tashi Lhunpo	Bkra shis lhun po
Tengyur	Bstan 'gyur
Thempangma	Them spangs ma
Thil	[M]thil
Tokden Jampal Gyatso	Rtogs ldan 'Jam dpal rgya mtsho
Trisong Detsen	Khri srong lde btsan
Tsalpa	Tshal pa

Tsari	Tsā ri
Tsongkhapa Losang Drakpa	Tsong kha pa Blo bzang grags pa
Umapa Pawo Dorjé	Dbu ma pa Dpa' bo rdo rje
Yeshé Dé	Ye shes sde

Bibliography

Abbreviations

BDRC   Buddhist Digital Resource Center (bdrc.io)

Pedurma   The comparative editions of the Tibetan canons, the Kangyur and Tengyur, referred to in Tibetan as *Dpe bsdur ma*, published between 2006 and 2009 in Beijing by the Tibetan Tripiṭaka Collation Bureau (Bka' bstan dpe sdur khang) of the China Tibetology Research Center (Krung go'i bod rig pa zhib 'jug ste gnas). Citations are by volume and page numbers.

Tōh   Catalogue numbers for texts in the Dergé canon of Buddhist scriptures as found in *A Complete Catalogue of the Tibetan Buddhist Canons* (Sendai, Japan: Tohoku Imperial University, 1934).

Tibetan Texts Cited

A mes zhabs Ngag dbang kun dga' bsod nams. *Gsang 'dus chos byung. Dpal gsang ba 'dus pa'i dam pa'i chos byung ba'i tshul legs bshad ngo mtshar rin po che'i bang mdzod* [*Precious Treasury of Wondrous Excellent Explanations: A History of the Glorious Guhyasamāja*]. Collected Works, vol. *da*: 475–792. Kathmandu: Sakya International Academy, 2000.

Bod rgya tshig mdzod chen mo [*Great Tibetan-Chinese Dictionary*]. Edited by Krang dbyi sun (Zhang Yisun) et al. Beijing: Mi rigs dpe skrun khang, 1993.

Bu ston Rin chen grub. *Chos 'byung chen mo. Bde bar gshegs pa'i bstan pa'i gsal byed chos kyi 'byung gnas gsung rab rin po che'i mdzod* [*History of Indian Buddhism*]. In Collected Works, vol. *ya* (26): 1b–212a. Lhasa: Zhol phar khang, n.d.

Co ne Grags pa bshad sgrub. *Legs bshad snying po. Grub mtha' bzhi'i lugs kyi bden gnyis kyi rnam gzhag legs par bshad pa'i snying po* [*Essence of Eloquence: A Presentation of the Two Truths in the Four Systems of Tenets*]. In Collected Works, 4:355–75 (print edition) 377–97 (BDRC digital edition). Beijing: China Tibetology Publishing House (Krung go'i bod rig pa dpe skrun khang). Digital edition available at bdrc.io (W1PD90129).

Dol po pa Shes rab rgyal mtshan. *Mdo lugs ma. Shes rab kyi pha rol tu phyin pa'i don mngon par rtogs pa'i rgyan gyi tshig le'ur byas pa'i 'grel pa mdo lugs ma* [*Sūtra-Based Commentary*]. In Collected Works, vol. 4. Edited by dpal brtsegs bod yig dpe snying zhib 'jug khang. Beijing: China Tibetology Publishing House (Krung go'i bod rig pa dpe skrun khang), 2011.

'Gos Lo tsā ba Gzhon nu dpal. *Deb ther sngon po* [*The Blue Annals*]. Edited by Lokesh Chandra. New Delhi: International Academy of Indian Culture, 1974.

Mkhas grub rje. *Rin po che'i snye ma. Rje rin po che'i gsang ba'i rnam thar rin po che'i snye ma* [*Sheaves of Precious Jewels: The Secret Biography of Jé Tsongkhapa*]. Collected Works of Jé Tsongkhapa, vol. *ka*: 113–36. Je Yabse Sungbum Project. Mundgod, India: Drepung Loseling Pethub Khangtsen Education Society, 2019.

———. *Yig chung nyer gcig* [*Twenty-One Short Pieces*]. Collected Works, vol. *ma*: 193–225. Je Yabse Sungbum Project. Mundgod, India: Drepung Loseling Pethub Khangtsen Education Society, 2019.

Nya dbon Kun dga' dpal. *Yid kyi mun sel. Bstan bcos mngon par rtogs pa'i rgyan 'grel ba dang bcas pa'i rgya 'grel bshad sbyar yid kyi mun sel* [*Dispelling the Darkness of the Mind*]. New Delhi: Ngawang Sopa, 1978.

Rgyal tshab Rje. *Zab mo'i lta khrid rin po che'i phreng ba* [*Precious Garland: A Guide to the Profound View*]. Collected Works, vol. *ka*: 189–97. Je Yabse Sungbum Project. Mundgod, India: Drepung Loseling Pethub Khangtsen Education Society, 2019.

Sgom chen Ngag dbang grags pa. *Lam gyi rim pa gsal 'debs su bya ba'i bskul ma* [*Exhortation by Way of Clearly Reviewing the Stages of the Path*]. Collected Works, vol. 2: 547–49. Gangs can khyad nor dpe tshogs 469. Lha sa: Ser gtsug nang bstan dpe rnying 'tshol bsdu phyogs sgrig khang, 2016. At bdrc.io (W1KG25311).

Shākya mchog ldan, Gser mdog paṇ chen. *Bzhed tshul rba rlabs kyi phreng ba* [*Garland of Waves of Views*]. In Collected Works, vol. 11. Thimphu: Kunzang Tobgyey, 1975.

———. *Dbu ma rnam nges. Dbu ma rnam par nges pa'i chos kyi bang mdzod lung dang rigs pa'i rgya mtsho* [*Ocean of Scriptural Statements and Reasoning: Treasury of Ascertainment of Mahāyāna Madhyamaka*]. In Collected Works, vols. 14–15. Delhi: Ngawang Topgyal, 1988.

Tsong kha pa. *Collected Works*. 18 vols. Je Yabse Sungbum Project. Mundgod, India: Drepung Loseling Pethub Khangtsen Education Society, 2019.

———. *Bdud rtsi'i sman mchog phreng ba* [*Garland of Supreme Medicinal Nectar*]. Vol. *ka*: 195–211.

———. *Dbu ma thal 'gyur ba'i lugs kyi lta khrid* [*Guide to the View According to Madhyamaka Prāsaṅgika*]. Vol. *tsha*: 517–25.

———. *Dgongs pa rab gsal. Dbu ma la 'jug pa'i rnam bshad dgongs pa rab gsal* [*Illuminating the Intent: An Exposition of Entering the Middle Way*]. Vol. *ma*.

———. *Dri ba lhag bsam rab dkar* [*Queries from a Sincere Heart*]. Vol. *kha*: 107–26.

———. *'Jam dbyangs kyi man ngag. Rje btsun 'jam pa'i dbyangs kyi man ngag rje red mda' ba la shog dril du phul ba* [*Mañjuśrī's Essential Points on the Path Sent to Master Rendawa as a Scroll*]. Vol. *pha*: 489–95.

———. *Legs bshad snying po. Drang ba dang nges pa'i don rnam par phye ba'i bstan bcos legs bshad snying po* [*Essence of Eloquence: Distinguishing the Provisional and the Definitive Meaning*]. Vol. *pha*: 299–464.

———. *Lam gtso rnam gsum* [*Three Principal Elements of the Path*]. Vol. *kha*: 286–87.

———. *Lam rim 'bring. Byang chub lam rim 'bring po* [*Middle-Length Treatise on the Stages of the Path to Enlightenment*]. Vol. *pha*: 1–297.

———. *Lam rim chen mo. Byang chub lam rim chen mo.* [*Great Treatise on the Stages of the Path to Enlightenment*]. Vol. *pa*: 1–726.

———. *Lam rim nyams mgur* [*Songs of Spiritual Experience*]. Vol. *kha*: 81–85.

———. *Lta ba'i yig chung* [*A Short Piece on the View*]. In *Gsang ba 'dus pa'i man ngag yig chung skor* [*Anthology of Brief Instructions on Guhyasamāja*]. Vol. *dza*: 373–456.

———. *Nā ro'i chos drug kyi dmigs skor lag tu lan tshul bsdus pa* [*Summary Guide to Visualization Practices for the Six Dharmas of Nāropa*]. Vol. *ta*: 365–91.

———. *Rim lnga gdan rdzogs* [*Five Stages in One Sitting*]. Vol. *nya*: 533–616.

———. *Rim lnga gsal sgron. Rim lnga rab tu gsal ba'i sgron me* [*A Lamp to Illuminate the Five Stages*]. Vol. *ja*: 1–455.

———. *Rtogs brjod 'dun legs ma* [*Realization Narrative*]. Vol. *kha*: 76–81.

———. *Sbas don kun gsal. Bde mchog bsdus pa'i rgyud kyi rgya cher bshad pa sbas pa'i don kun gsal ba* [*Illumination of the Hidden Meaning: Commentary on the Cakrasaṃvara Tantra Corpus*]. Vol. *nya*: 1–340.

———. *Sbas don lta ba'i mig 'byed. Bde mchog rim pa lnga pa'i bshad pa sbas pa'i don lta ba'i mig 'byed* [*Explanation that Opens the Eyes to See the Hidden Meaning of the Five Stages of Cakrasaṃvara Tantra*]. Vol. *tha*: 139–86.

———. *Sgrub le'i phyag rgya bzhi zhib tu gsungs pa rgyal tshab chos rjes zin bris su bkod pa* [*Detailed Description of the Four Mudrās from the Chapter on Accomplishment: Tsongkhapa's Teachings as Transcribed by Gyaltsab Jé*]. Vol. *dza*: 471–83.

———. *Sngags rim chen mo. Rgyal ba khyab bdag rdo rje 'chang chen po'i lam gyi rim pa gsang ba kun gyi gnad rnam par phye ba* [*Great Exposition of Secret Mantra*]. Vol. *ga*: 1–689.

———. *Yid ches gsum ldan. Zab lam nā ro'i chos drug gi sgo nas 'khrid pa'i rim pa yid ches gsum ldan.* [*Endowed with Three Convictions: A Guide to the Six Dharmas of Nāropa*]. Vol. *ta*: 276–363.

Other Works (cited by year)

Almogi, Orna. 2009. *Rong-zom-pa's Discourses on Buddhology: A Study of Various Conceptions of Buddhahood in Indian Sources with Special Reference to the Controversy Surrounding the Existence of Gnosis* (jñāna, ye shes) *as Presented by the Eleventh-Century Tibetan Scholar Rong-zom Chos-kyi-bzang-po.* Studia Philologica Buddhica Monograph Series 24. Tokyo: International Institute of Buddhist Studies.

Amar, Anandyn (Анандын Амар). 2015. *Монголын товч түүх* (*A Brief History of Mongolia*). In *Монголын эх түүх I боть* (*Ancient History of Mongolia, vol. 1*). Ulaanbaatar: Soyombo Printing.

Bat, D. 2012. *Агваанчойдор гуайн ярьсан "Монгол, Төвд Бурханы шашны аман түүх"* (*An Oral History of Buddhism in Mongolia and Tibet: Spoken by Mr. Agvaanchoidor*). Ulaanbaatar: National University of Mongolia.

Bernousky, Daniel. 2015. "Tibetan 'Magical Rituals' (las sna tshogs) from the Power of Tsongkhapa." *Revue d'Études Tibétaines* 31: 95–111.

Beyer, Stephan V. 1974. *The Buddhist Experience: Sources and Interpretations.* Belmont, CA: Dickenson Publishing.

Bingenheimer, Marcus. 2008. "The *Bhikṣuṇī Saṃyukta* in the Shorter Chinese *Saṃyukta Āgama.*" *Buddhist Studies Review* 25.1: 5–26.

Bodhi, Bhikkhu, trans. 2000. *The Connected Discourses of the Buddha: A New Translation of the Saṃyutta Nikāya.* Boston: Wisdom Publications.

Bötrül. 2012. *Distinguishing the Views and Philosophies: Illuminating Emptiness in a*

Twentieth Century Buddhist Classic. Translated by Douglas Samuel Duckworth. Albany: State University of New York Press.

Braarvig, Jens, ed. and trans. 1993. *Akṣayamatinirdeśasūtra.* 2 vols. Oslo: Solum Forlag.

Broido, Michael M. 1987. "Sa-skya Paṇḍita, the White Panacea and the Hva-shang Doctrine." *Journal of the International Association of Buddhist Studies* 10.2: 27–68.

Brunnhölzl, Karl. 2011b. *Gone Beyond: Volume Two.* Ithaca, NY: Snow Lion Publications.

———. 2011b. *Prajñāpāramitā, Indian "Gzhan stong pas," and the Beginning of Tibetan Gzhan stong.* Vienna: Arbeitskreis für Tibetische und Buddhistische Studien.

Buddhaghosa. 1991. *The Path of Purification: Visuddhimagga.* Translated by Bhikkhu Ñāṇamoli. Kandy: Buddhist Publication Society.

Chandra, Lokesh. 1963. *Materials for a History of Tibetan Literature.* 3 vols. Śata-Piṭaka Series, Indo-Asian Literatures 28–30. New Delhi: International Academy of Indian Culture.

Changkya Rölpai Dorjé. 2019. *Beautiful Adornment of Mount Meru: A Presentation of Classical Indian Philosophy.* Translated by Donald S. Lopez Jr. The Library of Tibetan Classics 24. Somerville, MA: Wisdom Publications.

Chimpa, Lama, and Alaka Chattopadhyaya. 1997. *Tāranātha's History of Buddhism in India.* Delhi: Motilal Banarsidass.

Collins, Steven. 1982. *Selfless Persons: Imagery and Thought in Theravada Buddhism.* Cambridge: Cambridge University Press.

Conze, Edward. 1951. *Buddhism: Its Essence and Development.* Oxford, England: Bruno Cassirer.

Cowherds, The. 2011. *Moonshadows: Conventional Truth in Buddhist Philosophy.* New York: Oxford University Press.

Dakpo Tashi Namgyal. 2019. *Moonbeams of Mahāmudrā, with "Dispelling the Darkness of Ignorance" by Wangchuk Dorje, the Ninth Karmapa.* Translated by Elizabeth Callahan. Boulder, CO: Snow Lion.

Dalai Lama. 2005. *The Universe in a Single Atom.* New York: Morgan Road Books.

Dalai Lama, His Holiness the, Dzong-ka-ba, and Jeffrey Hopkins. 2005. *Yoga Tantra: Paths to Magical Feats.* Ithaca, NY: Snow Lion.

Dalai Lama and Thubten Chodron. 2020. *In Praise of Great Compassion.* Somerville, MA: Wisdom Publications.

Damdinsuren, Tsendiin. 2008. *Академич Цэндийн Дамдинсурэн: дурсгалын түүвэр* (*Scholar Tsendiin Damdinsuren: The Memorial Collection*). Edited by L. Khurelbaatar. Ulaanbaatar: Academy of Sciences.

Davidson, Ronald M. 2002a. "Gsar ma Apocrypha: The Creation of Orthodoxy, Gray Texts, and the New Revelation." In *The Many Canons of Tibetan Buddhism,* edited by Helmut Eimer and David Germano, 203–24. Leiden: Brill.

———. 2002b. *Indian Esoteric Buddhism: A Social History of the Tantric Movement.* New York: Columbia University Press.

———. 2005. *Tibetan Renaissance: Tantric Buddhism in the Rebirth of Tibetan Culture.* New York: Columbia University Press.

de Jong, J. W. 1978. "Text-Critical Notes on the Prasannapadā." *Indo-Iranian Journal* 20.1–2: 25–59 and 20.3–4: 217–52.

Deguchi, Yasuo, Jay L. Garfield, and Graham Priest. 2013. "Does a Table Have Buddha-Nature? A Moment of Yes and No. Answer! But Not in Words or Signs: Reply to Siderits." *Philosophy East and West* 63.3: 387–98.

Demiéville, Paul. 1952. *Le Concile de Lhasa: Une Controverse sur le Quiétsme entre Boud-dhistes de l'inde et de la Chine au VIIIe Siècle de l'Ère Chrétienne.* Paris: Imprimerie Nationale de France.

Dhammajoti, Bhikkhu Kuala Lumpur. 2007. *Sarvāstivāda Abhidharma.* Hong Kong: Centre of Buddhist Studies, University of Hong Kong.

Duckworth, Douglas S. 2008. *Mipam on Buddha-Nature: The Ground of the Nyingma Tradition.* Albany: State University of New York Press.

Dudjom Rinpoche. 1991. *The Nyingma School of Tibetan Buddhism.* Translated by Gyurme Dorje and Matthew Kapstein. Boston: Wisdom Publications.

Eltschinger, Vincent. 2010. "Dharmakīrti." *Revue Internationale de Philosophie* 64.253 (3): 397–440.

———. 2013. "Buddhist Esotericism and Epistemology: Two Sixth-Century Innovations as Buddhist Responses to Social and Religio-Political Transformations." In *Periodization and Historiography of Indian Philosophy*, edited by Eli Franco, 171–274. Publications of the de Nobili Research Library 37. Vienna: Institut für Südasien-, Tibet- und Buddhismuskunde der Universität Wien.

Franco, Eli. 1997. *Dharmakīrti on Compassion and Rebirth.* Wiener Studien zur Tibetologie und Buddhismuskunde 38. Vienna: Arbeitskreis für Tibetische und Buddhistische Studien, Universität Wien.

Fuller, Paul. 2005. *The Notion of Diṭṭhi in Theravada Buddhism: The Point of View.* London: RoutledgeCurzon.

Garfield, Jay L. 2015. *Engaging Buddhism: Why It Matters to Philosophy.* New York: Oxford University Press.

Garfield, Jay L., and Graham Priest. 2003. "Nāgārjuna and the Limits of Thought." *Philosophy East and West* 53.1: 1–21.

Gethin, Rupert. 1997. "Wrong View (*micchā-diṭṭhi*) and Right View (*sammā-diṭṭhi*) in the Theravāda Abhidhamma." In *Recent Researches in Buddhist Studies: Essays in Honour of Professor Y. Karunadasa*, edited by K. L. Dhammajoti, Asanga Tilakaratne, and Kapila Abhayawansa, 211–29. Columbo: Y. Karunadasa Felicitation Committee.

———. 1998. *The Foundations of Buddhism.* Oxford: Opus OUP.

Gombrich, Richard. 2003. "Vedānta Stood on Its Head: *Sakkāya* and *Sakkāyadiṭṭhi*." In *Second International Conference on Indian Studies: Proceedings*, edited by Renata Czekalska and Halina Marlewicz, 227–38. Cracow Indological Series 4–5. Krakow: Ksiegarnia Akademicka.

———. 2009. *What the Buddha Thought.* London & Oakville: Equinox.

Gombojav, S. (С. Гомбожав). 1959. "Монголчуудын төвд хэлээр зохиосон зохиолын зүйл" ("Writings Written in Tibetan by Mongolians"). In *Олон улсын монгол хэл бичгийн эрдэмтдийн анхдугаар их хурал* (*Proceedings of the First International Congress of Mongolian Linguists*), vol. 1. Ulaanbaatar, 1959.

Gómez, Luís O. 1983. "The Direct and Gradual Approaches of the Zen Master Mahāyāna." In *Studies in Ch'an and Hua-yen*, edited by Robert M. Gimello and Peter N. Gregory, 69–167. Honolulu: University of Hawai'i Press.

———. 1987. "Purifying Gold: The Metaphor of Effort and Intuition in Buddhist Thought and Practice." In *Sudden and Gradual: Approaches to Enlightenment in Chinese Thought*, edited by Peter N. Gregory, 67–165. Kuroda Studies in East Asian Buddhism 5. Honolulu: University of Hawai'i Press.

Gray, David B. 2007. *The Cakrasamvara Tantra: A Study and Annotated Translation*. New York: American Institute of Buddhist Studies / Columbia University Press.

———. 2011. "Imprints of the 'Great Seal': On the Expanding Semantic Range of the Term *Mudrā* in Eighth through Eleventh Century Indian Buddhist Literature." *Journal of the International Association of Buddhist Studies* 34.1–2: 421–81.

———. 2012. *The Cakrasamvara Tantra: Editions of the Sanskrit and Tibetan Texts*. New York: American Institute of Buddhist Studies / Columbia University Press.

———. 2017. *Tsong Khapa's Illumination of the Hidden Meaning: Maṇḍala, Mantra, and the Cult of the Yoginīs (An Annotated Translation of Chapters 1–24)*. New York: American Institute of Buddhist Studies / Columbia University Press.

———. 2019. *Tsong Khapa's Illumination of the Hidden Meaning: Yogic Vows, Conduct, and Ritual Praxis (An Annotated Translation of Chapters 25–51)*. New York / Boston: American Institute of Buddhist Studies / Wisdom Publications.

Harrison, Paul. 2006. "*Vajracchedikā Prajñāpāramitā*: A New English Translation of the Sanskrit Text Based on Two Manuscripts from Greater Gandhāra." In *Buddhist Manuscripts Vol. 3: Manuscripts in the Schøyen Collection*, edited by Jens Braarvig, 133–159. Oslo: Hermes Publishing.

Harvey, Peter. 2009. "Theravāda Philosophy of Mind and the Person: *Anatta-lakkhaṇa Sutta, Mahā-nidāna Sutta*, and *Melindapañha*" In *Buddhist Philosophy: Essential Readings*, edited by William Edelglass and Jay Garfield, 265–75. New York: Oxford University Press.

Herrmann-Pfandt, Adelheid. 2008. *Die lHan kar ma: Ein früher Katalog der ins Tibetische übersetzten buddhistischen Texte. Kritische Neuausgabe mit Einleitung und Materialien*. Denkschriften, Österreichische Akademie der Wissenschaften, philosophisch-historische Klasse 367. Beiträge zur Kultur- und Geistesgeschichte Asiens 59. Vienna: Verlag der Österreichischen Akademie der Wissenschaften.

Higgins, David. 2013. *The Philosophical Foundations of Classical rDzogs Chen in Tibet: Investigating the Distinction Between Dualistic Mind* (sems) *and Primordial Knowing* (ye shes). Vienna: Arbeitskreis für Tibetische und Buddhistische Studien, Universität Wien.

Hirakawa, Akira. 1990. *A History of Indian Buddhism*, translated by Paul Groner. Honolulu: University of Hawai'i Press.

Hopkins, Jeffrey. 1999. *Emptiness in the Mind-Only School of Buddhism*. Berkeley: University of California Press.

———. 2008. *Tsong-kha-pa's Final Exposition of Wisdom*. Ithaca, NY: Snow Lion Publications.

Jackson, David P. 1994. *Enlightenment by a Single Means: Tibetan Controversies on the "Self-Sufficient White Remedy."* Beiträge zur Kultur- und Geistesgeschichte Asiens 12. Vienna: Verlag der Österreichischen Akademie der Wissenschaften.

Jackson, Roger R. 2019. *Mind Seeing Mind: Mahāmudrā and the Geluk Tradition of Tibetan Buddhism*. Studies in Indian and Tibetan Buddhism. Boston: Wisdom Publications.

———. 2020. "Tsongkhapa as Dzokchenpa." *Indian International Journal of Buddhist Studies* 21: 81–116.

Jinpa, Thupten. 2002. *Self, Reality and Reason in Tibetan Philosophy: Tsongkhapa's Quest for the Middle Way*. London: RoutledgeCurzon.

———. 2019. *Tsongkhapa: A Buddha in the Land of Snows*. Boulder, CO: Shambhala Publications.

————, trans. 2022. *Stages of the Path and the Oral Transmission: Selected Teachings of the Geluk School.* The Library of Tibetan Classics 6. Somerville, MA: Wisdom Publications.

Kamalaśīla, Ācārya. 1988. *The Stages of Meditation: Middle Volume.* Translated by Geshe Lhundub Sopa, Elvin W. Jones, and John Newman. Madison, WI: Deer Park Books.

Kano, Kazuo, and Hōdō Nakamura. 2009. "Japanese Translation and Critical Edition of bCom ldan rig ral's *Byams pa dang 'brel ba'i chos kyi byung tshul.*" *Acta Tibetica et Buddhica* 2: 117–39.

Kano, Kazuo, and Xuezhu Li. 2014. "Critical Edition and Japanese Translation and Critical Edition of the Saṃskrit Text of the *Munimatālaṃkāra* Chapter 1. *Ekayāna* Portion (fol. 67v2–70r4): Parallel Passages in the *Madhyamakāloka.*" *Mikkyo Bunka* [*Journal of Esoteric Buddhism*] 232 (March): 138–103 [7–42].

Kapstein, Matthew T. 2013. "Chinese and Indian Buddhists at Samyé." In *Sources of Tibetan Tradition*, edited by Kurtis R. Schaeffer, Matthew T. Kapstein, and Gray Tuttle, 142–50. New York: Columbia University Press.

Karmay, Samten G. 1988. *The Great Perfection: A Philosophical and Meditative Teaching of Tibetan Buddhism.* Leiden: E. J. Brill.

Kaschewsky, Rudolf. 1967. *Das Leben des Lamaistischen Heiligen Tsongkhapa Blo-bzaṅ-grags-pa (1357–1419) Dargestellt und erläutert anhand seiner Biographie. Quellort allen Glückes.* Inaug.-Diss. Bonn: Rheinische Friedrich-Wilhelms-Universität.

Kellner, Birgit. 2020. "Using Concepts to Eliminate Conceptualization: Kamalaśīla on Non-Conceptual Gnosis (*Nirvikaplpajñāna*)." *Journal of the International Association of Buddhist Studies* 43: 39–80.

Kimura, Takayasu, ed. 2007–9. *Pañcaviṃśatisāhasrikā Prajñāpāramitā* (1–1, 1–2). GRETIL edition input by Klaus Wille (Göttingen). Tokyo: Sankibo Busshorin.

Kolts, Russel, and Thubten Chodron. 2015. *An Open-Hearted Life: Transformative Methods for Compassionate Living from a Clinical Psychologist and a Buddhist.* Boulder, CO: Shambhala Publications.

Köppl, Heidi I. 2008. *Establishing Appearances as Divine: Rongzom Chözang on Reasoning, Madhyamaka, and Purity.* Ithaca, NY: Snow Lion Publications.

Kragh, Ulrich. 1998. "Culture and Subculture: A Study of the Mahāmudrā Teachings of Sgam po pa." M.A. research paper (special). Copenhagen University.

La Vallée Poussin, Louis de. 1970. *Madhyamakavṛttiḥ: Mūlamadhyamakakārikās (Mādhyamikasūtras) de Nāgārjuna avec la Prasannapadā Commentaire de Candrakīrti.* St. Petersburg: Imperial Academy of Sciences, 1903–13. Reprint Osnabrück: Biblio Verlag.

Longchen Rabjampa. 2014. *The Practice of Dzogchen: Longchen Rabjampa's Writings on the Great Perfection.* Introduced, translated, and annotated by Tulku Thondup. Edited by Harold Talbott. Boulder, CO: Snow Lion.

Longchenpa. 2017–18. *The Trilogy of Rest.* 3 vols. Translated by the Padmakara Translation Group. Boulder, CO: Shambhala Publications.

Luvsantseren, Geshé (Г. Лувсанцэрэн). 1976. *Review of Mongolian Literature, Book 2* (17th–18th Centuries) (*Монголын уран зохиолын тойм, Хоёрдугаар дэвтэр,* [XVII–XVIII зууны γe]), Ulaanbaatar.

Mathes, Klaus-Dieter. 2015. *A Fine Blend of Mahāmudrā and Madhyamaka: Maitrīpa's Texts on Non-Conceptual Realization* (Amanasikāra). Vienna: Verlag der Öster-reichischen Akademie det Wissenschaften.

McClintock, Sara L. 2002. *Omniscience and the Rhetoric of Reason: Śāntarakṣita and*

Kamalaśīla on Rationality, Argumentation, and Religious Authority. Studies in Indian and Tibetan Buddhism. Boston: Wisdom Publications.

Meinert, Carmen. 2003. "Structural Analysis of *the bSam gtan mig sgron*: A Comparison of the Fourfold Correct Practice in the *Āryavikalpapraveśanāmadhāraṇī* and the Contents of the Four Main Chapters of the *bSam gtan mig sgron.*" *Journal of the International Association of Buddhist Studies* 26.1: 175–95.

Mipham. 2004. *Speech of Delight: Mipham's Commentary on Śāntarakṣita's Ornament of the Middle Way.* Translated by Thomas Doctor. Ithaca, NY: Snow Lion Publications.

Mullin, Glenn H. 1996. *Tsongkhapa's Six Yogas of Naropa.* Ithaca, NY: Snow Lion Publications.

———. 1997. *Readings on the Six Yogas of Naropa.* Ithaca, NY: Snow Lion Publications.

Myagmarsuren, G. (Г. Мягмарсүрэн). 2021. *Бодь мөрийн зэргийн дээж бичиг* (*The Uppermost Manuscript of the Collected Lamrim Scriptures*). Ulaanbaatar: Bembi San Printing Company.

Nakamura, Hōdō. 2010–2011. "Traditions of the Commentaries Ascribed to Asaṅga and Vasubandhu on the *Abhisamayālaṃkāra*: Their Relationship with the Commentaries Ascribed to Daṃṣṭrasena on the *Prajñāpāramitā*-Literature." *Journal of Indian and Buddhist Studies* (*Indokagu Bukkyogaku Kenkyu*) 59.3: 1262–66 (2011) and 188–92 (2010).

———. 2014. "Ārya-Vimuktisena's *Abhisamayālaṃkāravṛtti*, The Earliest Commentary on the *Abhisamayālaṃkāra*: A Critical Edition and a Translation of the Chapters Five to Eight with an Introduction and Critical Notes." PhD diss., Universität Hamburg.

Nalanda Translation Committee, under the direction of Chögyam Trungpa. 1982. *The Life of Marpa the Translator.* Boulder, CO: Prajna Press.

Namdol, Gyaltsen, ed. and trans. 1985. *Bhāvanākrama of Ācārya Kamalaśīla.* Bibliotheca Indo-Tibetica 9. Sarnath: Central Institute of Higher Tibetan Studies.

Nattier, Jan. 1999. *Once Upon a Future Time: Studies in a Buddhist Prophecy of Decline.* Berkeley: Asian Humanities Press.

Newland, Guy. 1992. *The Two Truths.* Ithaca, NY: Snow Lion Publications.

Obermiller, E., trans. 1986 [1932]. *The History of Buddhism in India and Tibet by Bu–ston.* Delhi: Sri Satguru Publications.

Pensa, Corrado. 1967. *L'Abhisamayālamkāravrtti di Ārya-Vimuktisena.* Rome: Istituto Italiano per il Medio ed Estremo Oriente.

Pettit, John Whitney. 1999. *Mipham's Beacon of Certainty.* Studies in Indian and Tibetan Buddhism. Boston: Wisdom Publications.

Roberts, Peter Alan, trans. 2011. *Mahāmudrā and Related Instructions: Core Teachings of the Kagyü Schools.* The Library of Tibetan Classics 5. Boston: Wisdom Publications.

Sakya Pandita Kunga Gyaltshen. 2002. *A Clear Differentiation of the Three Codes: Essential Distinctions among the Individual Liberation, Great Vehicle, and Tantric Systems.* Translated by Jared Douglas Rhoton. Albany: State University of New York Press.

Sanderson, Alexis. 1988. "Śaivism and the Tantric Traditions." In *The World's Religions,* edited by S. Sutherland et al., 660–704. London: Routledge & Kegan Paul.

———. 1994. "Vajrayana: Origin and Function." In *Buddhism into the Year 2000,* 87–102. Bangkok and Los Angeles: Dhammakaya Foundation.

Schaeffer, Kurtis R., and Leonard W. J. van der Kuijp. 2009. *An Early Survey of Buddhist Literature: The Bstan pa rgyas pa rgyan gyi nyi 'od of Bcom ldan ral gri.* Harvard Oriental Series 64. Cambridge, MA: Harvard University Press.

Schmithausen, Lambert. 1987. *Ālayavijñāna: On the Origin and the Early Development of a Central Concept of Yogācāra Philosophy* (Parts 1 & 2). Tokyo: The International Institute for Buddhist Studies.

Schopen, Gregory. 2005. "The Phrase *sa pṛthivīpradeśaś caityabhūto bhavet* in the *Vajracchedikā*: Notes on the Cult of the Book in Mahāyāna." In *Figments and Fragments of Mahāyāna Buddhism in India*, 25–62. Honolulu: University of Hawai'i Press.

Seyfort Ruegg, David. 1989. *Buddha Nature, Mind and the Problem of Gradualism in a Comparative Perspective: On the Transmission and Reception of Buddhism in India and Tibet*. London: School of Oriental and African Studies, University of London.

Shastri S. D. 1994. *Pramāṇavārtikam*. Dharmakirti Nibandhavali, vol. 1. Varanasi: Bauddha Bharati.

Siderits, Mark and Shoryu Katsura. *Nāgārjuna's Middle Way: Mulamadhyamakakārikā*. Classics of Indian Buddhism. Boston: Wisdom Publications, 2013.

Sopa, Geshe Lhundub, with Dechen Rochard. 2017. *Steps on the Path to Enlightenment: A Commentary on Tsongkhapa's Lamrim Chenmo, vol. 5: Insight*. Somerville, MA: Wisdom Publications.

Sparham, Gareth. 2001. "Demons on the Mother: *Objections to the Perfect Wisdom Sūtras in Tibet.*" In *Changing Minds*, edited by Guy Newland, 193–214. Ithaca, NY: Snow Lion Publications.

Thakchoe, Sonam. 2007. *The Two Truths Debate: Tsongkhapa and Gorampa on the Middle Way*. Boston: Wisdom Publications.

Thondup Rinpoche, Tulku. 1986. *The Hidden Teachings of Tibet: An Explanation of the Terma Tradition of the Nyingma School of Buddhism*. London: Wisdom Publications.

———. 2014. *The Practice of Dzogchen: Longchen Rabjam's Writings on the Great Perfection*. Ithaca, NY: Snow Lion Publications.

Thurman, Robert A. F. 1982. *The Life and Teaching of Tsong Khapa*. Dharamsala: Library of Tibetan Works and Archives.

———. 1984. *The Central Philosophy of Tibet: A Study and Translation of Jey Tsong Khapa's Essence of True Eloquence*. Princeton, NJ: Princeton University Press.

Tsangnyön Heruka. 2016. *The Hundred Thousand Songs of Milarepa*. Translated by Christopher Stagg. Boulder, CO: Shambhala.

Tsongkhapa. 1980. *Compassion in Tibetan Buddhism*. Edited and translated by Jeffrey Hopkins. Ithaca, NY: Snow Lion Publications.

———. 2000. *The Great Treatise on the Stages of the Path to Enlightenment, Volume 1*. Translated by the Lamrim Chenmo Translation Committee. Edited by Joshua W. Cutler. Ithaca, NY: Snow Lion Publications.

———. 2001. *The Splendor of an Autumn Moon: The Devotional Verse of Tsongkhapa*. Translated and introduced by Gavin Kilty. Boston: Wisdom Publications.

———. 2002. *The Great Treatise on the Stages of the Path to Enlightenment, Volume 3*. Translated by the Lamrim Chenmo Translation Committee. Edited by Joshua W. Cutler. Ithaca, NY: Snow Lion Publications.

———. 2004. *The Great Treatise on the Stages of the Path to Enlightenment, Volume 2*. Translated by the Lamrim Chenmo Translation Committee. Edited by Joshua W. Cutler. Ithaca, NY: Snow Lion Publications.

———. 2006. *Ocean of Reasoning: A Great Commentary on Nāgārjuna's Mūlamadhyamakakārikā*. Translated by Geshe Ngawang Samten and Jay L. Garfield. Oxford: Oxford University Press.

————. 2013. *A Lamp to Illuminate the Five Stages: Teachings on Guhyasamāja Tantra.* Translated by Gavin Kilty. The Library of Tibetan Classics 15. Boston: Wisdom Publications.

————. 2021a. *Illuminating the Intent: An Exposition of Candrakīrti's Entering the Middle Way.* Translated by Thupten Jinpa. The Library of Tibetan Classics 19. Somerville, MA: Wisdom Publications.

————. 2021b. *The Middle-Length Treatise on the Stages of the Path to Enlightenment.* Translated by Philip Quarcoo. Somerville, MA: Wisdom Publications.

————. n.d. "In Praise of Dependent Origination." Translated by Thupten Jinpa. https://tibetanclassics.org/wp-content/uploads/2020/09/In-Praise-of-Dependent-Origination.pdf.

Tucci, Giuseppe. 1986 [1956, 1958]. *Minor Buddhist Texts, Parts I & II.* Delhi: Motilal Banarsidass.

————. 1988. *Rin-chen-bzaṅ-po and the Renaissance of Buddhism in Tibet around the Millennium.* Translated by Nancy Kipp Smith and Thomas J. Pritzker, edited by Lokesh Chandra. New Delhi: Aditya Prakashan.

Vaidya, P. L., ed. 1960. *Madhyamakaśāstra of Nāgārjuna, with the Prasannapadā by Candrakīrti.* Buddhist Sanskrit Texts 10. Darbhanga, Bihar: Mithila Institute.

————, ed. 1961. *Rāṣṭrapālaparipṛcchā.* In *Mahāyāna-Sūtra-Saṃgraha, Part I,* 120–64. Buddhist Sanskrit Texts 17. Darbhanga, Bihar: Mithila Institute.

van der Kuijp, Leonard W. J. 2013. "Some Remarks on the Textual Transmission and Text of Bu ston rin chen grub's *Chos 'byung,* a Chronicle of Buddhism in India and Tibet." *Revue d'Études Tibétaines* 25 (April): 115–93.

van Schaik, Sam. 2015. *Tibetan Zen: Discovering a Lost Tradition.* Boston: Snow Lion.

Vose, Kevin A. 2009. *Resurrecting Candrakīrti: Disputes in the Tibetan Creation of Prāsaṅgika.* Boston: Wisdom Publications.

Wallace. B. Alan. 1998. *The Bridge of Quiescence: Experiencing Tibetan Buddhist Meditation.* Chicago and LaSalle, IL: Open Court.

Yakherds. 2021. *Knowing Illusion: Bringing a Tibetan Debate into Contemporary Discourse,* vol. 1. New York: Oxford University Press.

Yuyama, Akira. 1992. "*Pañcāśati-,* '500' or '50'? With special reference to the Lotus Sūtra," *The Dating of the Historical Buddha/Die Datierung des Historischen Buddha,* Part 2, edited by Heinz Bechert, 208–33. Göttingen: Vandenhoek & Ruprecht.

Zajonc, Arthur, ed. 2004. *The New Physics and Cosmology: Dialogues with the Dalai Lama.* New York: Oxford University Press.

Zalta, Edward N. 2017. "Karl Popper." *The Stanford Encyclopedia of Philosophy.* Edited by Edward N. Zalta. Spring 2017 edition. https://plato.stanford.edu/archives/spr2017/entries/popper/

Zava Damdin Losang Tayang (Зава Дамдин Лувсандаян). 2014. *Их Монгол оронд Бурханы шашин дэлгэрсэн түүх "Алтан дэвтэр"* (*Golden Chronicle: A History of the Holy Dharma in the Land of Mongolia. Byang phyogs hor gyi yul du dam pa'i chos rin po che tshul gyi gtam rgyud bkra shes chos dung bzhad pa'i sgra dbyangs*). Translated by Geshé S. Gantumtur. Ulaanbaatar: Gandantegchenling Monastery.

Index

About the Contributors

BATAA Mishig-Ish chairs the Department of Religious Studies at the Institute of Philosophy of the Mongolian Academy of Sciences. He received a PhD in Asian studies from Ritsumeikan University, Japan, in 2013 and an MA in Asian religions and an MA in political science from the University of Hawaii at Manoa, Honolulu, in 2000 and 2001 respectively. He also studied as a monk at Gandantegchenling and Dashichoiling monasteries in Ulaanbaatar from 1989 to 1996. From 2002 to 2019 he taught as an associate professor at the National Academy of Governance. He was also a senior analyst on religious and cultural affairs at the National Security Council of Mongolia and served as an advisor on religious and cultural affairs to the president of Mongolia from 2011 to 2018. He heads the Tritiya Dharmachakra Foundation (TDF) for promoting Buddhist studies and research in Mongolia. The foundation also organizes symposiums on Buddhist and contemporary sciences in collaboration with universities in Mongolia, and it produced the documentary *The Dalai Lama and Mongolian Buddhism*. Dr. Bataa is also director of the board of trustees of Orgil Secondary School in Ulaanbaatar. The editor of several publications of conference proceedings on Buddhism, he has also published two books on contemporary Buddhism in Mongolia for Mongolian readers. Dr. Bataa is considered an expert on government-religious relations.

Born in 1950, **Thubten Chodron** graduated with a BA in history from the University of California, Los Angeles (Phi Beta Kappa), in 1971 and did graduate studies in education at the University of Southern California while working as a teacher in Los Angeles. In 1977 she was ordained as a Buddhist nun by Kyabjé Ling Rinpoche, and in 1986 she received bhikṣuṇī ordination in Taiwan. She studied and practiced for many years under the guidance of His Holiness the Dalai Lama, Tsenzhap Serkong Rinpoché, Zopa Rinpoché, and other masters. She has directed the spiritual program at Istituto Lama Tzong Khapa in Italy and Dorje Pamo Monastery in France and was resident teacher at Amitabha Buddhist Centre in Singapore and the Dharma Friendship Foundation in Seattle.

Bhikṣuṇī Chodron co-organized the conference "Life as a Western Buddhist Nun" and participated in the conferences of Western Buddhist teachers with H. H. the Dalai Lama in 1993 and 1994. Keen on interfaith dialogue, she attended the Jewish delegation's visit to Dharamsala, India, in 1990, and the Second Gethsemani Encounter in 2002. She participated in several of the early Mind-Life conferences and regularly attends the annual Western Buddhist Monastic Gatherings. She engages in Dharma outreach to people who are incarcerated and was on the board of Youth Emergency Services, which serves homeless youth.

In 2003, Bhikṣuṇī Chodron founded Sravasti Abbey, a Buddhist monastic community in Washington State, and is currently its abbess and resident teacher. She has authored many books, including *Open Heart, Clear Mind*; *Buddhism for Beginners*; and *Working with Anger*, and is working with H. H. the Dalai Lama on the ten-volume Library of Wisdom and Compassion series. Well known for her warm, humorous, and lucid approach, Bhikṣuṇī Chodron teaches worldwide, emphasizing the practical application of the Buddha's teachings.

Jay L. Garfield directs the Buddhist Studies Program, the South Asian Studies Program, and the Tibetan Studies in India Program at Smith College, in Northampton, Massachusetts. He is also visiting professor of Buddhist philosophy at Harvard Divinity School, professor of philosophy at Melbourne University, and adjunct professor of philosophy at the Central Institute of Higher Tibetan Studies in India. The site academic influence.com has identified him as one of the fifty most influential philosophers in the world over the past decade.

Garfield's research addresses topics in the foundations of cognitive science and the philosophy of mind; metaphysics; the history of modern Indian philosophy; topics in ethics, epistemology, and the philosophy of logic; the philosophy of the Scottish enlightenment methodology in cross-cultural interpretation; and topics in Buddhist philosophy, particularly

Indo-Tibetan Madhyamaka and Yogācāra. He is the author or editor of over thirty books and over two hundred articles, chapters, and reviews. His most recent books are *Getting Over Ourselves: How to Be a Person Without a Self* (2022), *Knowing Illusion: Bringing a Tibetan Debate into Contemporary Discourse* (with the Yakherds, 2021), *Buddhist Ethics: A Philosophical Exploration* (2021), *What Can't Be Said: Paradox and Contradiction in East Asian Thought* (with Yasuo Deguchi, Graham Priest, and Robert Scharf, 2021), *The Concealed Influence of Custom: Hume's* Treatise *From the Inside* Out (2019), and *Minds Without Fear: Philosophy in the Indian Renaissance* (with Nalini Bhushan, 2017).

David B. Gray is Bernard J. Hanley Professor of Religious Studies at Santa Clara University, in Santa Clara, California, where he teaches a wide range of courses on Asian religions. His research explores the development of tantric Buddhist traditions in South Asia and their dissemination in Tibet and East Asia, with a focus on *yoginītantra*, a genre of Buddhist literature focused on female deities and yogic practices involving the subtle body. His publications include numerous articles and book chapters, an edited volume, as well as *The Cakrasamvara Tantra: A Study and Annotated Translation* (2007), *The Cakrasamvara Tantra: Editions of the Sanskrit and Tibetan Texts Translation* (2012), *Illumination of the Hidden Meaning (Chapters 1–24): Maṇḍala, Mantra, and the Cult of the Yoginīs* (2017), and *Illumination of the Hidden Meaning, Part II: Chapters 25–51, Yogic Vows, Conduct, and Ritual Practice* (2019).

Roger Jackson is John W. Nason Professor of Asian Studies and Religion, Emeritus, at Carleton College, where he taught the religions of South Asia and Tibet for nearly three decades. He has also taught at the University of Michigan, Fairfield University, McGill University, and Maitripa College. He has a BA from Wesleyan University and an MA and PhD from the University of Wisconsin, Madison, where he studied under Geshé Lhundub Sopa. His books include *Is Enlightenment Possible? Dharmakīrti and rGyal tshab rje on Knowledge, Rebirth, No-Self and Liberation* (1993); *Tibetan Literature: Studies in Genre* (with José Cabezón, 1996); *Buddhist Theology: Critical Reflections by Contemporary Buddhist Scholars* (with John Makransky, 1999); *Tantric Treasures: Three Collections of Mystical Verse from Buddhist India* (2004); *The Crystal Mirror of Philosophical*

Systems (with Geshe Sopa et al., 2009); *Mind Seeing Mind: Mahāmudrā and the Geluk Tradition of Tibetan Buddhism* (2019), which received the 2020 Toshihide Numata Award for the "outstanding book in any area of in Buddhist studies"; and *Rebirth: A Guide to Mind, Karma, and Cosmos in the Buddhist World* (2022). He was editor in chief of the *Journal of the International Association of Buddhist Studies* from 1985 to 1993 and coedited the *Indian International Journal of Buddhist Studies* from 2006 to 2018. His book *Saraha: Poet of Blissful Gnosis* will be published in 2024, and his current focus is the place of Buddhism in the Beat literary and spiritual movement in North America in the mid-twentieth century.

Gavin Kilty spent fourteen years in India studying Buddhism with Tibetan teachers, including eight years at the Institute of Buddhist Dialectics established by His Holiness the Dalai Lama in Dharamsala, where he completed the major part of the Tibetan monastic curriculum in the medium of the Tibetan language. He now works full-time as a translator of Tibetan texts, primarily for Thupten Jinpa's Institute of Tibetan Classics and the Tsadra Foundation. His published translations include *Ornament of Stainless Light: An Exposition of the Kālacakra Tantra* by Khedrup Norsang Gyatso (2004); *Mirror of Beryl: A Historical Introduction to Tibetan Medicine* by Desi Sangyé Gyatso (2009); *A Lamp to Illuminate the Five Stages: Teachings on Guhyasamāja Tantra* by Tsongkhapa (2012), winner of the 2017 Shantarakshita Award for Excellence in Translation presented by the Tsadra Foundation; *Tales from the Tibetan Operas* (2019); *The Life of My Teacher: A Biography of Kyabjé Ling Rinpoché* by the Dalai Lama (2017); *The Splendor of an Autumn Moon: Devotional Verse of Tsongkhapa* (2001), *Understanding the Case against Shukden: The History of a Contested Practice* by the Association of Geluk Masters et al. (2019); *The Light of Samantabhadra: An Explanation of Dharmakīrti's Commentary on Valid Cognition* by Gorampa Sönam Sengé (2023); and *The Fourteenth Dalai Lama's Stages of the Path*, compiled by Dagyab Kyabgön Rinpoché (2022).

Donald S. Lopez Jr. is the Arthur E. Link Distinguished University Professor of Buddhist and Tibetan Studies at the University of Michigan. He is the author, translator, and editor of numerous works in the field of Buddhist studies, and he has written extensively on the European encounter with Buddhism. His recent books include *Dispelling the Darkness: A Jesuit's Quest for the Soul of Tibet* (with Thupten Jinpa); *Gendun Chopel: Tibet's Modern Visionary*; *Seeing the Sacred in Samsara: An Illustrated Guide to the Eighty-Four Mahasiddhas*; *Two Buddhas Seated Side by Side: A Guide to the Lotus Sūtra* (with Jacqueline Stone); and, as translator, *Beautiful Adornment of Mount Meru: A Presentation of Classical Indian Philosophy*. Among anthologies, he is the editor of several volumes in the Princeton Readings in Religions series (which he founded). He is also the editor of the Buddhism volume of the *Norton Anthology of World Religions* and the editor of *Buddhist Scriptures* for Penguin Classics. In 2008, he was the first scholar of Buddhism to deliver the Terry Lectures at Yale. In 2014, *The Princeton Dictionary of Buddhism* (edited with Robert Buswell) was awarded the Dartmouth Medal of the American Library Association for best reference work of the year. In 2000, he was elected to the American Academy of Arts and Sciences.

Guy Newland holds a BA (1977), MA (1983), and PhD (1988) from the University of Virginia; his doctorate is in the history of religions. Since 1988, he has been a professor at Central Michigan University. He is the author of *The Two Truths* (1992), *Appearance and Reality* (1999), and *Introduction to Emptiness* (2008). He edited *Changing Minds* (2001), a festschrift for Jeffrey Hopkins. Together with Joshua Cutler, he edited the three-volume translation of Tsongkhapa's *Great Treatise on the Stages of the Path to Enlightenment* (2000, 2002, 2004); he later translated and edited the Dalai Lama's teachings on that text, published as *From Here to Enlightenment* (2012). As a member of the scholarly collective known as the Cowherds, he coauthored *Moonshadows: Conventional Truth in Buddhist Philosophy* (2011) and *Moonpaths: Ethics and Emptiness* (2015). In 2016, Newland published the personal memoir *A Buddhist Grief Observed*. Among the outstanding Tibetan scholars with whom he has been honored to work, he is especially grateful to Geshé Palden Drakpa of Drepung Loseling, who inspired and guided him in the study of Madhyamaka.

Dechen Rochard is a practicing Buddhist since 1984 and a disciple of His Holiness the Dalai Lama. She was ordained as a novice nun by him in Bodhgaya in 1986 and remained within the monastic order for twelve years. After completing several three-month solitary retreats in the United

Kingdom during her early years as a nun, she enrolled at the Institute of Buddhist Dialectics, Dharamsala, where she completed the first ten years of the geshé studies program. In 1997 she returned to England as a laywoman and worked part-time as a Buddhist prison chaplain for several years. Throughout this period, she studied Theravāda Buddhism and Sanskrit at the University of Bristol. She also continued studying Madhyamaka under the guidance of Geshé Lhundub Sopa for over a decade, during which time she transcribed and edited his oral commentary on the "Insight" chapter of Tsongkhapa's *Lamrim Chenmo*, published as volume 5 of *Steps on the Path to Enlightenment* (2017). Having obtained a BA in philosophy in 1979, she completed a PhD in Buddhist philosophy at the University of Cambridge in 2013. Since 2014 Dechen has been working for the Dalai Lama Foundation, translating volume 2, *The Mind* (2020), and volume 4, *Philosophical Topics* (2023), of *Science and Philosophy in the Indian Buddhist Classics*. She is an honorary research fellow in the Department of Religion and Theology, University of Bristol, and a fellow of the Dalai Lama Centre for Compassion, Oxford. She teaches Buddhist philosophy and practice in the UK and abroad and currently lives in Bristol.

Geshé Ngawang Samten obtained his masters from the Central Institute of Higher Tibetan Studies, Sarnath, (CIHTS) and subsequently the *geshé lharampa* degree from Ganden Monastic University, India. He worked as associate professor in the Research Department and later as professor in the Department of Buddhist Philosophy at CIHTS. Since 2001 he has been the director and vice chancellor of the same institute. He has been a visiting professor at Amherst College, Smith College, and Hampshire College in the United States, at the University of Tasmania in Australia, and at the Tibet Center Institute in Austria. He served as an active member on important committees of the Central Tibetan Administration, Dharamsala, and on various ministries of the Indian government, Indian national academic bodies, and Indian universities. He has critically edited and translated numerous classical works of Indian and Tibetan masters and has contributed articles to special publications and books. In 2009 he was awarded the *Padma Shri*, one of the highest Indian civilian national honors, by the president of India in recognition of his contribution to education and literature, and in 2016, the Indian government presented him with the *Vesak Samman* in recognition of his outstanding contribution to Indian philosophy and culture.

Gareth Sparham received a BA in English (Hons) from McGill University and PhD in Asian studies from the University of British Columbia. He studied formally at the Rigs lam slob grwa (Institute of Buddhist Dialectics) in Dharamsala from 1974 until 1986 and remained closely associated with the institute until 1998. He then taught Tibetan and Sanskrit at the University of Michigan and the University of California, Berkeley, for twelve years, leaving to focus on translating Indian and Tibetan Perfection of Wisdom literature from Tibetan and Sanskrit into English. He has translated many works of Tsongkhapa into English, including those in *Ocean of Eloquence* (1993), *The Fulfillment of All Hopes* (1999), *Tantric Ethics* (2005), and *Golden Garland of Eloquence* (2008–13), and has contributed the entry on Tsongkhapa to the *Stanford Encyclopedia of Philosophy* and to *Oxford Bibliographies Online*.

What to Read Next from Wisdom Publications

The Middle-Length Treatise on the Stages of the Path to Enlightenment
Tsongkhapa
Translated by Philip Quarcoo

"It is thrilling at long last to have a complete translation of the *Middle-Length Treatise on the Stages of the Path to Enlightenment*. Philip Quarcoo's accurate and readable rendering brings Jé Rinpoché's lucid presentation alive."—Roger R. Jackson, John W. Nason Professor of Asian Studies and Religion, emeritus, Carleton College

Illuminating the Intent
An Exposition of Candrakīrti's Entering the Middle Way
Tsongkhapa
Translated by Thupten Jinpa

This work is perhaps the most influential explanation of Candrakīrti's seventh-century classic *Entering the Middle Way* (*Madhyamakāvatāra*).

A Lamp to Illuminate the Five Stages
Teachings on Guhyasamāja Tantra
Tsongkhapa
Translated by Gavin Kilty

"Tsongkhapa's *Lamp to Illuminate the Five Stages* stands as one of the greatest literary contributions to the genre of highest yoga tantra ever written. In his translation of this extremely profound text, Gavin Kilty has successfully captured both its meaning and eloquence with such precision and grace that it will stand as the benchmark to which future translations of similar material must aspire."—David Gonsalez, translator of *Source of Supreme Bliss*

Illumination of the Hidden Meaning (volumes 1 and 2)
Tsongkhapa
Translated by David B. Gray

An annotated translation of Tsongkhapa's *Illumination of the Hidden Meaning* (*sbas don kun gsal*), a magnificent commentary on the *Cakrasamvara Tantra*. This is the first English translation of this important work, which marked a milestone in the history of the Tibetan understanding and practice of the Indian Buddhist tantras.

The Life and Teachings of Tsongkhapa
Robert Thurman

A must-read for students of Tibetan Buddhism, *The Life and Teachings of Tsongkhapa* provides a thorough exploration of the great teacher's wisdom.

Stages of the Path and the Oral Transmission
Selected Teachings of the Geluk School
Translated by Thupten Jinpa

"Because so many of its doctrinal works have been translated into English, it is often assumed that the Geluk tradition is concerned above all with scholastic philosophy. However, like all Tibetan traditions, the Geluk has a rich canon of devotional works, meditation manuals, and practical instructions for the vision of reality. The most famous of those works are collected in this remarkable volume, works composed by some of the greatest masters and saints of the Land of Snows."—Donald Lopez, Arthur E. Link Distinguished University Professor of Buddhist and Tibetan Studies, University of Michigan

Steps on the Path to Enlightenment (5 volumes)
A Commentary on Tsongkhapa's Lamrim Chenmo
Geshe Lhundub Sopa with David Patt

"An indispensable companion to Tsongkhapa's elegant and elaborate Great Exposition on the Stages of the Path."—*Buddhadharma*

Nāgārjuna's Middle Way
Mūlamadhyamakakārikā
Translated by Mark Siderits and Shōryū Katsura

"Authoritative, vivid, and illuminating."—Graham Priest, author of
Logic: A Very Short Introduction

Mind Seeing Mind
Mahamudra and the Geluk Tradition of Tibetan Buddhism
Roger R. Jackson

"Roger Jackson's *Mind Seeing Mind* is an outstanding achievement, vast
in scope and profound in its engagement with Tibetan Buddhist contemplative and philosophical traditions. From the origins of the Mahāmudrā
teaching in India, through its refinement and development among the
Kagyü masters of Tibet, to its transmission to Jé Tsongkhapa and his
Gelukpa successors down to the present day, Jackson guides the reader
on a journey resembling the exploration of a great river from its turbulent headwaters to the spreading streams of its delta. *Mind Seeing Mind*
is a model study of the historical and doctrinal literature of Buddhism in
Tibet."—Matthew T. Kapstein, École Pratique des Hautes Études, Paris,
and the University of Chicago

Science and Philosophy in the Indian Buddhist Classics
(4 volumes)
Conceived and Introduced by His Holiness the Dalai Lama
Edited by Thupten Jinpa

"*Science and Philosophy in the Indian Buddhist Classics* offers a rare gift of
wisdom from the ancient world to the modern reader. The editors have
curated a rich treasure of the philosophy and maps of the mind that have
their origins in the early centuries of Indian thought, were preserved in
translation for centuries in Tibet, and now are brought to all of us in this
translation."—Daniel Goleman, author of *Emotional Intelligence*

About Wisdom Publications

Wisdom Publications is the leading publisher of classic and contemporary Buddhist books and practical works on mindfulness. To learn more about us or to explore our other books, please visit our website at wisdomexperience.org or contact us at the address below.

Wisdom Publications
132 Perry Street
New York, NY 10014 USA

We are a 501(c)(3) organization, and donations in support of our mission are tax deductible.

Wisdom Publications is affiliated with the Foundation for the Preservation of the Mahayana Tradition (FPMT).